THE EDEN STORY
A History of Paradise, from Its Demise to Its New Rise

WILLEM J. OUWENEEL

PAIDEIA PRESS

PAIDEIA
PRESS

The Eden Story: A History of Paradise, from Its Demise to Its New Rise

This English edition is a publication of the Reformational Publishing Project (www.reformationalpublishingproject.com) and Paideia Press (P.O. Box 500, Jordan Station, Ontario, Canada L0R 1S0). Copyright © 2020 by Paideia Press. All rights reserved. Except for brief quotations in critical publications or reviews, no part of this book may be reproduced in any manner without prior written permission from Paideia Press at the address above.

Unless otherwise indicated, Scripture quotations are from the ESV® Bible (The Holy Bible, English Standard Version®). Copyright © 2001 by Crossway, a publishing ministry of Good News Publishers. Used by permission. All rights reserved.

Scripture quotations or references marked as NKJV are taken from the New King James Version®. Copyright © 1982 by Thomas Nelson, Inc. Used by permission. All rights reserved.

Scripture quotations or references marked as NIV are taken from the Holy Bible, New International Version®, NIV®. Copyright © 1973, 1978, 1984, 2011 by Biblica, Inc.™ Used by permission of Zondervan. All rights reserved worldwide. www.zondervan.com. The "NIV" and "New International Version" are trademarks registered in the United States Patent and Trademark Office by Biblica, Inc.™

ISBN 978-0-88815-252-7

Printed in the United States of America

THE EDEN STORY

A History of Paradise, from Its Demise to Its New Rise

Table of Contents

Chapter 1   **From Garden to Garden**   1
- 1.1   The Garden
- 1.2   The Sanctuary
- 1.3   *Pardēs, Paradeisos*
- 1.4   Eden
- 1.5   *Qodesh, Hagios*
- 1.6   Beginnings
- 1.7   Dining
- 1.8   Ultimate Enjoyment
- 1.9   Our Daily Meals

Chapter 2   **The First Three Edens**   23
- 2.1   The King's Garden
- 2.2   A Celestial Eden
- 2.3   Music
- 2.4   An Earthly Eden
- 2.5   The City of Man
- 2.6   The Third Eden
- 2.7   Adam and Noah
- 2.8   Babel

Chapter 3   **The Tabernacle**   45
- 3.1   East or West?
- 3.2   The Universe, the Land, and the Tent
- 3.3   God's Longing
- 3.4   Seven Words
- 3.5   Additional Similarities
- 3.6   Eden and the Tabernacle

	3.7	More Similarities	
	3.8	*Yom Kippur*	
	3.9	The Temple of Solomon	
Chapter 4		**The Promised Land**	63
	4.1	Visiting the Land	
	4.2	Israel and Egypt	
	4.3	Seven Parallelisms	
	4.4	The Planting and the Voice	
	4.5	The Sabbath Rest	
	4.6	A Land of Trees	
	4.7	Milk and Honey	
	4.8	Four Main Trees	
	4.9	In Exile	
Chapter 5		**The Garden of Joseph**	83
	5.1	Two Gardens	
	5.2	A Third "Garden"?	
	5.3	The Cherubim	
	5.4	Eve and the Two Marys	
	5.5	The Second Eve	
	5.6	The Seven Tents	
	5.7	Christ and the *Shekhinah*	
	5.8	Christ As the Tree of Life	
Chapter 6		**Church Life**	101
	6.1	Cathedrals and Church Huts	
	6.2	The Temple of God	
	6.3	Pentecost	
	6.4	The Hundred and Twenty	
	6.5	A New Eden	
	6.6	The Lord's Supper	
	6.7	Passover and the Lord's Supper	
	6.8	Eden and Eternal Life	
	6.9	Conquering the Land	

Chapter 7		**The Hereafter**	**121**
	7.1	"Going to Heaven"	
	7.2	The Jewish *Gan Eden*	
	7.3	New Insights	
	7.4	Old Testament Hints	
	7.5	"Eternal Tents" and Abraham's "Bosom"	
	7.6	Edenic Features	
	7.7	"With Me In Paradise"	
	7.8	The Father's House	
	7.9	The Third Heaven	
Chapter 8		**The Ultimate Eden**	**141**
	8.1	A Simple Grave	
	8.2	Springtime	
	8.3	Seven Seasons	
	8.4	Edenic Dwellings	
	8.5	A Tree and a Tent	
	8.6	Five Features of Eden	
	8.7	The Sixth Feature of Eden	
	8.8	The Seventh Feature of Eden	
	8.9	Explanation	

Appendix 1: Eden in Ezekiel 31 — **161**

Appendix 2: Seven Trees, Seven (Anti-)Edenic Events — **165**

Appendix 3: Seven Edenic Feminine Names — **175**

Appendix 4: Edenic Music — **179**

Bibliography — **183**

Scripture Index — **187**

Subject Index — **205**

Foreword

There is a remarkable word in the prophecy of Joel, which I like to quote from the Bible translation called The Message:

> Blow the ram's horn trumpet in Zion! Trumpet the alarm on my holy mountain! Shake the country up! God's Judgment's on its way—the Day's almost here! A black day! A Doomsday! Clouds with no silver lining! Like dawn light moving over the mountains, a huge army is coming. There's never been anything like it and never will be again. Wildfire burns everything before this army and fire licks up everything in its wake. Before it arrives, the country is like the Garden of Eden. When it leaves, it is Death Valley. Nothing escapes unscathed (2:1–3).

This is just about the saddest prophecy in the Bible about Eden that I know: we read here about the Garden of Eden, which turns into some Death Valley after a devastating fire or army has overrun it. Joel says this here only by way of comparison. But redemptive history has known many *real* Edens, all of which have experienced evil fires and armies (in the figurative sense) that exist in the world, and what the latter can do to the magnificent things that God has prepared. They all have been hurt, and often badly wounded by the powers of darkness, and in particular by human failure:

- The celestial Eden was ruined by the fall of Satan and his angels.
- The first earthly Eden had to be evacuated as a consequence of

Adam and Eve's fall.
- Noah laid out a new Eden in a new world, and ruined it by his drunkenness.
- Israel's tabernacle in the wilderness was in many ways a copy of Eden, and was eventually replaced by the temple of Solomon; perhaps it was destroyed by the Philistines or the Babylonians, that is, as a consequence of Israel's failure.
- In fact, the Promised Land was another Eden, prepared by God for his people—but because of Israel's apostasy it fell into the hands of the Assyrians (partly), the Babylonians, and so many other powers afterward, until as late as the twentieth century.
- In a sense, the New Testament church began its existence in another Eden: the Garden of Joseph, where Jesus was buried and arose, and manifested himself to the first of his followers. How soon, unfortunately, evil entered this church as well.
- We are waiting for the ultimate Eden. Let me quote The Message again:

All around us we observe a pregnant creation. The difficult times of pain throughout the world are simply birth pangs. But it's not only around us; it's *within* us. The Spirit of God is arousing us within. We're also feeling the birth pangs. These sterile and barren bodies of ours are yearning for full deliverance. That is why waiting does not diminish us, any more than waiting diminishes a pregnant mother. We are enlarged in the waiting. We, of course, don't see what is enlarging us. But the longer we wait, the larger we become, and the more joyful our expectancy (Rom. 8:22–25).

I will have much to say about each of these successive Edens. No matter how many previous Edens have been ruined, God's people never give up hope. No matter how mighty the dark powers may be, no matter how many failures humanity has heaped one upon the other, God will eventually reach his goal: his ultimate Eden, as described in Revelation (MSG):

Are your ears awake? Listen. Listen to the Wind Words, the Spirit blowing through the churches. I'm about to call each conqueror to dinner. I'm spreading a banquet of Tree-of-Life fruit, a supper plucked from God's orchard [Paradise] (2:7).

Then the Angel showed me Water-of-Life River, crystal bright. It flowed from the Throne of God and the Lamb, right down the middle of the street. The Tree of Life was planted on each side of the River, producing twelve kinds of fruit, a ripe fruit each month. The leaves of the Tree are for healing the nations. Never again will anything be cursed. The Throne of God and of the Lamb is at the center (22:1–3).

I experienced the momentary temptation to write also about all the *false* Edens that many Western thinkers have tried to introduce, or have announced or promised, beginning with Plato's "philosopher kings," all the way through Romanticism and Marxism, and the modern Edens promised by the new Marxists (Marcuse, Adorno) and others. I withstood the temptation because such a discussion really requires a separate book. I am happy to limit myself here to the real Edens.

This book wishes to tell the story of Eden, from the beginning—even *before* Genesis 2!—until the very end of the new heavens and the new earth. It will be a sad story with a happy ending. It is a drama, but not a tragedy, because tragedies always end in a tragical way. It is not a comedy, either, because en route there will be little reason to laugh, except in this sense: "Heaven-throned God breaks out laughing. At first he's amused at their [i.e., the God-deniers' and Messiah-defiers'] presumption; then he gets good and angry. Furiously, he shuts them up: 'Don't you know there's a King in Zion? A coronation banquet is spread for him on the holy summit'" (Ps. 2:4–6 MSG).

To be sure, this "banquet" is not literally in the original text—but what a beautiful way of describing the ultimate Eden!

"Eat!" said the serpent to Eve in the first earthly Eden, and Eve said it to Adam (Gen. 3:1–6). "Take, eat!" said Jesus the last night of his earthly life (Matt. 26:26). "Come, buy and eat!" the Lord will say in the end, followed by this Edenic promise:

> For you shall go out in joy
>   and be led forth in peace;
> the mountains and the hills before you
>   shall break forth into singing,
>   and all the trees of the field shall clap their hands.
> Instead of the thorn shall come up the cypress;
>   instead of the brier shall come up the myrtle;
> and it shall make a name for the LORD,
>   an everlasting sign that shall not be cut off (Isa. 55:1, 12–13).[1]

Loerik (near Houten, Netherlands), Summer 2019
Willem J. Ouweneel

---

[1] Bible quotations in this book are usually from the English Standard Version (ESV).

Abbreviations

Bible Versions

AMP	Amplified Bible
AMPC	Amplified Bible, Classic Edition
ASV	American Standard Version
CEB	Common English Bible
CEV	Contemporary English Version
CJB	Complete Jewish Bible
CSB	Christian Standard Bible
DARBY	Darby Translation
DRA	Douay-Rheims 1899 American Edition
EHV	Evangelical Heritage Version
ERV	Easy-to-Read Version
ESV	English Standard Version
EXB	Expanded Bible
GNT	Good News Translation
GNV	1599 Geneva Bible
GW	God's Word Translation
HCSB	Holman Christian Standard Bible
KJV	King James Version
MSG	The Message
NABRE	New American Bible (Revised Edition)
NASB	New American Standard Bible
NIV	New International Version
NLT	New Living Translation
NKJV	New King James Version
OJB	Orthodox Jewish Bible
TPT	The Passion Translation

1
From Garden to Garden

*And the LORD God planted a garden in **Eden**, in the east,*
  and there he put the man whom he had formed.
And out of the ground the LORD God made to spring up
  every tree that is pleasant to the sight and good for food.
The tree of life was in the midst of the garden,
  and the tree of the knowledge of good and evil.
*A river flowed out of **Eden** to water the garden,*
  and there it divided and became four rivers . . .
The LORD God took the man
  *and put him in the garden of **Eden** to work it and keep it.*
                                        Genesis 2:8–10, 15

1.1 The Garden

The greater part of my mother's ancestry comes from the eastern part of the Netherlands, from a rural region called the Achterhoek. The man who wrote about this area in the most expert, but also most idyllic, romantic way, was a farmer's son, who wanted to be a pastor but became a headmaster, a church elder, and the historian and folklorist of his region. His name was Hendrik Willem Heuvel (1864–1926), and his most famous book was *Oud-Achterhoeksch Boerenleven*[1] ("Ancient Farmers' Life in the Achterhoek," seen through the dreamy eyes of a twelve years old boy). It is one of my favorite books; I am very happy that I could function as the chairman of an editorial board that recently published an annotated edition (in Dutch) of this

---
1 Heuvel (1927).

classical work.[2]

As a young boy, Heuvel viewed the region of his birth as the most paradisal part of the world.[3] "Paradisal" is the proper term because, as a good Protestant boy, young Heuvel associated the idyllic land of his youth with the Garden of Eden. After his fall, Adam had to leave his Paradise, and in the same way, Heuvel argued, *every* happy young human being reaches the point where they must leave behind the gorgeous, well-protected "Eden" of their youth in order to face the responsibilities and vicissitudes of adult life.

Almost at the beginning of his book Heuvel wrote:

From very far, we gaze through the gate of our lost Eden! How do those sounds of a gray past move our hearts. *At some time, every human being lives in Eden's Garden, but he must leave that place, in order to work the field, which bears thorns and thistles.* However, in hours of musing, Eden pops up for us as a green island, deeply in the subconscious. There, the tree of life is still rustling at the shore of God's river; there, the dewy morning of one's sunny youth still spreads its scent (italics added).

Much later in the book we read: "Just as Adam woke up in Eden's Garden on the first morning, thus it was with me, who still felt something of that mysterious wonderland, from which my soul had come forth."

Still later we read about a certain place near Heuvel's parental farm called "the Hay Meadow":

There lies the emerald green field in the luster of the morning sun. The dew glistens on grass and shrubs. The early haze hovers as a fine blur over the awakening landscape. It is still so quiet, so lovely quiet. A single bird is softly humming. From a far distance, we hear the crow of a rooster or the lowing of a cow. Far away,

---

2   Heuvel (2020).
3   Large parts of this idyllic world have been ruined through massive agricultural clearing of the wild areas of the Achterhoek; this has increased the prosperity of the population but decreased the beauty of the region.

through openings in the thickets, we look into other meadows, where the white hazes are already getting thinner. And I felt like Adam in Eden's youth. Oh, if I, only for an hour, could again enjoy all that sweetness of those golden hours of life's daybreak, when everything was still so new, so virginally fresh, as those bedewed meadows!

Of course, Heuvel knew about the ancient parallels of Eden's Garden found in other cultures. At one place in his masterwork, he compares the hay gleaners of his youth with the shepherds and shepherdesses of "Arcadia," the utopian, idyllic, unspoiled, harmonious wilderness idealized by the ancient world, and often described as the counterpart of the biblical Eden. But Arcadia is mentioned only once; time and again, Heuvel returns in his thoughts to the "Eden" of his youth, which he, as he grew up, had to leave both literally and mentally.

I do not wish to theologically dissect Heuvel's presentations of Eden, but limit myself to picking up this one idea, lying in the background of his thinking: the life of one individual is, as it were, a reflection of the entire world's history. It begins with the Paradise or our early youth—at least if this was a *happy* youth—the place that every human being must learn to leave in order to eat their bread by the sweat of their brow in adult life. But one can never quench the thirst in one's soul: the longing for the waters, as well as the flowers and the fruits of Eden, the smells and the sounds of Paradise. Some people *will* indeed reach Eden by the grace of God—others will never reach it because of their own stubbornness. For some, the cherubim at the entrance of Eden become friends and companions—for others, the flaming swords of these cherubim will forever remain a hindrance to re-entering Paradise.

1.2 The Sanctuary

As we will see in this book, Eden is not only a Garden but also a Sanctuary, because God honored the place with his presence (Gen. 3:8). And wherever God is, we are on holy ground. Both the tabernacle in Sinai's wilderness and the temple at Jerusalem were copies—or more modestly, glimpses, shadows—of Eden in many details, as we will see (chapter 3). Just as God dwelt in Eden, he dwelt in the tabernacle and the temple, where people could have fellowship with him. Protestantism has highly spiritualized these things—and, to my mind, in many respects rightly so—but Roman Catholicism has endeavored to remain much closer to the paradisal earthly splendor of the Jerusalem temple.

My friend Hendrik Willem Heuvel, though a Protestant, felt this every time he entered a Catholic church building: ". . . that colorful altar over there, where, through painted windows, the golden sunlight in such a movingly beautiful way extols all those holy things." And elsewhere, about another Catholic church building: ". . . in that dim, colorful sanctuary, with the silent statues and the flickering little lights before the high altar, there is something wondrously mysterious, which attracts me." But also certain high church traditions within Protestantism desire their church services to be a foretaste of the Paradise to come, of Eden restored, the divine Sanctuary of the future. They do so through beautiful garments, splendid church buildings, magnificent music and singing, as I experienced, for instance, in St. Paul's Cathedral (London, UK) or in the Washington National Cathedral. Other Protestant movements may have preferred to spiritualize these things, but as a matter of principle they reach out for the same Eden to come.

This is what this book is about: Paradise lost, Paradise regained, to use the terms of English poet John Milton (d. 1674). A Sanctuary lost, that is, a place where God dwelt with people, and where they had fellowship with him, and ultimately, thank God, also a Sanctuary regained: "The One on the Throne will pitch his tent [or, tabernacle][4] there for them: no more hunger, no more thirst, no more scorching heat. The Lamb on the Throne will shepherd them, will lead them to spring waters of Life. And God will wipe every last tear from their eyes" (Rev. 7:15–17 MSG). Or again about this tent (or tabernacle): "Behold, the tabernacle [or, tent] of God [is] with men, and he shall tabernacle with them, and they shall be his people, and God himself shall be with them, their God" (21:3 DARBY).

---

4   The English word "tabernacle" comes from Latin *tabernaculum*, "tent," the term used in the Vulgate. The Hebrew term is *mishkan*, "dwelling-place" (from *sh-k-n*, "to dwell"). The Greek term is *skēnē*, "tent."

We have an agglomerate of notions here: Garden, Paradise, Sanctuary, tabernacle, temple, but also the Promised Land, parts of which called to mind the "garden of the Lord" (Gen. 13:10); or the holy mountain (Zion), which one day will be like Eden: "The wolf and the lamb shall graze together; the lion shall eat straw like the ox, and dust shall be the serpent's food. They shall not hurt or destroy in all my holy mountain" (Isa. 65:25; cf. also the link between "Eden" and the "holy mountain" in Ezek. 28:13–14). Even heaven, the celestial part of God's creation (Gen. 1:1), will share in the Eden to come: God "stretches out the heavens like a curtain, and spreads them like a tent [tabernacle] to dwell in" (40:22).

Eden is a central theme in the Bible, from the first to the last page. There is an Eden at the beginning: "And the Lord God planted a garden in Eden, in the east, and there he put the man whom he had formed. And out of the ground the Lord God made to spring up every tree that is pleasant to the sight and good for food. The tree of life was in the midst of the garden" (Gen. 2:8–9). There is also an Eden at the end of the Bible: "To the one who conquers I will grant to eat of the tree of life, which is in the paradise of God" (Rev. 2:7), and:

> Then the angel showed me the river of the water of life, bright as crystal, flowing from the throne of God and of the Lamb through the middle of the street of the city; also, on either side of the river, the tree of life with its twelve kinds of fruit, yielding its fruit each month. The leaves of the tree were for the healing of the nations. No longer will there be anything accursed, but the throne of God and of the Lamb will be in it, and his servants will worship him. They will see his face, and his name will be on their foreheads. And night will be no more. They will need no light of lamp or sun, for the Lord God will be their light, and they will reign forever and ever (22:1–5).

This book is about how humanity lost Eden, but also how the ideal of Eden was perpetuated throughout the ages in the hearts of God's people: after Noah's Flood, in the Promised Land as such, in the tabernacle and the temple, in the person of Jesus Christ, in the church (seen through God's eyes), in the Johannine notion of eternal life, in the Messianic kingdom, and in the new heavens and the new earth. The first humans were rightly driven away from the first Eden. But from the outset, God had a better Eden in view for them. Humanity is on its way to that better Eden, in which it shares through repentance and faith. And in the meantime, we sometimes catch glimpses of it—like young Heuvel in the paradise of his youth, and like all of us do, if we are just open for it. This is because we all have not only our Marahs, but also our Elims along the way (Exod. 15:22–27), as we are travelling to the new heavens and the new earth.

1.3 Pardēs, Paradeisos

It may seem rather dull to enter now into a bit of linguistics. However, we cannot avoid looking at some crucial terms. First, the term "paradise." It comes from the assumed Proto-Iranian term *paridayjah*, which referred to a luxury garden owned by Persian nobility. In Hebrew, the derived term became *pardēs*. In the Old Testament, it occurs three times: "... Asaph, keeper of the royal park [*pardēs*]" (Neh. 2:8 NIV). Solomon says, "I made myself gardens [*gannot*] and parks [*pardēsim*], and planted in them all kinds of fruit trees" (Eccl. 2:5). The young man in Solomon's Song tells his beloved:

> "My sister, my bride, you are a locked garden [*gan*]—a locked garden [*gan*] and a sealed spring. Your branches are a paradise [*pardēs*] of pomegranates with choicest fruits, henna with nard—nard and saffron, calamus and cinnamon, with all the trees of frankincense, myrrh and aloes, with all the best spices. You are a garden [*gannim*[5]] spring, a well of flowing water streaming from Lebanon" (Song 4:12–15 HCSB).

I have given this latter quotation in full because it gives us such a beautiful idea of a pleasure garden; we will come back to it later (e.g., in §4.6).

None of these three passages is a reference to the real biblical Eden; the first two speak of literal parks or orchards, and the third one refers to a figurative park. But at least they give us the essential

---

5 Hebrew *gan* has two plurals: *gannot* (Eccl. 2:5) and *gannim* (Song 4:15).

features of a paradise, especially the third quotation.

> (a) It is an enclosed place, a locked garden,[6] not accessible to intruders (who would dare to tread the royal park without the king's permission?), and thus a place of rest and enjoyment.
> (b) It is characterized by springs and wells, by flowing rivers, like the four rivers in the Garden of Eden (Gen. 2:10–14), and the river of the water of life in the New Jerusalem (Rev. 22:1). They serve to quench people's thirst and give them refreshment.
> (c) It is a place full of trees that produce fruits, which taste good and are good for people's health (cf. Gen. 2:9).
> (d) It is a place full of fragrant plants, which spread the most wonderful odors.

I add two obvious features, which do not follow directly from the three passages mentioned:

> (e) Paradise is a landscape that is a splendid sight to behold, a piece of pure art.
> (f) Paradise is a place of music, which we will later derive from Ezekiel 28:13, which speaks (in one interpretation) of "timbrels and pipes" (see §2.3).

Notice how in this way all the senses are involved with "paradise": seeing, hearing, smelling, and tasting, and not least of all: feeling—the refreshing waters over one's body, the fruits in the hand and the bite in the mouth, the moss and the grass to lie down upon, the flowers to be picked. The more literally one tries to imagine such a material paradise, the easier it will be to grasp the spiritual meanings. No one will properly understand spiritual seeing, hearing, smelling, tasting, and feeling who has never properly seen with their eyes, heard with their ears, smelled with their nose, tasted with their tongue, and felt with their hands. Like the prophet says, "On this mountain the Lord of hosts will make for all peoples a feast of rich food, a feast of well-aged wine, of rich food full of marrow, of aged wine well refined" (Isa.

---

6   The word *gan*, "garden," itself comes from the root *g-n-n*, "to cover, surround, defend."

25:6).

In Jewish apocalyptic writings, and later in the Talmud, *pardēs* became the term for the Garden of Eden. In the Septuagint, the Greek *paradeisos* (derived from *pardēs*) rendered the Hebrew *gan*, "garden," in Genesis 2 and 3, referring to the Garden of Eden. The Latin Vulgate used *paradisus* in Genesis 2 and 3, and from there, the term was adopted in all Western languages.[7] In summary, "paradise" is a term for any park, orchard, or pleasure garden, and especially for the Garden of Eden, both in the original literal meaning and the later figurative meanings. In the Old Testament, the literal meaning is found in Genesis 2 and 3, and the figurative meaning (the celestial Garden of Eden) is found in Ezekiel 28:13, which speaks of the angelic prince of Tyre:

> You were in Eden, the garden of God; every precious stone was your covering, sardius, topaz, and diamond, beryl, onyx, and jasper, sapphire, emerald, and carbuncle; and crafted in gold were your settings and your engravings. On the day that you were created they were prepared. You were an anointed guardian cherub. I placed you; you were on the holy mountain of God; in the midst of the stones of fire you walked.[8]

Later, we will come back to the details of this fascinating passage (§§2.1 and 2.2).

In the New Testament, the Greek word *paradeisos* occurs three times, just like *pardēs* in the Old Testament. Jesus said to the criminal on the cross: "Truly, I say to you, today you will be with me in paradise" (Luke 23:43). The apostle Paul says,

> I know a man in Christ [Paul is referring to himself] who fourteen years ago was caught up to the third heaven—whether in the body or out of the body I do not know, God knows. And I know that this man was caught up into paradise—whether in the body or out of the body I do not know, God knows—and he heard things that cannot be told, which man may not utter (2 Cor. 12:2–4).

---

7   *Paradise, paradis, paradijs, paradiso, paraíso,* and so on.
8   For an extensive exegesis of this passage, see Ouweneel (2019).

Jesus says to the overcomer in Ephesus: "To the one who conquers I will grant to eat of the tree of life, which is in the paradise of God" (Rev. 2:7).

None of these three passages is easy to understand. The latter one is the least difficult because Jesus is obviously referring to the heavenly Garden of Eden to come in the eternal state, as in Revelation 22:1–2. In Luke 23, Jesus seems to refer to the intermediate state of the believer (the period between physical death and resurrection), but this would be quite unusual (see chapter 7). And in the middle passage, the only help we receive is that "paradise" here might be related to the "third heaven," whatever this may be. All these matters will have to be discussed later.

1.4 Eden

The meaning of "Eden" (Heb. *eden*) that is commonly given is "delight." The Septuagint renders it as *tryphē*, which means "luxury, splendor." The word *eden* is derived from a general Semitic root '-d-n, with connotations such as tenderness and softness, but also verdure, greenery. Eden represents the delight that humans may enjoy between the magnificent verdure of trees of all kinds: trees of beauty, trees of sweet fruits, trees of sweet smell. As we saw, the primary idea of "paradise" is an orchard of splendid trees.

Already the Eden of Genesis 2 is, besides waters, primarily a place of trees:

> And the LORD God planted a garden in Eden, in the east, and there he put the man whom he had formed. And out of the ground the LORD God made to spring up every tree that is pleasant to the sight and good for food. The tree of life was in the midst of the garden, and the tree of the knowledge of good and evil. A river flowed out of Eden to water the garden, and there it divided and became four rivers (vv. 8–10).[9]

The prophet Ezekiel speaks repeatedly of Eden (chapters 28, 31, and 36). The "trees of Eden" have his special attention:

---

9 For the biblical idea of a "garden" as an idealistic place of delight, see Berg (1988).

The cedars in the garden of God could not rival it [= the cedar[10]], nor the fir trees equal its boughs; neither were the plane trees like its branches; no tree in the garden of God was its equal in beauty. I made it beautiful in the mass of its branches, and all the trees of Eden envied it, that were in the garden of God. . . . On the day the cedar went down to Sheol I caused mourning; I closed the deep over it, and restrained its rivers, and many waters were stopped. I clothed Lebanon in gloom for it, and all the trees of the field fainted because of it. I made the nations quake at the sound of its fall, when I cast it down to Sheol with those who go down to the pit. And all the trees of Eden, the choice and best of Lebanon, all that drink water, were comforted in the world below. They also went down to Sheol with it, to those who are slain by the sword; yes, those who were its arm, who lived under its shadow among the nations. "Whom are you thus like in glory and in greatness among the trees of Eden? You shall be brought down with the trees of Eden to the world below. You shall lie among the uncircumcised, with those who are slain by the sword" (Ezek. 31:8-9, 15-18).

This special emphasis on the "tree" reminds us of that other "tree": "Christ redeemed us from the curse of the law by becoming a curse for us—for it is written, 'Cursed is everyone who is hanged on a tree'" (Gal. 3:13). "He himself bore our sins in his body on the tree, that we might die to sin and live to righteousness. By his wounds you have been healed" (1 Pet. 2:24; see also Acts 5:30; 10:39; 13:29).

Not only did Jesus die on a tree, but his cross was very nearby a garden, like a new Eden: "Now in the place where he was crucified there was a garden, and in the garden a new tomb in which no one had yet been laid" (John 19:41; see chapter 5). The history of Eden begins with two trees in a garden, and halfway through Scripture, we find another "tree" in a literal garden. The garden where Adam and Eve died spiritually (cf. Gen. 2:17) formed the counterpart of that other garden, the new Eden, where the "last Adam" (1 Cor. 15:45) died *and arose*. The first encounter of the risen Christ was with Mary Magdalene in that very garden: "Jesus said to her, 'Woman, why are

---

10 The cedar refers either to Assyria or to Egypt; see the Appendix.

you weeping? Whom are you seeking?' Supposing him to be the *gardener*, she said to him, 'Sir, if you have carried him away, tell me where you have laid him, and I will take him away'" (John 20:15). Here the term "gardener" represents much more than just a simple mistake by Mary: Jesus was the *Master* of Eden, just as he was the Master of this new garden. The "delight" of Eden was lost by Adam's fall; the new Eden means new delight, even much better delight than Adam ever lost.

In addition to old and new Eden, there are various other Edens, especially this one: the Messianic kingdom. The first Adam, together with his wife, was called to rule the earth (Gen. 1:26, 28), but he lost this rule through his fall. The last Adam will rule in the Messianic kingdom, and again the trees will be prominent: ". . . the Spirit is poured upon us from on high, and the wilderness becomes a fruitful field, and the fruitful field is deemed a forest" (Isa. 32:15). "I will put in the wilderness the cedar, the acacia, the myrtle, and the olive. I will set in the desert the cypress, the plane and the pine together" (41:19). Even old Eden is brought back to memory: "[T]he LORD comforts Zion; he comforts all her waste places and makes her wilderness like Eden, her desert like the garden of the LORD; joy and gladness will be found in her, thanksgiving and the voice of song" (51:3). See also 55:13, "Instead of the thorn shall come up the cypress; and it shall make a name for the LORD, an everlasting sign that shall not be cut off."

Actually, as we will see, there are still more Edens than these three in redemptive history. As I said, the tabernacle (with its beautiful "almond tree," Exod. 25:33–34) and the temple (with its palm trees, 1 Kings 6:29, 32, 35; 7:36) were copies of Eden. Also the Promised Land was, and is, a reminiscence of Eden: "And Lot lifted up his eyes and saw that the Jordan Valley was well watered everywhere like the *garden of the* LORD, like the land of Egypt, in the direction of Zoar" (Gen. 13:10). And last but not least, there is the restored Eden in the new heavens and the new earth, in which the tree of life will be prominent (Rev. 2:7; 22:1–2).

1.5 *Qodesh, Hagios*
In the biblical sense, every "paradise" is a sanctuary because, first, God dwells there; second, it is accessible only to the initiated (it is

"set apart," "separated" from the profane[11]); and third, everything in there is dedicated, consecrated to God. This is the very sense of the Hebrew *qodesh* and the Greek *hagios*, "holy, sacred." Where God dwells we are dealing with "holy ground" (Exod. 3:5; cf. Deut. 33:16). When God spoke to Adam, both before and after the Fall, Adam was on holy ground (Gen. 2:16–17; 3:9–19). When God "walked" in the Garden (Gen. 3:8), the same expression is used as in Leviticus 26:11–12, "I will make my *dwelling* [Heb. *mishkan*[12]] among you, and my soul shall not abhor you. And I will *walk* among you and will be your God, and you shall be my people." This is God's promise if Israel would keep his Torah: he would "dwell" (*sh-k-n*) among them and "walk" (*h-l-kh*) among them. The two verbs belong together, and thus Eden was God's first sanctuary on this earth: a house where he "dwelt," and a garden in which he "walked."

We can go one step further. I quoted Isaiah 40:22, which says that God "stretches out the heavens like a curtain, and spreads them like a tent [tabernacle] to dwell in" (40:22). We may take this to mean that, according to God's plan, the entire "heaven and earth," created in Genesis 1:1, that is, the entire cosmic universe, should become the "tent (tabernacle)" in which God could dwell. The Garden of Eden was only the prototype, the show model, the pattern for the Garden to come, which will encompass the entire new heaven and new earth.

God had commanded the first humans to fill the *earth* and subdue it (Gen. 1:28). After the planting of Eden he seemed to limit the command: "The LORD God took the man and put him in the garden of Eden to work it and keep it" (Gen. 2:15). Many have taken this to mean that humanity was supposed to win the entire earth as a sanctuary for God, starting from Eden. After the Fall, however, the command was widened again but in a very different sense: "[T]he LORD God sent him out from the garden of Eden to work the *ground* [the soil of the earth] from which he was taken" (3:23)—but now he could only do so with great pain and trouble (vv. 17–19). Man began to work the *earth*, but it was no longer a place where God could dwell; it was a

---

11 Cf. the "wall ... to make a separation between the holy and the common" in the new temple of Ezekiel (42:20).

12 This is also the word for "tabernacle," a word that literally means "tent" (see note 4), whereas the literal meaning of *mishkan* is "dwelling."

place estranged from God. Man began to work the earth, not as an extension of Eden but in separation from it. It took quite some time before we hear in the Bible about new places where God could find a habitation, namely, among a people redeemed from slavery.

1.6 Beginnings

Where does the history of Eden begin? One might suppose that it begins in Genesis 2—but this is not the answer of the rabbis. The Talmud says,

> Seven things were created before the world was created, and these are they: The Torah [i.e., the Mosaic Law], repentance, the Garden of Eden, Gehenna [i.e., hell], the Throne of Glory, the Temple, and the name of the Messiah. . . . The Garden of Eden, as it is written, "And the Lord God planted a garden in Eden from aforetime."[13]

Such a tradition, not preserved in the Mishnah, is called a *baraitha*, and this one is particularly well-known in rabbinical Judaism. The underlying idea is that certain things "are indispensable pre-requisites for the orderly progress of mankind upon earth."[14] I sum them up in four groups, together with the Bible verses on which their pre-existence is based.

(a) and (b) The *Torah* ("the beginning of his way," Prov. 8:22 CJB[15]) is God's supreme guideline for humanity, and *repentance* ("Before . . . you had formed the earth . . . you say, 'Return, O children of man!'," Ps. 90:2–3) is needed whenever the Torah has been trespassed.

(c) and (d) The *Garden of Eden* ("planted . . . from the beginning," Gen. 2:8 DRA) and *Gehenna* ("ordained of old," Isa. 30:33 KJV[16]) are mentioned together as representing the two options for humanity's eternal destination: eternal bliss or eternal perdition.

---

13 Bab. Talmud: Pesahim 54a (Soncino-ed., 265); see also Nedarim 39b (Soncino-ed., 124).
14 See Pesahim 54a (Soncino-ed., 265), footnote.
15 The text refers to "Wisdom," but the rabbis equated the two: the Torah is God's eternal wisdom.
16 The text speaks of *Topheth* (see the esv textual note), a "burning place," though to be a reference to the eternal fire of God's judgment.

(e) and (f) The *Throne of Glory* ("established from the beginning," Ps. 93:2 CSB) and the *Temple* ("A glorious throne set on high from the beginning is the place of our sanctuary," Jer. 17:12) indicate that the final goal of creation is the kingdom of God.

(g) The *Messiah* ("whose coming forth is from of old," Micah 5:2) will be the Ruler in the future kingdom God, which is therefore called the Messianic kingdom.

Crucial to this line of thinking is the meaning of *miqqedem* ("[from] of old"), which we find in several of the verses quoted. The term may refer back to a historical past (Ps. 74:12; 77:5, 11; 143:5; Isa. 45:21; 46:10; Hab. 1:12). But *qedem* definitely *can* mean "eternity," as in the expression "the eternal God" (Deut. 33:27, Heb. *Elohey qedem*). Certainly in Proverbs 8:23 the expression refers to the eternity preceding creation. And if one prefers expressions such as "ancient" or "of old," we may say that the Messiah mentioned in Micah 5:2 dates from ancient times, *long before creation existed*, and that perhaps the same may be assumed for the other six things summed up in the *baraitha* we mentioned. At least, the thought is attractive that, before God created the Garden of Eden, he already had in his mind that other, more glorious, celestial Eden toward which redemptive history is moving throughout the centuries.

The idea of certain matters existing, beside God, already before, or from, the foundation of the world is not foreign to the New Testament. Apart from the pre-existence of Christ ("[Father,] you loved me before the foundation of the world," John 17:24), we think of the eternal election and predestination of believers "before the foundation of the world" (e.g., Eph. 1:3–5). The KJV, and others in its wake, render Revelation 13:8 as follows: "... the Lamb slain from the foundation of the world." That is, in God's eternal, anticipatory counsel the atonement was a fact from eternity; in the "scroll" it was written about him (Ps. 40:7; Heb. 10:7). In the very quality of *Lamb*, Christ "was foreknown before the foundation of the world" (1 Pet. 1:19–20). "If the serpent bites before it is charmed, there is no advantage to the charmer" (Eccl. 10:11). When the serpent "bit" in paradise, the "charming" had already occurred in God's eternal counsel, and thus was as real as when it occurred on earth within the course of time.

To me, such thoughts seem to be basically the same as those of the rabbis, who believed that certain things must have been well-established in the mind of God before the world was created. The LORD thought of the Garden of Eden even before any trees and rivers had been created at all. He thought of the ultimate Paradise, and even took all precautions in case humanity would fall into sin and would have to be driven from the first Eden. What God had in mind *before* the world began, will be definitely realized by the time world history has reached its *consummation*. He is the God "declaring the end from the beginning and from ancient times things not yet done, saying, 'My counsel shall stand, and I will accomplish all my purpose'" (Isa. 46:10). God "declares" the ultimate Eden from the first Eden.

Traces of the *baraitha* we mentioned are also found in various Jewish works apart from the Bible and the Talmud. Thus, the Midrash Tehillim (a homiletic-typological Jewish exegetical book on the Psalms), commenting on Psalm 31:19 ("Oh, how abundant is your goodness [or, your good (treasure)], which you have stored up for those who fear you"), thinks here of Paradise with all the treasures of reward for the righteous, and such "from the beginning": "that which was prepared beforehand here from the time when I took counsel to make Paradise."[17]

From before the foundation of the (physical) world are also the seven archangels, known from rabbinic tradition (perhaps referred to in Rev. 8:2, "the seven angels who stand before God"). Only two of these archangels are known in the Bible: the archangel Michael (Dan. 10:13, 21; 12:1; Jude 9; Rev. 12:7) and the angel Gabriel (never called an archangel; Dan. 8:16; 9:20–21; Luke 1:19, 26). According to an ancient Jewish tradition, each of the seven angels is placed over a certain domain of cosmic reality. Ethiopic Enoch (20:5, 7) tells us that Michael "is set over the best part of mankind [i.e., Israel[18]] and over chaos" (a strange combination), while Gabriel is set "over Paradise and the serpents and the cherubim."[19] The serpents and cherubim are added possibly because they occur in Genesis 3 (vv. 1–4, 13–14, 24).

---

17 Apocalypse of Baruch 4:3; see http://www.pseudepigrapha.com/pseudepigrapha/2Baruch.html.

18 In Dan. 10:21 Michael is referred to as the angelic "prince" of Israel, contrasted with the angelic "princes" of Persia and Greece (vv. 13, 20).

19 http://read.thebookofenoch.info/tboe.pdf.

If there is any truth in this ancient tradition, we may be impressed to know that it was Gabriel, the one supposedly set over Paradise, who received the divine order to announce the births of John the Baptist and of Jesus (Luke 1:19, 26), the latter being the Messiah who was going to restore Paradise to humanity. As Jesus says in the same Gospel: "Blessed are those servants whom the master finds awake when he comes. Truly, I say to you, he will dress himself for service and have them recline at table, and he will come and serve them" (12:37; see the next section).

1.7 Dining

This is where our story begins: at "the beginning." Not the beginning of Genesis 1:1 (the beginning of creation), but the beginning of John 1:1, where—whatever "beginning" in the past we may think of—the Word (Logos) *was*, and the Word was with God, and the Word was God. Literally, it says that the Word was "turned toward" God,[20] that is, not only existing next to him but accompanying him, in personal fellowship with him. This notion is strengthened in verse 18, where "the only and one Son, who himself is God" (CSB, NIV), is seen in the "lap, bosom" (Gk. *kolpos*) of the Father. This reminds us of Jesus' disciple who was reclining at table on the "bosom" of Jesus (John 13:23). The parallel is striking,[21] and certainly suggests that John 1:18, too, wishes to evoke the picture of persons reclining at table, and dining together, one person being the honorable guest of the other one (lying on his "bosom").

This is remarkable. One of the first things we hear about God is about the Father and the Son reclining at table. Redemptive history begins with a (figurative) dinner! If Paradise was indeed in God's heart and mind already before the foundation of the world, does it go too far to suggest that behind John 1:18 lies this pre-creational Paradise? The very least we can say is that the place at the bosom of the Father was a place of glory, and of love, the eternal glory and love that the Son enjoyed with the Father before the foundation of the world (John 17:5, 24)—a place of delight (Eden!). Do we not see in

---

20 It is the preposition *pros* plus the accusative.
21 In spite of the different prepositions: *eis ton kolpon* and *en tōi kolpōi*, respectively; see Morris (1971, 114n118).

the eternal Wisdom of Proverbs 8 none other than the pre-incarnate Christ whom we hear say: ". . . then I was beside him [i.e., God], like a master workman [or, a nursling], and I was daily his delight [Heb. *sha'ashu'im*], rejoicing before him always" (v. 30)?

The very first thing that God tells Adam about Eden refers to eating: "You may surely eat of every tree of the garden" (Gen. 2:16). The last thing the Bible tells us is about eating: ". . . on either side of the river, [there was] the tree of life with its twelve kinds of fruit, yielding its fruit each month. . . . Blessed are those who wash their robes, so that they may have the right to the tree of life . . . [I]f anyone takes away from the words of the book of this prophecy, God will take away his share in the tree of life" (Rev. 22:2, 14, 19). And a little earlier: "To the one who conquers I will grant to eat of the tree of life, which is in the paradise of God" (2:7). Jesus himself said of his faithful followers: "Truly, I say to you, he [i.e., the Master himself] will dress himself for service and have them recline at table, and he will come and serve them" (Luke 12:37). "[P]eople will come from east and west, and from north and south, and recline at table in the kingdom of God" (13:29; cf. Matt. 8:11). "I assign to you, as my Father assigned to me, a kingdom, that you may eat and drink at my table in my kingdom" (22:29–30). "On this mountain the LORD of hosts will make for all peoples a feast of rich food" (Isa. 25:6). "I tell you I will not drink again of this fruit of the vine until that day when I drink it new with you in my Father's kingdom" (Matt. 26:29).

Of course, this is all figurative language—yet obviously referring to real matters. There was a real heavenly supper before the foundation of the world. There will be a real heavenly supper after the consummation of the world. Between these two, Christians enjoy the Lord's Supper—a little meal reminiscent of those great dinners at the beginning and the end of redemptive history. Every time we celebrate it, our thoughts may move back to Jesus hanging on the tree ("For as often as you eat this bread and drink the cup, you proclaim the Lord's death *until he comes*," 1 Cor. 11:26). But our thoughts may also move to the lost tree of life in Eden, and to the regained tree of life in the world to come.

1.8 Ultimate Enjoyment

Let me finish this first chapter with four quotations from the book of Ecclesiastes, which describe eating and drinking as the symbol of utter enjoyment and ultimate bliss, and thus offers us an implicit description of the delights of Eden. I also add the matrimonial blessings, as the New Jerusalem is explicitly called the bride of the Lamb (Rev. 21:9–10).

"There is nothing better for a person than that he should eat and drink and find enjoyment in his toil. This also, I saw, is from the hand of God, for apart from him who can eat or who can have enjoyment?" (2:24–25).

"I perceived that there is nothing better for [people] than to be joyful and to do good as long as they live; also that everyone should eat and drink and take pleasure in all his toil—this is God's gift to man" (3:12–13).

> "Behold, what I have seen to be good and fitting is to eat and drink and find enjoyment in all the toil with which one toils under the sun the few days of his life that God has given him, for this is his lot. Everyone also to whom God has given wealth and possessions and power to enjoy them, and to accept his lot and rejoice in his toil—this is the gift of God. For he will not much remember the days of his life because God keeps him occupied with joy in his heart" (5:18–20).

"I commend joy, for man has nothing better under the sun but to eat and drink and be joyful, for this will go with him in his toil through the days of his life that God has given him under the sun" (8:15).

"Enjoy life with the wife whom you love, all the days of your vain life that he has given you under the sun, because that is your portion in life and in your toil at which you toil under the sun" (9:9; cf. Prov. 5:18–19).

These are simple descriptions of a good life: a good marriage, good food and drink—for what more does a person wish? We might even be amazed to find them in Holy Scripture. But in thinking this way, we are forgetting that these basic blessings are reminiscences of the Garden of Eden, as well as of the ultimate Eden of God. When it comes to the meaning of "Eden," *Delight*, we could hardly think of more basic delights in our daily lives than good marital life and good eating and drinking.

In summary, I conclude that the basic Edenic delights are expressed especially in these five metaphors:

(a) A *garden* (§1.1).
(b) A *sanctuary* (§1.2).
(c) *Eating* and *drinking* (see, e.g., §§1.7 and 4.6–4.8).
(d) *Marital life*, hence the frequent bridal metaphor (see, e.g., §§1.3, 5.8, 8.3, and 8.7).
(e) *Music* (see §2.3).

1.9 Our Daily Meals

If eating and drinking belong to the most specific metaphors of the delights of Eden, I must add here something about our daily meals. The apostle Paul prophesied

> that in later times some will depart from the faith by devoting themselves to deceitful spirits and teachings of demons, through the insincerity of liars whose consciences are seared, who forbid marriage and require abstinence from foods that God created to be received with thanksgiving by those who believe and know the truth. For everything created by God is good, and nothing is to be rejected if it is received with thanksgiving, for it is made holy by the word of God and prayer (1 Tim. 4:1–5).

Forbidding marriage (that is, forbidding sexuality) as well as the use of (certain) foods is a demonic trick of robbing God's people of some of the greatest foretastes of Eden. Marriage and meals are gifts of God, "to be received with thanksgiving," for they are "made holy (or hallowed, sanctified) by the word of God and prayer."

Why do we actually pray before our meals? We do not have a direct divine commandment in the Bible to do so, but we do have the example of the Lord Jesus himself. At the institution of the Lord's Supper, he "gave thanks" (Luke 22:17, 19). He did not "bless" the bread (in spite of the wrong rendering of Matt. 26:26 in many translations), but he spoke a "blessing," that is, he praised God. The "cup of blessing" (1 Cor. 10:16) is not a cup *that* we bless, but a cup *for which* we "bless" (praise) God. No celebration of the Lord's Supper is conceivable without blessing (praising, honoring, worshiping) God. This is self-evident. But the interesting thing is that, at common meals, Jesus did the very same thing: "... Then he ordered the crowds to sit down on the grass, and taking the five loaves and the two fish, he looked up to heaven and said a blessing" (Matt. 14:19), that is, he thanked and praised God. And of Jesus' stay in Emmaus we read: "When he was at table with them, he took the bread and blessed and broke it and gave it to them" (Luke 24:30).

Both at the Lord's Supper and at common meals Jesus did this one thing: he thanked and praised God. Properly speaking, we do not pray, "Bless this food," but: "Blessed are you, Lord," as the Jews still do before every meal: *Baruch attah, Adonai Eloheinu, melech ha'olam, hamotzi lechem min ha'aretz*, "Praised are you, Lord, our God, King of the world, who causes bread to come forth from the earth."

This correspondence between the Lord's Supper and common meals does not belittle the Lord's Supper; on the contrary, it rather elevates our common meals. To return to 1 Timothy 4, our daily food is sanctified by the Word of God and prayer. Or, to put it this way, by God's Word and our prayer of praise, each meal becomes an Edenic event, a foretaste of the everlasting Edenic bliss. Through praising God before our meal, we invite him, as it were, to join us during this moment of Edenic fellowship.

If I am not mistaken, during Israel's wilderness journey *each* Israelite meal that included meat had to have the character of a sacrificial meal. That is to say, the cow, sheep, goat, or fowl that was to be eaten had to be brought to the tabernacle first, to be sacrificed by the priest as a so-called peace offering (Lev. 3 and 7). The fat of the animal was offered upon the altar of burnt offering, as "food" (Lev. 3:11, 16; Heb. *lechem*, lit. "bread") for the LORD himself. The breast and the thigh of cow, sheep, or goat was for the priest (7:30–34), and the rest of the meat was for the offerer and his family. Thus, in every meal, the LORD himself took part, as well as the priests, as well as the offerer and his family. Each meal was a *holy* event because of this sacrificial character. After Israel had arrived in the Promised Land, this rule could no longer be maintained because most of the people lived too far away from the sanctuary. But in the wilderness, what a precious thing this was! A person offered their animal to the Lord, and the Lord gave back most of it to the offerer. The offerer and family ate their steaks, their chops, their cutlets, their prime rib, their veal, and their mutton, as a gift of the Lord. They ate from him, before him, with him—and they rejoiced in him.

This is what we do still today. Take your time as a family for breakfast, lunch, and dinner, to eat together praising God, enjoying not only your food and drink but also each other's company, socializing, sharing, chatting, laughing together, talking with and listening to each other. The Dutch have an adjective for this, *gezellig* (noun: *gezelligheid*), which is unique in the world. It can be expressed only vaguely in English terms such as "cozy, snug, comfortable ('comfy'), intimate, warm." *Gezelligheid* is the most Edenic word in the Dutch language!

It often amazed me that the following ordinary request is found in such a lofty prayer as the Lord's Prayer: "Give us this day our daily bread" (Matt. 6:11), until I realized that this request ties in with the petition, "Your kingdom come" (v. 10). It is as the man who said to Jesus, "Blessed is everyone who will eat bread in the kingdom of God!" (Luke 14:15). Eat your daily bread (and your vegetables, and your meat, your milk, and your honey) with thanksgiving and praise, and think of God's kingdom to come!

2
The First Three Edens

... You were in Eden, the garden of God ...
On the day that you were created they were prepared.
You were an anointed guardian cherub. I placed you;
you were on the holy mountain of God [or, of the gods]. ...
Ezekiel 28:13–14

2.1 The King's Garden

No monarchy in the world could imagine a royal palace without a magnificent garden around it, or behind it. I grew up in the city of Apeldoorn (Netherlands), where we as children sang to the elderly Queen Wilhelmina. Actually, since her abdication in 1948 she was not the Queen anymore, but just "Princess" Wilhelmina. We sang to her on her birthday (August 31). I still see her sitting in front of the palace, in a chair, a small lady covered with fur. What was behind the palace we could only guess—but we knew it had to be beautiful. At a later stage, I once had the privilege of visiting that magnificent royal park.

Long afterward, my wife and I lived with our young family near another royal palace, near the town of Soestdijk (in the province of Utrecht). Wilhelmina's daughter, Queen Juliana, lived here with her family. Every time we drove by, we watched the flagpole: if the flag was raised, we knew that the Queen was at home. Again, we saw only the front of the palace, and we could only guess what was behind it: another magnificent royal park. It was only many years later, after Juliana had passed away (2004), that the public was allowed to see the park in all its splendor. We loved it! And we tried to imagine how the monarch had once walked around there, enjoying the silence and the beauty, coming to inner rest and harmony.

There are no royal palaces without royal parks (and, to be sure, no presidential palaces without presidential parks). In the Bible it is the same. The Old Testament speaks several times of a "king's garden" (2 Kings 25:4; Neh. 3:15; Jer. 39:4; 52:7), a park in which the king could walk, relax, and repose. The book of Esther tells us about the "garden of the king's palace" (1:5), or the "palace garden" (7:7–8). Some kings loved to be buried there in their garden, like king Manasseh, who "was buried in the garden of his house, in the garden of [king] Uzza" (2 Kings 21:18). He was succeeded by his son Amon, who after his death was buried in the same "garden of Uzza" (v. 26). Unfortunately, we do not know anything else about this garden, or about this Uzza. But I imagine that it must have been wonderful.

If God's earthly creation is a reflection and counterpart of the celestial world, we could not imagine God's celestial palace[1] without a celestial garden. Indeed, the Old Testament tells us about such a celestial Eden, as we will see in the next section.

2.2 A Celestial Eden

One of the most remarkable passages about Eden in the Old Testament is the one in Ezekiel 28, where God says to the one who, in my view, is none other than the angelic prince of Tyre:

> You were the signet of perfection, full of wisdom and perfect in beauty. You were in Eden, the garden of God; every precious stone was your covering, sardius, topaz, and diamond, beryl, onyx, and jasper, sapphire, emerald, and carbuncle; and crafted in gold were your settings and your engravings. On the day that you were created they were prepared. You were an anointed guardian cherub. I placed you; you were on the holy mountain of God [or, of the gods]; in the midst of the stones of fire you walked. You were blameless in your ways from the day you were created, till un-

---

[1] Interestingly, the Hebrew word *hekal* can mean both "palace" and "temple"; translators must always choose which rendering fits the context best.

righteousness was found in you. In the abundance of your trade you were filled with violence in your midst, and you sinned; so I cast you as a profane thing from the mountain of God [or, of the gods], and I destroyed you, O guardian cherub, from the midst of the stones of fire. Your heart was proud because of your beauty; you corrupted your wisdom for the sake of your splendor. I cast you to the ground; I exposed you before kings, to feast their eyes on you, ... (vv. 12–19).

As for the translation "mountain of the gods," the Dutch NBG translation is one of a few translations that have this rendering; some translations place it in a footnote. For this picture of the "mount of the gods," see Psalm 82, especially verse 1: "God has taken his place in the divine council; in the midst of the gods he holds judgment." In the Middle East, the pagans had their own "mountain of the gods," namely, Mount Zaphon.[2] This is an ancient name for Jebel Aqraa ("Bald Mountain"), the highest mountain in Syria, on the Mediterranean coast. It was a holy site of the Canaanites because it was believed to be the mountain where the god Baal dwelt (cf. Baal-zephon in Exod. 14:2), and where he assembled with the other gods; Baal-Zaphon is known to have been worshiped at Tyre. Zaphon seems to be the mountain referred to in Isaiah 14:13 (note ESV: "the mount of assembly in the remote parts of Zaphon[3]"; MSG: "the assembly of angels that meets on sacred Mount Zaphon"; see also the NIV). Psalm 48:2 (EXB note) is very interesting: "Mount Zion is like the high mountains of Zaphon [comparing Yahweh's mountain with the mountain of Baal]; it is the city of the Great King." That is, the pagans may have their holy mountain, where the gods assemble, but God's people have their own holy mountain. It may not be as high and impressive as Mount Zaphon, but the true God of gods dwells there in his holy temple.

Ezekiel 28:14 ("the holy mountain of God/the gods") is either

---

2 Cf. Mount Ida in Asia Minor, Mount Olympus in Greece, and even Mount Brocken in Germany.

3 The Hebrew word *zaphon* also means "north"; some have been suggested that in Psalm 89:12 actually four mountains are intended: Mount Zaphon, Mount ... [of the South], Mount Tabor, and Mount Hermon.

a reference to Mount Zaphon, the mountain of the gods (but could God's celestial Eden be located there?), *or* it is a reference to God's own "mountain," a kind of celestial Zion, in a sense comparable to that of Hebrews 12:22 ("... you have come to Mount Zion, to the city of the living God, the heavenly Jerusalem"). The good angels meet on God's "mountain" (compare 1 Kings 22:19, "I saw the LORD sitting on his throne, and all the host of heaven [i.e., the angels] standing beside him on his right hand and on his left"). Mount Zaphon, or its celestial counterpart in the invisible world, is the meeting place of the "gods," the bad angels, the angelic princes worshiped by the pagan nations. Psalm 82:1 refers to a celestial place where both God and the angelic princes assemble.

This passage cannot be properly understood if we do not have some knowledge of the angelic princes in general.[4] We meet the "princes" (Heb. *sarim*, not humans but angelic figures) of Persia and Greece in Daniel 10:13 and 20, where at the same time the archangel Michael is described as the angelic prince of Israel (v. 21). In Isaiah 14 we meet the angelic prince of Babylon in verses 12-15 (the descriptions of the earthy king of Babylon and that of his angelic prince merge in this chapter). Similarly, I cannot doubt that we meet the angelic prince of Tyre in Ezekiel 28, the invisible power behind the earthly king. To my mind, its angelic character is clear from verse 14 ("an anointed guardian cherub") and verse 16 ("O guardian cherub").

There is a Jewish tradition that Tyre represents the Roman Empire,[5] which would greatly enhance the significance of this lamentation on the "prince" of Tyre. The parallels between Babylon and Rome are even stronger than those between Tyre and Rome;[6] to close this triangle, there are clear parallels between Isaiah 14:12-15 (Babylon) and Ezekiel 28:12-19 (Tyre). First, both princes were on the "mount of assembly," or "the mountain of the gods," that is, the place where the "gods" (angelic princes) meet. Second, both princes were driven by pride, and both princes were cast from heaven, or cast from the

---

4   See extensively, Ouweneel (2019); cf. the extensive commentary by Block (1998, 99–121), which seems to lack any understanding of this aspect of the passage.

5   Pesiqta Rabba 14, 15, on Ezek. 27:27.

6   Ouweneel (2019, Appendix 10).

mountain of the gods. It is no wonder that some church fathers have thought here of the fall of Satan (cf. Luke 10:18; 1 Tim. 3:6). This is not too far off, but it seems more correct to say that the angelic prince of Babylon and the one of Tyre, if they are not identical, are prominent servants of Satan: "angels of Satan" (cf. Matt. 25:41; Rev. 12:7, 9). But I add to this that, in the book of Revelation, Satan himself can indeed be described as the angelic prince behind and beyond the Roman Empire (compare Rev. 12 and 13).

One of the remarkable things is that the celestial habitation of the angelic prince is described as "Eden, the garden of God" (v. 13). In Jewish thought, this celestial Eden is perhaps the strongest foundation for the idea of a celestial Eden as the abode of the righteous in the hereafter. But this is certainly not the meaning in Ezekiel 28. Rather, here "Eden" seems to be another name for "the holy mountain of the gods" (v. 14). Before there were any humans in an earthly Eden there were angels in a celestial Eden, including Lucifer. And the result was the same: certain angels fell into sin, and the first humans did too. Both were driven out of their respective Edens.

The angelic prince is called a *cherub*, a term with an unclear etymology. In the Bible, it is a designation of beings that often seem to be only figurative, like the cherubim on the mercy seat (Exod. 25:18–22) and the cherubim in Ezekiel's vision (Ezek. 10). But in places like Genesis 3:24 and the present passage, we apparently must think of more concrete, angelic personalities. The connection between the latter two passages goes even further: the cherubim of Genesis 3:24 wield their swords to guard the access to the tree of life, while the cherub of Ezekiel 28 is also a guardian cherub. However, the latter cherub does not stand at the entrance of the garden, like those in Genesis 3, but walks around *in* the garden. The function seems to be similar, namely, protecting the garden. But in the former case, the cherubim are more servants, whereas in the latter case, the cherub gives us more the impression of being a royal lord-protector; he is after all the (angelic) "king (or prince) of Tyre" (28:2, 12). This royal impression of the cherub is enhanced by his splendid appearance with many jewels and gold.

2.3 Music

For "settings and engravings" (Ezek. 28:13 ESV), other translations have "tabrets (timbrels, tambourines)" and "pipes." The great expositor Rabbi David Kimchi (d. 1235) indeed defended this rendering. If it is correct,[7] they add an element that could hardly be lacking in any presentation of Paradise. Interestingly, music is not mentioned in connection with the tabernacle, although the tambourines were certainly not lacking in Israel (Exod. 15:20). Even before David introduced the temple music—to be played in the temple yet to be built by his son—we hear about harp, tambourine, flute, lyre, castanets, cymbals, trumpets, horns, and other musical instruments (1 Sam. 10:5; 18:6; 2 Sam. 6:5; 1 Chron. 13:8). If the tabernacle was a copy of Eden, as we will see in the next chapter, the temple was even more so because of the added music.

In Amos 6:5, King David is described as a man who invented "instruments of music." Apparently, it was his initiative to fill the temple that was to be built under his son Solomon with music, dancing, and singing. I like to think that he was the man who composed Psalm 150: "Praise him with trumpet sound ... with lute and harp ... with tambourine and dance ... with strings and pipe[8] ... with sounding cymbals ... with loud clashing cymbals!" When David brought up the ark of the covenant to the "city of David," we hear about the first regular music:

> David also commanded the chiefs of the Levites to appoint their brothers as the singers who should play loudly on musical instruments, on harps and lyres and cymbals, to raise sounds of joy... . The singers ... were to sound bronze cymbals; [others] were to

---

7   The commentaries are very unsure. The Septuagint does not have any musical instruments here; the Vulgate has *foramina*, which might be rendered "pipes"; but in the Nova Vulgata they have disappeared. The KJV (1611) has *tabrets and pipes*, Luther's German translation (1545) has *Pauken und Pfeifen*, Louis Segond's French translation (1880) has *tambourins* and *flutes*, the Dutch States' Translation (1637) has *trommelen en pijpen*.

8   The KJV reads "organs," and the ancient Dutch States Translation does, too—a great encouragement for the early Protestant churches to introduce the organ into their services!

play harps according to Alamoth; but [others again] were to lead with lyres according to the Sheminith.⁹ Chenaniah, leader of the Levites in music, should direct the music, for he understood it. [Others] should blow the trumpets before the ark of God.... So all Israel brought up the ark of the covenant of the LORD with shouting, to the sound of the horn, trumpets, and cymbals, and made loud music on harps and lyres (1 Sam. 15:16–28).

Later we read of a more organized musical playing and singing in view of the still future temple service:

David and the chiefs of the service also set apart for the service the sons of Asaph, and of Heman, and of Jeduthun, who prophesied with lyres, with harps, and with cymbals.... [One group] prophesied under the direction of the king. [A second group] prophesied with the lyre in thanksgiving and praise to the LORD. ... [A third group] were all under the direction of their father in the music in the house of the LORD with cymbals, harps, and lyres for the service of the house of God. Asaph, Jeduthun, and Heman were under the order of the king (1 Chron. 25:1–6).

Indeed, when the temple of Solomon was consecrated, we read:

And when the priests came out of the Holy Place (for all the priests who were present had consecrated themselves, ... and all the Levitical singers, ... arrayed in fine linen, with cymbals, harps, and lyres, stood east of the altar with 120 priests who were trumpeters; and it was the duty of the trumpeters and singers to make themselves heard in unison in praise and thanksgiving to the LORD), and when the song was raised, with trumpets and cymbals and other musical instruments, in praise to the LORD, 'For he is good, for his steadfast love endures forever,' the house, the house of the Lord, was filled with a cloud, so that the priests could not stand to minister because of the cloud, for the glory of the LORD

---

9   Regarding the terms *Alamoth* and *Sheminith*, are these references to high- and low-pitched music, respectively? Or to various ways of playing or singing?

filled the house of God (2 Chron. 5:11–14).

Later we will see in which sense, and to what extent, the temple was a copy of Eden; for now, I have limited myself to the "tabrets" and "pipes," which, if we understand the text correctly, were already present in the celestial Garden of Eden, described by Ezekiel. At any rate, harps will not be lacking in the eschatological Eden, according to the book of Revelation (5:8; 14:2; 15:2), not to mention the many trumpets in the book. And in the Gospels, Jesus himself describes the joys of the house of the prodigal son's father as a place of "music and dancing" (Luke 15:25; also cf. 7:32).

2.4 An Earthly Eden

The second Eden of which we read in the Bible is, of course, the Garden of Eden in Genesis 2 and 3. Elsewhere I have described the cause, the course, and the consequences of the fall of Adam and Eve into sin.[10] Now we wish to discuss particularly the primary intention and goal of the Garden.

There is a peculiarity in the Hebrew language that exists in Greek as well, namely, that there is one word for "earth" and "land," *'erets* (sometimes *'arets*) in Hebrew, and *gē* in Greek. This fact often leads to embarrassment for translators because it is not always clear whether they should render these words as "earth" or as "land." For instance, is it "all the tribes (peoples) of the earth," or "all the tribes of the land [of Israel]" in Revelation 1:7? The difficulty begins immediately in Genesis 1, enhanced by the fact that the second term, "land," can have (at least) two different meanings, namely, the dry land in contrast with the waters, *or* land in the sense of country (e.g., the Holy Land). In verse 1, *'erets* means "earth" in its widest sense: the globe. But in verse 10, God calls the dry [land] *'erets*, which is usually rendered "earth" but is more properly rendered "land" in the sense of the dry areas distinguished from the waters. The other meaning, "land" in the sense of "country" is meant in the phrases "the whole land of Havilah" (Gen 2:13), "the whole land of Cush," and "the land of Nod." (4.16). These are three different meanings of *'erets* in the first chapters of Genesis.

---

10 Ouweneel (2008, chapters 10–14; 2018, chapters 8–10).

The reason I mention these things is that for the Hebrew reader, there is apparently little difference between *'erets* in the sense of "earth" and *'erets* of the "land" (a piece of the earth) where one actually lives. If God told the first humans, "[F]ill *ha'arets* and subdue it" (Gen. 1:28), they understood that nobody could expect the two of them, or even the tenth generation descended from them, to fill the entire habitable world immediately. They began at the place that *for them* was *ha'arets*, and this was the Garden, a piece of land that was an example, a display model as it were, for the earth in its entirety. Just as God created the earth in Genesis 1:1, so too he was the One who planted a garden "in Eden, in the east" (2:8). "In the east" is Hebrew *miqqedem*, which can also be rendered as "(from) of old," or "from (or, at) the beginning" (DRA, WYC; see §1.6). This makes the parallel with Genesis 1:1 even more evident: in the beginning God created the earth, and: at the beginning God planted the garden. In Genesis 1, God was delighted to have created the world, so to speak: "And God saw everything that he had made, and behold, it was very good" (v. 31). In Genesis 2, God planted a garden of delight (*Eden*), and again, it was very good.

The Garden of Eden stood for the earth as a whole. The first humans were "to work it and to keep it," that is, Eden (Gen. 2:15), and from there they were to fulfill the command of 1:28, that is, to fill the entire earth and subdue it. However, what the Fall accomplished was something very different, almost the opposite: the first man had to "work the ground from which he was taken" (3:23; cf. 2:7), but from now on he could do so only *in separation from Eden*. God's plan had been that humanity would conquer the world, beginning in Eden. The consequence of the Fall, however, was a mastering of the world without any further access to Eden. Such a world is necessarily cold and dark; true "delight" is left behind. Before the Fall, humanity's task was to begin in Eden and conquer the entire earth. After the Fall, humanity's task was to survive in a cold and dark world and *find its way back to Eden*. Its task was to regain a paradise lost, to quote Milton again.

In a sense, one could say that, after Adam's fall, the earth was figuratively again "without form and void, and darkness was over the face of the deep"—but also that, again, "the Spirit of God was hovering" over this *tohu wabohu* (as the Hebrew text says in Gen. 1:2). This is why the conversion of any individual human being is like a repetition of what happened in Genesis 1:3, "God said, 'Let there be light,' and there was light." The apostle Paul expresses this in a marvelous way: "God, who said, 'Let light shine out of darkness,' has shone in our hearts to give the light of the knowledge of the glory of God in the face of Jesus Christ" (2 Cor. 4:6). The divine light that enabled the first Eden to emerge from the darkness is also the light that will bring forth the last Eden: "[T]he city [i.e., the New Jerusalem] has no need of sun or moon to shine on it, for the glory of God gives it light, and its lamp is the Lamb" (Rev. 21:23).

2.5 The City of Man

If people have been driven out of Eden, and have been driven far away from it, what can they do? What they *should* do is endeavor to find their way back to Eden in a manner that is intended by, and pleasing to, God. In a sense, this is reached only at the end of redemptive history: "To the one who conquers [i.e., overcomes all the spiritual dangers and hindrances] I will grant to eat of the tree of life, which is in the paradise of God" (Rev. 2:7).

What can godless people do in the meantime? Seek God's face, and wonder how, in his grace and mercy, he might take repentant people back to Eden? This is one option. The other option for people is to shrug their shoulders, and endeavor to be satisfied with the present cold and dark world by making it as pleasant as possible. That is, *Eden* ("delight") has been lost, so let us try to create our own, man-made delight. The answer is the "city of (natural) man." This is the name that Augustine gave to the city that forms the devilish counterpart of the City of God. The Garden is lost, a city is built: "Then Cain went away *from the presence of the* LORD and settled in the land of Nod, east of Eden. Cain knew his wife, and she conceived and bore Enoch. When he built a city, he called the name of the city after the name of his son, Enoch" (Gen. 4:17). Cain does not just leave the region; he goes away "from the presence of the LORD." He settled in a land with the name of Nod, which means "wandering," in fact named after himself because he had become a "fugitive and a wanderer [Heb. *nod*]" (vv. 12–14).

Remarkably enough, it is added that the land where Cain settled was "east of Eden," that is, on the side where the cherubim were blocking the way to Eden. Cain turned his back to Eden, so to speak; he set himself a new goal: a city that should take the place of the garden. If we cannot have the garden, let us have the city!

Spiritually and figuratively speaking, Cain's offspring is the *serpent's* offspring (3:15). Among the descendants of his son Enoch—not to be confused with the godly Enoch of 5:18–24—we find these four characteristics (vv. 20–22):

(a) Jabal represents "those who dwell in tents and have livestock"—the beginning of economy, and thus of an ordered society.
(b) Jubal represents "all those who play the lyre and pipe"—the beginning of the arts, and of culture in the wider sense.
(c) Tubal-cain "was the forger of all instruments of bronze and iron"—the beginning of technology.
(d) Their sister's Naamah represents what her name means: "sweet, pleasant."

In itself, there is nothing wrong with economy, society, the arts, culture, technology, and feminine sweetness, and not even with the idea of a city as such. But *everything* is wrong with these things in the "city of man," the city built by people who are far from Eden, and do not know the longing for it, or who even despise it: the *city without God*. Livestock is not the problem—Abel had livestock, too (vv. 2, 4). Lyre and pipe are not the problem—they will be in the new Eden. Bronze is not the problem—the feet of the Son of Man are like it (Rev. 1:15; 2:18). Pleasantness is not the problem—in fact, that is the name of Eden itself. The problems with these things begin where they function in a world without God. Then they come devilish.[11]

The rabbis understood this: a Midrash says that Jabal was responsible for the first idolatrous temples that were built. Rashi says that Jubal's music was used in idolatry (as a counterpart of the music in Solomon's temple). Others said that Tubal-cain's technology was

---

[11] Adherents of the Two Kingdom theology would erroneously say that these become "neutral"; see extensively, Ouweneel (2017).

used in warfare, as may be seen in Lamech's bluster: "I have killed a man for wounding me, a young man for striking me. If Cain's revenge is sevenfold, then Lamech's is seventy-sevenfold" (Gen. 4:23–24).

The apex of this development was found in the person of Nimrod, the "mighty hunter before the LORD" (Gen. 10:9). He began by building cities, and ended by building kingdoms, not to say empires: "The beginning of his kingdom was Babel, Erech, Accad, and Calneh, in the land of Shinar. From that land he went into Assyria and built Nineveh, Rehoboth-Ir, Calah, and Resen between Nineveh and Calah; that is the great city" (vv. 10–12). Notice what happens here: Nimrod was apparently doing what God had commanded the first humans to do: to fill the earth and subdue it (1:28). But the difference is tremendous: God wished humanity to fill the earth and subdue it *from Eden*, starting here, and from there "work" the entire earth. Nimrod, as a spiritual Cain—from the serpent's offspring—fills the earth and subdues it *in separation of Eden*, and even in opposition to it. God wanted the earth to be filled with the scent of Eden, whereas Nimrod filled the earth with the stench of the serpent.

I repeat: there is nothing wrong with a city as such. The first *good* city mentioned in the Bible is Salem, a city under the blessings of Melchizedek (Gen. 14:18–20; cf. Heb. 7), precursor of the city of Jerusalem (which presumably is identical with it). At the end of redemptive history, city and garden will even coalesce: the "river of the water of life, bright as crystal," will be "flowing from the throne of God and of the Lamb through the middle of the street of the city [i.e., the New Jerusalem]; also, on either side of the river, the tree of life with its twelve kinds of fruit, yielding its fruit each month" (Rev. 22:1–2). The serpent's offspring built a city as a *replacement* for Eden, and it is still doing so every day in all "neutral" or outrightly wicked politics and culture; God will build the "city of God" (cf. Ps. 46:4; 87:3) as the *fulfillment* of Eden.

2.6 The Third Eden

Bible readers have often noticed clear similarities between the work of creation in the beginning and Noah's Flood. And even more, these similarities can be extended to Israel's exodus from Egypt, where God again made a new beginning with humanity. Humanly speaking, after

Adam's failure God made a new start with Noah. And after Babel's failure (Gen. 11), God "tried" again with Israel. Let us briefly look at these three beginnings: Adam, Noah, and Israel, and the three Edens associated with them. I am going to mention seven similarities.

First, in all three cases there was special election: Adam was chosen from all creatures, Noah was chosen from all humanity (Gen. 6:7–9, 18), and Israel was chosen from all the nations (Deut. 7:6–7). God picks the objects of his favor with care, and was all the more "disappointed" (to use an anthropomorphism) when they failed time and again: "He expected good grapes to grow there, but there were only rotten ones" (Isa. 5:2 ERV).

Second, in all three cases we hear about the *tehom*, the "deep" (AMP: the "primeval ocean that covered the unformed earth"; NABRE: the "abyss"). At creation: "The earth was without form and void, and darkness was over the face of the *tehom*" (Gen. 1:2). At the beginning of the Flood: "[A]ll the fountains of the *tehom* burst forth, and the windows of the heavens were opened" (7:11). At the exodus, after Israel's passage through the Red Sea, the people sing: "At the blast of your nostrils the waters piled up; the floods stood up in a heap; the *tehomot* congealed in the heart of the sea" (Exod. 15:8). The *tehomot* are the chaos powers, dark abyssal monsters, which always attempt to hinder God's work. However, they are fully under God's control: "When the waters saw you, O God, when the waters saw you, they were afraid; indeed, the *tehomot* trembled" (Ps. 77:16; cf. 104:6–9).

Third, in all three cases the story begins with dry land emerging from the waters: at the second day of creation (Gen. 1:6–7), after the Flood (8:7, 13–14), and at the passage through the Red Sea (Exod. 14:16, 21, 29; 15:19). The general principle is that the waters have to retreat, and that the dry land is for God's people.

Fourth, in all three cases the people involved were immediately placed under God's commandments: God told Adam what to do and what not to do (Gen. 1:28; 2:16–17), and he did the same with Noah (8:17; 9:1–17), and especially with Israel (Exod. 19–20), to whom he gave the Torah. God almost never manifests himself to human beings without giving them orders immediately: "Be fruitful and multiply" (Gen. 1:28), "Make yourself an ark" (6:14), "Go from your country" (12:1), "I am God Almighty; walk before me, and be blameless" (17:1),

"Do not come near; take your sandals off your feet" (Exod. 3:5), "[I]f you will indeed obey my voice and keep my covenant, you shall be my treasured possession among all peoples" (19:5). And so on.

Fifth, in all three cases there is a specific path to travel to reach Eden. There were six days of God's work of creation until Adam appeared and the garden was planted. There were forty days of rain over the earth and a total of 150 days of "waters prevailing on the earth" (Gen. 7:17, 24) during Noah's Flood before the waters subsided, and a "new world" appeared. And it took forty years to go from the Red Sea to the Promised Land.

Sixth, in all three cases God is preparing an Eden, in spite of all the hindrances and counter-powers. God's work in Genesis 1 leads to the planting of the Garden of Eden in chapter 2. Noah's Flood leads to a "new earth," cleansed from humanity's sin, and thus also to a "new Eden" in the form of Noah's vineyard (Gen. 9:20; see below). And Israel's exodus brought them eventually to the Promised Land, another "new Eden," resembling the "garden of the LORD" (Gen. 13:10), a land of "delight":

> For the LORD your God is bringing you into a good land, a land of brooks of water, of fountains and springs, flowing out in the valleys and hills, a land of wheat and barley, of vines and fig trees and pomegranates, a land of olive trees and honey, a land in which you will eat bread without scarcity, in which you will lack nothing, a land whose stones are iron, and out of whose hills you can dig copper. And you shall eat and be full, and you shall bless the LORD your God for the good land he has given you (Deut. 8:7–10).

Seventh, in all three cases the people involved very soon fell into grave sin: Adam ate of the tree (Gen. 3), Noah drank too much of the vine (9:20–21), and Israel ate and drank at its first—wicked—party: "[T]hey rose up early the next day and offered burnt offerings and brought peace offerings [to the golden calf]. And the people sat down to eat and drink and rose up to play" (Exod. 32:6). Eating and drinking are wonderful, even paradisal in nature—but apart from God, in rebellion, they can be most awful. Wrong eating and drinking even *led* to the Flood:

They were eating and drinking and marrying and being given in marriage, until the day when Noah entered the ark, and the flood came and destroyed them all. Likewise, just as it was in the days of Lot—they were eating and drinking, buying and selling, planting and building, but on the day when Lot went out from Sodom, fire and sulfur rained from heaven and destroyed them all.... [S]o will it be on the day when the Son of Man is revealed (Luke 17:27–30).

2.7 Adam and Noah

We will deal with Israel's exodus and the Promised Land in chapter 4. If we now limit ourselves to Adam's Eden and Noah's "Eden," we notice even more similarities than we have found up to this point. I am going to mention twelve of them.

First, in Genesis 1 God blessed the animals (v. 22), and afterward the first humans (v. 28), and in Genesis 9 he blessed Noah and his sons (v. 1), and all the animals with him (vv. 9–10).

Second, God told Adam, "Be fruitful and multiply and fill the earth and subdue it.... Behold, I have given you every plant yielding seed that is on the face of all the earth, and every tree with seed in its fruit. You shall have them for food" (1:28–29), and he told Noah, "Be fruitful and multiply and fill the earth.... Every moving thing that lives shall be food for you. And as I gave you the green plants, I give you everything" (9:1, 3, 7). In particular, such virtually identical phrases clearly suggest the new beginning God is making with humanity after the Flood.

Third, God made his covenant with Adam (if we may read Hos. 6:7 this way), and he made his covenant with Noah (9:8–17). At least we can say that God entered into a special relationship of love and fellowship with both, as well as with the creatures inferior to them.

Fourth, three sons of Adam are mentioned: Cain, Abel, and Seth, of whom one, Cain, was cursed (4:11), and three sons of Noah are mentioned: Shem, Ham, and Japheth, of whom one, Ham, was cursed in his son Canaan (9:25). At the same time, there was also blessing (3:21; 9:26).

Fifth, Adam became a man who worked the "ground [Heb. *ad-amah*] from which he was taken" (2:7; 3:23); Noah "began to be a man of the soil, and he planted a vineyard" (9:20). Do not underestimate a simple vineyard as a new Eden! Wine is what "cheers God and men" (Judg. 9:13); wine is given "to gladden the heart of man" (Ps. 104:15). That is, Noah's vineyard was definitely another place of "delight." And we may add, the Promised Land is a land of grain, wine, and oil (Num. 18:12; Deut. 7:13; 11:14; 12:17; 14:23; 18:4; 28:51). Israel as a nation is also compared with a vineyard, from which the Lord expected to harvest good grapes (Isa. 5:1–7).[12]

Sixth, Adam's fall and Noah's fall were strikingly similar. Both took forbidden fruit. In the case of the first humans, this meant that the forbidden tree "was good for food, and that it was a delight to the eyes, and that the tree was to be desired to make one wise" (Gen. 3:6). How much more paradisal could one have it? There was only one problem with this fruit: God had forbidden it. It is somewhat comparable with Noah's situation. The wine as such was forbidden; contrary to usage by common people, "is it not for kings to drink wine?" (Prov. 31:4). It is a royal drink. But drinking *too much* wine is an egregious sin: for drunkards there is no place in the kingdom of God (1 Cor. 5:11; 6:10; 15:34; Gal. 5:21; Eph. 5:18; cf. 1 Thess. 5:7; 1 Tim. 3:3; 1 Pet. 4:3; Rev. 17:2, 6).

Seventh, after their fall, both Adam and Noah were exposed in their nakedness:

> Then the eyes of both [i.e., Adam and Eve] were opened, and they knew that they were naked. And they sewed fig leaves together and made themselves loincloths. . . . And he [i.e., Adam] said, "I heard the sound of you [i.e., God] in the garden, and I was afraid, because I was naked, and I hid myself." He said, "Who told you that you were naked? Have you eaten of the tree of which I commanded you not to eat?" (Gen. 3:7, 10–11).

"And Ham, the father of Canaan, saw the nakedness of his father

---

12 The same chapter of Isaiah also describes the bad use of wine, though: "Woe to those who rise early in the morning, that they may run after strong drink, who tarry late into the evening as wine inflames them! They have lyre and harp, tambourine and flute and wine at their feasts, but they do not regard the deeds of the Lord, or see the work of his hands" (vv. 11–12).

and told [mockingly] his two brothers outside" (9:22).

Eighth, both Adam and Noah were properly covered after their fall. Nakedness is here a matter of shame, of "exposure" after one has sinned, so that a proper covering is needed: "And the LORD God made for Adam and for his wife garments of skins and clothed them [Adam and Eve]" (3:21). "Then Shem and Japheth took a garment, laid it on both their shoulders, and walked backward and covered the nakedness of their father. Their faces were turned backward, and they did not see their father's nakedness" (9:23).

Ninth, after Adam's fall there was a sacrifice, though a sacrifice that was only implied in the "garments of [animal] skins" with which God covered Adam and Eve (3:21). After the Flood, Noah brought a sacrifice as a basis for God's dealings with the cleansed earth (8:20–22).

Tenth, after Adam's fall the sign of God's covenant faithfulness was the tree of life, to which a redeemed humanity will one day be brought back (Rev. 2:7; 22:1–2). After Noah's Flood, the sign of God's covenant faithfulness was the rainbow (9:13), which appears in the book of Revelation as well (4:3; 10:1).

Eleventh, there is a clear eschatological significance in both cases: the fallen Adam points forward to the "last Adam," in whom creation will be restored. And Noah's new world points forward to the new heavens and earth:

> [T]he heavens existed long ago, and the earth was formed out of water and through water by the word of God, and ... by means of these the world that then existed was deluged with water and perished. But by the same word the heavens and earth that now exist are stored up for fire, being kept until the day of judgment and destruction of the ungodly.... [T]he day of the Lord will come like a thief, and then the heavens will pass away with a roar.... But according to his promise we are waiting for new heavens and a new earth in which righteousness dwells (2 Pet. 3:5–13).

Twelfth, after the creation of the world, the place of blessing was narrowed down to the Garden of Eden. After Noah's Flood, the place of blessing was narrowed down to Shem and his offspring: "Blessed be the LORD, the God of Shem; and let Canaan be his servant. May God enlarge Japheth, and let him dwell in the tents of Shem; and let Canaan be his servant" (Gen. 9:26–27). Notice the following:

(a) Shem is the "father" of the chosen people of Israel (10:21–31; 11:10–27), and this explains his special blessing.

(b) The name Shem means "name," reminding us of the God of Israel, who is often reverently called by Jews *HaShem*, "the Name."

(c) Shem will subdue Canaan, and in this prediction the conquest of the *land* of Canaan (the land of the offspring of the man Canaan) is included as well.

(d) There is also blessing for Japheth, but only "in the tents of Shem" (cf. Gen. 12:3; John 4:22). The great Jewish Bible expositor Rashi emphasized that it is *God* who dwells in the "tents" of Shem, namely, in the tabernacle (a literal tent) and the temple of Solomon. Thus, the entire episode points forward to the next Eden—actually to at least three "Edens": the tabernacle, the Promised Land, and the temple of Solomon.

2.8 Babel

The city of Babel (Gen. 11:1–9) is literally the apex of all the wonderful cities that Cain's—that is, the serpent's—spiritual descendants had built so far (4:17; 10:10–12). The city entailed their refusal to "fill" the earth again (9:1): instead of dispersing, they concentrated at one spot in order to challenge heaven, and thus defy God, with their tower. They did not take rocks, but made bricks, for the tower was to be their own handiwork: "Come, let us build *ourselves* [not for God] a city and a tower with its top in the heavens, and let us make a name for *ourselves* [not for God], lest we be dispersed over the face of the whole earth [i.e., against God's command]" (Gen. 11:4).

We can say that the book of Genesis is full of hints about the people and the land of Israel, which will become reality first in Exodus, but hints that already cast their shadow forward. This is such an example. Moses told Israel, "Hear, O Israel: you are to cross over the Jordan today, to go in to dispossess nations greater and mightier than you, cities great and fortified *up to heaven*" (Deut. 9:1; cf. 1:28; Num. 13:28; Jer. 51:53 about Babylon). The faithful people of God always encounter the fortresses of humanity, built in order to challenge God and prove their (supposed) superiority. They are "fortified up to heaven" in order to defy the God of heaven. These constitute a clenched fist raised to heaven, like the rebellious in Israel, who also sinned "with a high hand" (Num. 15:30).

The faithful have a deep longing for Eden to come some day, but the wicked always want their Eden *here and now*, not a garden but a city, not a place of humble service to God but a place of rebellion and apostasy. If the *faithful* long for a "city" it is the city of God. Abraham encountered the wicked cities of the Canaanites, of which Sodom and Gomorrah were some impressive examples. But we read of him:

> [H]e was looking forward to the city that has foundations, whose designer and builder is God.... [The patriarchs] died in faith, not having received the things promised, but having seen them and greeted them from afar, and having acknowledged that they were strangers and exiles on the earth. For people who speak thus make it clear that they are seeking a homeland.... [T]hey desire a better country, that is, a heavenly one. Therefore God is not ashamed to be called their God, for he has prepared for them a city (Heb. 11:10–16).

Interestingly, we read that "the Lord *came down* to *see* the city and the tower, which the children of man had built" (Gen. 11:5). Later, we read that the Lord went "*down* to *see*" what was going on in Sodom and Gomorrah (18:21), and still later the Lord "saw" Israel's misery (Exod. 2:25), and he said to Moses,

> I have surely *seen* the affliction of my people who are in Egypt and have heard their cry because of their taskmasters. I know their sufferings, and I have *come down* to deliver them out of the hands of the Egyptians and to bring them up out of that land to a good and broad land, a land flowing with milk and honey (3:8).

Notice the connections: Babel exalted itself to heaven, but God came down to look at Babel, and later at Sodom and Gomorrah, to see their wickedness and to destroy their false, man-made imitations of

Eden.[13] But he also came down to look at Israel in their affliction, and to lead them to a new and genuine Eden, prepared by his own hand for his beloved people.

In the Bible, Babel always stands for a corrupt, human, though outwardly "religious" order of things, which defies the true God and seeks glory only for itself. Nebuchadnezzar, the king of Babylon (i.e., Babel), said, "Is not this great Babylon, which I have built by my mighty power as a royal residence and for the glory of my majesty?" (Dan. 4:30). This is also the language of the Babel of Genesis 11. Behind this boasting was, and is, the angelic prince of Babylon, whom we encounter in Isaiah 14:12–15 (see §2.2). In the end, this is none other than Satan himself, "the great dragon . . . that ancient serpent, who is called the devil and Satan, the deceiver of the whole world" (Rev. 12:9; cf. 20:2).

Indeed, first, the serpent deceived the first humans in Genesis 3, and drove the first humans to their fall, and as a consequence drove them out of Eden. Second, he is also the power that we meet in Babel and in ancient Babylon, called the "dragon" in Jeremiah 51:34 (KJV).[14] Third, he is the angelic prince of Egypt, who is called a "dragon" too, especially at the passage through the Red Sea (Isa. 51:9; cf. Ps. 74:13). Fourth, he is also the dragon[15] in Revelation, including the great Babylon in chapters 17 and 18.

These are all forms of one and the same Satanic power, which drove the first humans out of Eden and will do everything it can to hinder the arrival of any new Eden of God. This is why Jesus Christ not only had to break the power of sin and death, but also the works of Satan: "The reason the Son of God appeared was to destroy the works of the devil" (1 John 3:8b).

---

13 Lot was attracted to Sodom because the region reminded him of Eden (Gen. 13:10–13).

14 Notice how in v. 34 it is Babel's king who "swallows" Judah like a dragon, but in v. 44 it is Bel (Babylon's chief god, i.e., its angelic prince) out of whose mouth Judah is taken again; the two are basically one.

15 Heb. *tannin* can mean both "serpent" (Exod. 7:9–12) and "dragon" (Ps. 74:13; Jer. 51:34); for a picture of (the angelic prince of) Egypt, see Isa. 27:1; Ezek. 29:3; 32:2.

Since . . . the children [of Abraham] share in flesh and blood, he himself likewise partook of the same things, that through death he might destroy the one who has the power of death, that is, the devil, and deliver all those who through fear of death were subject to lifelong slavery (Heb. 2:14–15).

"And the great dragon was thrown down, that ancient serpent, who is called the devil and Satan, the deceiver of the whole world—he was thrown down to the earth, and his angels were thrown down with him" (Rev. 12:9).

There can be no genuine and lasting Eden as long as the old serpent is not permanently thrown into the lake of fire and sulfur (20:10). Notice the figurative language here: in the eternal state, in addition to God there will be only a garden and a lake, each with a figurative animal. That is, every person who has ever lived on this earth will be either blessed in the garden together with the Lamb, or burning in the lake together with the ancient serpent.

3
The Tabernacle

Make a Lampstand of pure hammered gold.
Make its stem and branches, cups, calyxes, and petals all of one piece.
Give it six branches, three from one side and three from the other;
put three cups shaped like almond blossoms,
each with calyx and petals, on one branch, three on the next, and
so on—the same for all six branches.
On the main stem of the Lampstand, make four cups shaped like almonds, with calyx and petals,
a calyx extending from under each pair of the six branches, the entire Lampstand fashioned from one piece of hammered pure gold.

Exodus 25:31–36 (MSG)

3.1 East or West?

For some time now, my wife and I have lived in the town of Houten, just south of Utrecht (Netherlands). In the ancient center of the town stands the village church, dating from a time when Houten was still very small (its ancient history goes back to Roman times, as archeology has shown). The church building in its present form dates from 1678, which by European standards is not very old. But parts of the south wall consist of tuff rock from the tenth or eleventh century, and the foundation of the wall consists of bricks from the Roman era. On the west side of the church, as in so many ancient churches, we find the church tower, which also contains the main entrance to the church. If you walk through this entrance, down the aisle in the main part of the building, you are walking in the direction of the chancel, which is on the east side of the church. Just outside the village church of Houten, at the entrance, there is a sign that tells the visitor that, if you enter the church, you will walk in the direction of the rising of the sun.

Since the eighth century, most church buildings were built with this west-to-east orientation.[1] This is the case with the St. Peter Basilica in Rome, with the Westminster Abbey in London, with the Notre Dame Cathedral in Paris, but also with the modern Washington National Cathedral. Several reasons have been given for this custom. Perhaps Christians followed the example of Jews in the Western world, who would face east toward Jerusalem when praying. Or Christians faced the East when praying because it was from there that they expected Christ to return (Matt. 24:27). Or did they follow the idolatrous sun worshippers, who face the sunrise when praying? Many European churches were built precisely on the spots of ancient pagan temples or altars. Under one of the oldest churches in Rome, the San Clemente, a sanctuary has been found dedicated to the sun god Mithras.

One thing is certain: the common church orientation is the very opposite of the orientation of the tabernacle and the temple. Is this an omen? If our oldest church locations were once pagan sanctuaries, has the devil played a trick on us by making of our churches opposites of Eden?

As for the Garden of Eden in Genesis 2–3, this is perhaps less clear. If we translate, "And the LORD God planted a garden in Eden, in the east [Heb. *miqqedem*]" (Gen. 2:8), the east might be the region where the garden was planted. But if we translate "eastward" (KJV) or "toward the east" (NASB), this seems to suggest the east-to-west orientation of the garden. This is corroborated by chapter 3:24, "at the east of the garden of Eden he placed the cherubim and a flaming sword that turned every way to guard the way to the tree of life," where the

---

1   Notice that "to orientate" comes from Latin *oriens*, which means "rising," viz., the rising of the sun, that is, the east side. In ancient times, "orientation" meant finding the eastern direction, so that one would also know the other four directions.

entrance to the garden is on the east side. Eden had its entrance on the east side, whereas many of our ancient churches have their entrances on the west side.

This orientation is still more evident with the tabernacle. Exodus 27:13 shows that the entrance to the court of the tabernacle was on the east side. This is supported by the arrangement of the camp (see Numbers 2). If the entrance was on the east side, the tabernacle was more on the west side, and the Most Holy place was the farthest west. Here, the tribes of Ephraim, Manasseh, and Benjamin had their camps. This is why God is "enthroned upon the cherubim [standing on the ark]," that is, "before Ephraim and Benjamin and Manasseh" (Ps. 80:1–2), because these were camping nearest to the ark.

In the church of our town of Houten—and thousands of other churches—you enter on the west side, and you walk toward the sunrise. In the tabernacle, you enter on the east side, and you walk toward the sunset. But you could also put it this way: if the *Shekhinah* appeared to the people, it moved from west to east, from sunset to sunrise. This is the common orientation for the Israelite: he faces the east, and therefore has the midday sun at his right hand (so literally in Ps. 121:5), and has the Mediterranean Sea behind him (cf. Deut. 11:24; 34:2; Joel 2:20; Zech. 14:8, literally, the "hinder sea"; ASV: the sea behind you). Eden and the tabernacle faced the rising sun, the appearing light. And when I enter the church of Houten, and walk down the aisle, I do the same: I walk toward the rising light.

"Give ear, O Shepherd of Israel, you who lead Joseph like a flock. You who are enthroned upon the cherubim, shine forth. Before Ephraim and Benjamin and Manasseh, stir up your might and come to save us!" (Ps. 80:1–2).

"For as the lightning comes from the east and shines as far as the west, so will be the coming of the Son of Man" (Matt. 24:27).

3.2 The Universe, the Land, and the Tent

The tabernacle of Israel, so neglected in liberal theology, is one of the most remarkable Edens in the entire Old Testament.[2] As we saw in the first chapter, Eden is both a garden and a sanctuary. In the taber-

---

2 For many similarities between Eden and the tabernacle, see Morales (2012).

nacle, the sanctuary aspect is more prominent, but we will see that the garden element is not in the least lacking.

Already after Israel had passed through the Red Sea, it was singing of the sanctuary:

> You have led in your steadfast love the people whom you have redeemed; you have guided them by your strength to your holy abode [or, habitation, dwelling]. . . . You will bring them in and plant them on your own mountain, the place, O LORD, which you have made for your abode, the sanctuary, O LORD, which your hands have established (Exod. 15:13, 17).

Interestingly, the precise meaning of the text is not made clear. God's holy abode could be the *entire* Promised Land, or it could be the temple that Israel was going to build in the Promised Land (although only after several centuries, under King Solomon, at the initiative of his father David). There is no doubt that indeed the entire Land is holy: "And the LORD will inherit Judah as his portion in the holy land [Heb. *admath haqqodesh*, holy ground[3]], and will again choose Jerusalem" (Zech. 2:12; Masoretic text 2:16). Some translations also have "holy land" in Psalm 78:54, "And he brought them to his holy land [Heb. *gevul qodshow*], to the mountain which his right hand had won" (ESV); others render the expression concerned more precisely as "holy territory" (CSB), or "the border of his sanctuary" (KJV), or "the border of his holy land" (NIV), but the effect is the same: the *entire* Promised Land is *Holy* Land. This is because the land belongs to God (Lev. 25:23; cf. Exod. 19:5), and because the LORD dwells there; the land is his home, and he *feels* at home there.[4] In this land, God "walks" among his people (Lev. 26:12) as he once "walked" in Eden (Gen. 3:8).

If world history in fact began with a "holy *'erets*," "holy earth" (although this expression is not used anywhere), we are now dealing

---

3 The same expression appears in Exod. 3:5.

4 The story goes that when he was in Jerusalem, President Reagan wished to make a phone call to God. When they told him that the cost was fifty cents, he exclaimed that in Washington, London, or Moscow he had to pay seven dollars! Ah, was the answer, but here you pay the local rate.

with a "holy *'erets*" in the narrower sense of *'erets*, the "holy land." Or broader still, if the entire universe is like a tent stretched out (Ps. 104:2; Isa. 40:23) as one immense abode (dwelling-place) of God, we will now find a literal tent (Latin: *tabernaculum*), in which God will make his abode. Notice the narrowing down: from a universe, to the earth globe, to the Holy Land, to a small tent, which still fully deserves the designation "abode of the LORD":

> ... at the entrance of the tent of meeting before the LORD, where I will meet with you [i.e., Moses], to speak to you there. There I will meet with the people of Israel, and it shall be sanctified by my glory. I will consecrate the tent of meeting [i.e., the tabernacle] and the altar. Aaron also and his sons I will consecrate to serve me as priests. *I will dwell among the people of Israel* and will be their God. And they shall know that I am the LORD their God, who brought them out of the land of Egypt *that I might dwell among them*. I am the LORD their God (Exod. 29:42–46).

Perhaps we must narrow this still further. God's dwelling-place was between the cherubim on the so-called mercy seat, which was on the ark of the covenant. He told Moses, "There I will meet with you, and from above the mercy seat, from *between the two cherubim that are on the ark of the testimony*, I will speak with you about all that I will give you in commandment for the people of Israel" (Exod. 25:22). The fulfillment of this is found in Numbers 7:89, "And when Moses went into the tent of meeting to speak with the LORD, he heard the voice speaking to him from above the mercy seat that was on the ark of the testimony, from between the two cherubim; and it spoke to him." Imagine, he who fills the universe and beyond, has concentrated his presence, so to speak, on that one square cubit on the mercy seat! We know with Solomon that "heaven and the highest heaven cannot contain you" (1 Kings 8:27)—which is just as true as the fact that he is "the LORD of hosts, who is enthroned on the cherubim" (1 Sam. 4:4; 2 Sam. 6:2; 2 Kings 19:15; 1 Chron. 13:6; Ps. 80:1; 99:1; Isa. 37:16), namely, the two cherubim on the ark. They were the "cherubim of glory" (Heb. 9:5) because God's glory upon, or between, them.

Notice the connection with Genesis 3: there, cherubim watched the entrance of Eden so that no one could enter. On the mercy seat, the two cherubim were watching, too: they looked down, so to speak, at what lay under the mercy seat: the two tablets of stone, which contained God's holy demands (Deut. 10:1–5; 1 Kings 8:9). In both cases, the cherubim were sustainers of God's holiness. The big difference was this: there was no blood to open the gates of Eden again. But as for the tabernacle, one time a year the high priest sprinkled the blood of the sacrifices on the mercy seat (Lev. 16). If the cherubim now looked down, they still saw the tablets of stone; but they also the blood that atoned for all the people's trespassing God's holy demands.

3.3 God's Longing

God is not ashamed to dwell in a small, relatively simple tent; as he reminds David at a much later time: "I have not lived in a house since the day I brought up the people of Israel from Egypt to this day, but I have been moving about in a tent for my dwelling" (2 Sam. 7:6). How could he have been ashamed if at the same time he is the God who fills the universe?[5]

Indeed, as soon as Moses has ascended Mount Sinai to meet with the LORD, the very first thing the LORD tells him is this:

> Speak to the people of Israel, that they take for me a contribution. From every man whose heart moves him you shall receive the contribution for me. And this is the contribution that you shall receive from them: gold, silver, and bronze, blue and purple and scarlet yarns and fine twined linen, goats' hair, tanned rams' skins, goatskins, acacia wood, oil for the lamps, spices for the anointing oil and for the fragrant incense, onyx stones, and stones for setting, for the ephod and for the breastpiece. And let them make me a sanctuary, *that I may dwell in their midst*. Exactly as I show you concerning the pattern of the tabernacle, and of all its furniture, so you shall make it. . . . And see that you make them after the pattern for them, which is

---

5   Cf. the description of Christ, who is the One who "fills all in all" (Eph. 1:23; Col. 2:10), and of God who one day will be "all in all" (1 Cor. 15:28).

being shown you on the mountain (Exod. 25:2–9, 40).

Apparently, this was God's most urgent and burning desire: to have a tent in the midst of Israel in which he could dwell. What an astonishing truth! For a sacred people such a sacred place was appropriate. And if it was a sanctuary, a holy dwelling-place, it was at the same time intended to be like a Garden of Eden, another such holy place where God had once dwelt and walked among his people in utter delight, at least as long as his people walked according to his commandments.

The last words quoted ("after the pattern for them, which is being shown you on the mountain") are strongly emphasized in the letter to the Hebrews: the tabernacle priests

> serve a copy and shadow of the heavenly things. For when Moses was about to erect the tent, he was instructed by God, saying, "See that you make everything according to the pattern that was shown you on the mountain." But as it is, Christ has obtained a ministry that is as much more excellent than the old as the covenant he mediates is better, since it is enacted on better promises (Heb. 8:5–6).

Notice here the parallel between "heavenly things" and "pattern": the tabernacle had to be a copy of the "heavenly tabernacle," the sanctuary that we also find described in Revelation 13:6 (God's "tabernacle, and them that dwell in heaven," KJV) and 15:5 ("the temple of the tabernacle of the testimony in heaven," KJV). In summary:

(a) As there is a heavenly *tabernacle*, there is also an earthly tabernacle, which is a copy of it.
(b) As there is a heavenly *Eden*, there is also an earthly Eden, which (we may assume) is also a copy of it.
(c) As there is a heavenly *Jerusalem*,[6] there is also an earthly Jeru-

---

6   Cf. Gal. 4:26 (the "Jerusalem above"); Heb. 12:22 (the "heavenly Jerusalem"); Rev. 21:2 (the "new Jerusalem"), although the meaning is not always exactly the same (in Rev. 21–22, the new Jerusalem is the bride of the Lamb).

salem, which (we may assume) is also a copy of it.

Time and again, God's people lost their earthly sanctuary; they lost the tabernacle, they lost the first temple to the Babylonians, and the second temple to the Romans. However, if they repent, God has a heavenly sanctuary awaiting them. Time and again, God's people lost their earthly Eden—but if they repent, God has a heavenly Eden awaiting them. And time and again, God's people lost their earthly Jerusalem—but if they repent, God has a heavenly Jerusalem awaiting them. This will become full reality no earlier than in the "eternal state": the new heavens and the new earth. The story of Eden, which began in Genesis 2 if not in past eternity, will end there—in the everlasting glory of the celestial city *and* garden *and* sanctuary.

3.4 Seven Words

In Genesis 1, there is a noticeable emphasis on God's "speaking." Each of the seven days of creation begins with a command spoken by God, on the third there are two, and on the sixth day four such commands—ten in total. They remind us of the Ten Commandments, which are literally God's "ten words," the *'asereth haddevarim* (Exod. 34:28; Deut. 4:13; 10:4[7]). The Bible begins with God's "ten words" at creation, and on Sinai we hear again "ten words" from God (Exod. 20; Deut. 5). It is different in Genesis 2; here God is "forming," "breathing," "planting," "taking," and "putting," which involve a lot of activities. In chapter 1 the only activity is speaking (commanding), aside from the verb "to create" in verses 1, 21, and 27. In Genesis 2, God's *hands* are prominent, while in Genesis 1, God's *mouth* is prominent.

It can hardly be a coincidence that on Mount Sinai we hear seven "words" (commanding discourses) spoken by the LORD with respect to building the tabernacle. As the first world was prepared in seven days, each day with its own commands (Genesis 1), the tabernacle is prepared through seven commands. That is, each of the ten sayings in Genesis 1 begins with the Hebrew phrase *wayyomer Elohim*, "And God said." The seven commands in Exodus 25–31 each begin with the

---

[7] The Hebrew expression in these passages is *'asereth haddevarim*, but in rabbinic tradition this has become *'asereth haddivrot*, which means the same thing.

Hebrew phrases *wayyrdabber* YHWH, "And the LORD said," or *wayyomer* YHWH, "And the LORD spoke." These are the following.

First command (25:1): concerning the ark of the covenant, the table for bread, the golden lampstand, the actual tent, the bronze altar, the court, the oil for the lamp, the priests' garments, and the altar of incense. All these many things are included in the LORD's first command. If the first command indeed corresponds with the first day of creation, this may help us to understand the all-encompassing significance of what happened on this first day: "[T]here was light." And where there is light, there is everything we need, for God is light (1 John 1:5; cf. Rev. 21:23).

Second command (30:11): concerning the census tax.

Third command (30:17): concerning the bronze basin.

Fourth command (30:22): concerning the anointing oil.

Fifth command (30:34): concerning the incense.

Sixth command (31:1): concerning the calling of Oholiab and Bezalel.

Seventh command (31:12): concerning the Sabbath.

I do not wish to suggest that there are clear-cut parallels between each of these sayings and each of the days of creation, respectively. But at least it is quite remarkable, first, that on the sixth day two specific *human beings* are introduced, who will have to construct the tabernacle, just as on the sixth day of creation we see two human beings enter the scene.

Second, the seventh day of creation was the Sabbath, and the seventh command concerns this very Sabbath, even with an explicit reference to the seven days of creation. God told Israel through Moses:

> Above all you shall keep my Sabbaths, for this is a sign between me and you throughout your generations, that you may know that I, the LORD, sanctify you. . . . Six days shall work be done, but the seventh day is a Sabbath of solemn rest, holy to the LORD. . . . Therefore the people of Israel shall keep the Sabbath, observing the Sabbath throughout their generations, as a covenant forever. It is a sign forever between me and the people of Israel that *in six days the LORD made heaven and earth, and on the seventh day he rested and was refreshed* (31:13–17; cf. 20:11).

3.5 Additional Similarities

Please note some more similarities between the sevenfold work of creation and the sevenfold construction of the tabernacle.

First, on the fourth day the "lights" (Heb. *me'oroth*, from Heb. *or*, "light") are placed at the sky: the sun, the moon, and the stars. Ancient thinking knew seven non-starry celestial bodies ("planets") that could be observed with the naked eye and that seemed to move freely along the sky: the sun, the moon, Mercury, Venus, Mars, Jupiter, and Saturn. The singular word *maor* returns in the expression "oil for the light," that is, for the seven lamps of the lampstand—again seven (Exod. 25:6; 27:20; 35:8, 14, 28; 39:37). There are seven special lights at the sky, and there were seven lights in the tabernacle.

Second, Genesis 1:14 says that the sun, the moon, and the stars are "for seasons" (Heb. *lemo'adim*). This is quite a remarkable word in the Torah because the *mo'adim* are the "appointed times (or, feasts)" (from Heb. *ya'ad*, "to appoint"), the festival times of Israel set apart for the Lord (see especially Lev. 23; verse 2: "... *my* appointed feasts," with the emphasis on "my"[8]). These festivals are consistently calculated in terms of the sun and the moon, the great lights instituted on the fourth day of creation. As for the moon, because the first day of the month is always the time of the new moon, it is necessarily always full moon on the fifteenth day of the month (cf. Lev. 23:6 for the Passover, vv. 34 and 39 for the Feast of Booths). As for the sun, each festival begins at night, that is, at the moment when the sun sets.

Third, we find the Holy Spirit at work in Genesis 1:2 ("the Spirit of God was hovering over the face of the waters") as well as in the tabernacle work: "See, I have called by name Bezalel the son of Uri, son of Hur, of the tribe of Judah, and I have filled him with the Spirit of God, with ability and intelligence, with knowledge and all craftsmanship, to devise artistic designs, to work in gold, silver, and bronze, in cutting stones for setting, and in carving wood, to work in every craft" (Exod. 31:2–5). Not only this, but since the construction of the tabernacle, the Spirit's dwelling-place is exactly determined: since Exodus 40:34–38, the Holy Spirit, who is basically identical with the

---

8   Cf. Num. 28:3, "My offering, my food for my food offerings, my pleasing aroma, you shall be careful to offer to me at its appointed time."

Shekhinah, dwells in the tabernacle, namely, between the cherubim on the mercy seat (Exod. 25:22; Num. 7:89; 1 Sam. 4:4; 2 Kings 19:15; Ps. 80:1; 99:1).

Fourth, at the end of each work there is the conclusion that it is "good." After God's work of creation was finished, we read, "And God saw everything that he had made, and behold, it was very good" (Gen. 1:31). And after the construction of the tabernacle was finished, we read, "According to all that the LORD had commanded Moses, so the people of Israel had done all the work. And Moses saw all the work, and behold, they had done it; as the LORD had commanded, so had they done it" (Exod. 39:42–43a).

Fifth, there is a blessing for the first humans at the end of the work of creation (Gen. 1:28), and there is a blessing at the end of the work of the tabernacle: "Then Moses blessed them [i.e., the Israelites]" (Exod. 39:43b).

3.6 Eden and the Tabernacle

From the creation week we must now move more specifically to the parallelisms between the Garden of Eden and the tabernacle. We have already seen that, in fact, the Garden was a sanctuary because God dwelt and worked there. The tabernacle was the first specific structure in which the LORD, according to his own saying, wished to dwell. The essential point we must make here is that, although the first humans had to be driven out of the Garden because of their sin, God never gives us his ideal, which I call the Edenic ideal. He made a new beginning with Noah on a cleansed earth—but his "Eden" failed. God made a new beginning with a new "invention": God's own holy *people*, his "treasured possession" (Exod. 19:5; Deut. 7:6; 14:2; 26:18). He even gave them a new "Eden": the tabernacle—but again, God's enterprise failed, not because of any faults on his part but because of the rebellion of his people (Exod. 32).

Let us now look at the element in the tabernacle that reminds us most strongly of Paradise; this is no doubt the lampstand:

> You shall make a lampstand of pure gold. The lampstand shall be made of hammered work: its base, its stem, its cups, its *calyxes*, and its *flowers* shall be of one piece with it. And there shall be six

branches going out of its sides, three *branches* of the lampstand out of one side of it and three *branches* of the lampstand out of the other side of it; three cups made like *almond blossoms*, each with *calyx* and *flower*, on one *branch*, and three cups made like *almond blossoms*, each with *calyx* and *flower*, on the other *branch*—so for the six *branches* going out of the lampstand. And on the lampstand itself there shall be four cups made like *almond blossoms*, with their *calyxes* and *flowers*, and a *calyx* of one piece with it under each pair of the six *branches* going out from the lampstand. Their *calyxes* and their *branches* shall be of one piece with it, the whole of it a single piece of hammered work of pure gold (Exod. 25:31–36; notice my italics).[9]

The suggestion is quite understandable that this lampstand has the form of the tree of life with its branches, almond blossoms, calyxes, and flowers. This is an obvious suggestion, even though I am not aware of any explicit confirmation of it. No matter how this may be understood, at any rate the lampstand is a paradisal element, just as we find it again in the temple: "The cedar within the house was carved in the form of gourds and open flowers. . . . Around all the walls of the house he [i.e., Solomon] carved engraved figures of cherubim and palm trees and open flowers, in the inner and outer rooms" (1 Kings 6:18, 29). Almond blossoms, gourds, flowers, palm trees—they all remind us of that Garden, that place of "delight," with which the history of humanity began. And notice the cherubim that were depicted in the temple, as well as those standing on the mercy seat. There were cherubim at the entrance of the Garden of Eden, as we saw, and there were cherubim in the tabernacle and the temple.

3.7 More Similarities

There are more similarities. For instance, just as Adam and Eve were placed in the Garden "to work it and keep it" (Gen. 2:15), God ap-

---

9   In simpler language (ERV): "The lampstand must have six branches—three branches on one side and three branches on the other. Each branch must have three flowers. Make these flowers like almond flowers with buds and petals. Make four more flowers for the lampstand. These flowers must be made like almond flowers with buds and petals," and so on.

pointed the Levites in the tabernacle: "They shall keep guard over him [i.e., Aaron] and over the whole congregation before the tent of meeting, as they minister at the tabernacle. They shall guard all the furnishings of the tent of meeting, and keep guard over the people of Israel as they minister at the tabernacle" (Num. 3:7–8). In both passages we find the same Hebrew verb *sh-m-r*, "to keep (guard)." A holy place is a place to be guarded, protected, to keep it holy, consecrated to God. Just as God "dwelt" and "walked" in the Garden of Eden, so too he "dwelt" and "walked" among the Israelites (Gen. 3:8; Lev. 26:11–12).

There is even correspondence in the clothing. "And the LORD God made for Adam and for his wife garments [Heb. *kothnowth*] of skins and clothed them" (Gen. 3:21). "And Moses brought Aaron's sons and clothed them with coats [Heb. *kuttonoth*]" (Lev. 8:13). The words for "garments" and "coats" come from the same root, originally meaning "linen" (although not all coats were indeed made of linen), and in both cases the verb "to clothe" (Heb, *l-b-sh*) is the same. In a sense, it could be said that Adam was not only the king but also the priest in Eden, as the forerunner of the great King and Priest in the Eden to come. Hence the link between Adam, on the one hand, and Aaron with his sons, on the other hand.

Just as Adam was still without sin, it is remarkable that Aaron and his sons had to be "without blemish":

> Speak to Aaron, saying, "None of your offspring throughout their generations who has a blemish may approach to offer the bread of his God. For no one who has a blemish shall draw near, a man blind or lame, or one who has a mutilated face or a limb too long, or a man who has an injured foot or an injured hand, or a hunchback or a dwarf or a man with a defect in his sight or an itching disease or scabs or crushed testicles. No man of the offspring of Aaron the priest who has a blemish shall come near to offer the LORD's food offerings; since he has a blemish, he shall not come near to offer the bread of his God. He may eat the bread of his God, both of the most holy and of the holy things, but he shall not go through the veil or approach the altar, because he has a blemish, that he may not profane my sanctuaries, for I am the LORD who

sanctifies them" (Lev. 21:17-23).

As such, Adam and his sons were forerunners of the perfect and blameless kings and priests in the Eden to come: Christ "made us a kingdom, priests to his God and Father" (Rev. 1:6). "[Y]ou [i.e., the Lamb] were slain, and by your blood you ransomed people for God from every tribe and language and people and nation, and you have made them a kingdom and priests to our God, and they shall reign on the earth" (5:9-10); God's "servants will worship him [a priestly expression] ... and they will reign [as kings] forever and ever" (22:4-5).

3.8 Yom Kippur

To mention one more striking similarity, I remind the reader of what I said at the beginning of this chapter about east and west. When Adam and Eve were driven out of Eden, they went eastward: they left the Garden through the exit on the east side. The tabernacle also had its exit on the east side. However, on *Yom Kippur*, the Day of Atonement, the high priest took the opposite direction. He went westward, in the direction of the Most Holy chamber, first with the blood of the bullock, then with the blood of the first goat (Lev. 16). At the veil, he met with the cherubim that were depicted on it: "[Y]ou shall make a veil of blue and purple and scarlet yarns and fine twined linen. It shall be made with cherubim skillfully worked into it" (Exod. 25:31). The cherubim at Eden prevented Adam and Eve from entering the Garden. The cherubim on the veil prevented, so to speak, the priests from entering the Most Holy chamber throughout the year—with this sole exception: on *Yom Kippur*, the high priest was allowed to *pass* the cherubim in order to enter the Most Holy chamber and come into the presence of the Most High God. This could be done only through blood: sin drove humanity out of Eden, while the blood of the sacrifices, which atones for sins committed, can bring them into Eden again.[10]

This is what we read of Christ:

---

[10] Notice that in this typological language no torn veil is mentioned, neither here or in Heb. 10:19-22; there was a torn veil in the temple at Jesus' death (Luke 23:45), but no torn veil in the tabernacle is mentioned in Hebrews.

[W]hen Christ appeared as a high priest of the good things that have come, then through the greater and more perfect tent (not made with hands, that is, not of this creation) he entered once for all into the holy places, not by means of the blood of goats and calves but by means of his own blood, thus securing an eternal redemption. For if the blood of goats and bulls, and the sprinkling of defiled persons with the ashes of a heifer, sanctify for the purification of the flesh, how much more will the blood of Christ, who through the eternal Spirit offered himself without blemish to God, purify our conscience from dead works to serve the living God (Heb. 9:11–14).

Therefore, brothers, since we have confidence to enter the holy places by the blood of Jesus, by the new and living way that he opened for us through the curtain [or, veil], that is, through his flesh, and since we have a great priest over the house of God, let us draw near with a true heart in full assurance of faith, with our hearts sprinkled clean from an evil conscience and our bodies washed with pure water (10:19–22).

This is the Christian position: we are on our way to the "new Eden," which has been promised to the overcomers in the age to come (Heb. 6:5) and the world to come (2:5), just as Israel in the wilderness was on its way to the Promised Land, which to them was their "new Eden." But this is not all: we also have an "Eden" that is *permanently nearby*: the heavenly sanctuary, in which believers may enter with confidence in order to worship God and enjoy his presence, love, and fellowship. In Israel, it was only the high priest who had this privilege, and this only once a year. The believers of God's church, in the present age, *all* have this privilege, *all* the time; they may enter into God's sacred presence in order to worship him and enjoy his love and fellowship. Christians are too little conscious of this heavenly Eden *now*. They may look forward only to the Eden to come, or look forward far too little to the Eden to come. In either case, they may little appreciate this heavenly Eden, to which we have access *already now*. (Note his remarkable word "access" in Rom. 5:2 and in Eph. 2:18; 3:12, which seems to point to the same privilege.)

The LORD will dwell in the Eden to come, but he also dwells in the midst of his people *right now*:

> [W]e are the temple of the living God; as God said, "I will make my dwelling among them and walk among them, and I will be their God, and they shall be my people. Therefore go out from their midst, and be separate from them, says the Lord, and touch no unclean thing; then I will welcome you, and I will be a father to you, and you shall be sons and daughters to me, says the Lord Almighty (2 Cor. 6:16–18; cf. Exod. 25:8; Lev. 26:11–12; 2 Sam. 7:14; Isa. 52:11; Jer. 31:9; 32:38; Ezek. 37:27; Amos 3:13; 4:13).

3.9 The Temple of Solomon

The moment came, during the history of David and Solomon, when God

> forsook his dwelling [i.e., the tabernacle] at Shiloh, the tent where he dwelt among mankind.... He rejected the tent of Joseph; he did not choose the tribe of Ephraim, but he chose the tribe of Judah, Mount Zion, which he loves. He built his sanctuary like the high heavens, like the earth, which he has founded forever (Ps. 78:60, 67–69).

That is, Shiloh, the place where the tabernacle had stood for so many years (Josh. 18:1, 8–10; 19:51; Judg. 18:31; 1 Sam. 1:3, 24; 4:3), was located in the tribal area of Ephraim. After God had chosen David, from the tribe of Judah, it was time to have a sanctuary in the territory of Judah, namely, on Mount Zion.

Just as the tabernacle had Edenic features, the temple was going to have them as well. In §3.6 I mentioned some features of Solomon's temple from 1 Kings 6. I add verse 18 from chapter 7: "Likewise he made *pomegranates* in two rows around the one latticework to cover the capital that was on the top of the pillar, and he did the same with the other capital" (cf. vv. 20, 42). See verse 36 as well: "And on the surfaces of its stays and on its panels, he carved cherubim, lions, and *palm trees*, according to the space of each, with wreaths all around." We read in 2 Chronicles 3: "The nave he lined with cypress and covered it with fine gold and made *palms* and chains on it" (v. 5). "In front of the house he made two pillars thirty-five cubits high, with a capital of five cubits on the top of each. He made chains like a necklace and put them on the tops of the pillars, and he made a hundred *pomegranates* and put them on the chains" (vv. 15–16). "So Hiram finished the work that he did for King Solomon on the house of God: the 400 *pomegranates* for the two latticeworks, two rows of *pomegranates* for each latticework, to cover the two bowls of the capitals that were on the pillars" (4:11–13).

Almost by definition, such palm trees and pomegranates must be called paradisal elements.[11] When Israel embarked on its wilderness journey, it soon reached Elim, a lovely oasis, where the "twelve springs of water and seventy palm trees" (Exod. 15:27) were a tremendous promise and encouragement for a nation that still had a long way to go to reach its "Eden," the Promised Land, with its abundant water and lush palm trees. Every time Israel celebrated the Feast of Booths—the great harvest feast, foreshadowing *par excellence* the Messianic kingdom—the palm trees were another sign of the world to come: "[Y]ou shall take on the first day the fruit of splendid trees, branches of palm trees and boughs of leafy trees and willows of the brook, and you shall rejoice before the LORD your God seven days" (Lev. 23:40; cf. Neh. 8:15).

The first city they encountered in the Promised Land was Jericho, the "city of palm trees" (Deut. 34:3; cf. 2 Chron. 28:15). When Jesus was coming up from Jericho and was approaching Jerusalem, the people "took branches of palm trees and went out to meet him, crying out, 'Hosanna! Blessed is he who comes in the name of the LORD, even the King of Israel!'" (John 12:13). This was another great foreshadowing of the Messianic kingdom:

> After this I looked, and behold, a great multitude that no one could number, from every nation, from all tribes and peoples and languages, standing before the throne and before the Lamb, clothed in white robes, with palm branches in their hands, and crying out with a loud voice, "Salvation belongs to our God who sits on the

---

11 The same paradisal motif will be found in the eschatological temple (Ezek. 40:16, 22, 26, 31, 34, 37; 41:18–20, 25–26).

throne, and to the Lamb!" (Rev. 7:9–10).

Pomegranates are a "literal" element of paradise in the sense of Song 4:12–13, "A garden locked is my sister, my bride, a spring locked, a fountain sealed. Your shoots are an orchard [*pardēs, paradeisos*] of pomegranates with all choicest fruits." A most remarkable application of the pomegranate is that they were placed on the hem of the high priestly robe: "On its hem you shall make pomegranates of blue and purple and scarlet yarns, around its hem, with bells of gold between them, a golden bell and a pomegranate, a golden bell and a pomegranate, around the hem of the robe" (Exod. 28:33–34; cf. 39:24–26). This makes the pomegranate the fruit of the sanctuary *par excellence*; one could compare it with the "fruit unto holiness (or, sanctification)" in Romans 6:22 (KJV, ASV). Of course, this was exactly what the temple was: one large sanctuary. As far as I see, no fruit was more appropriate for such a place than the pomegranate.

4
The Promised Land

And Lot lifted up his eyes
and saw that the Jordan Valley was well watered everywhere
like the garden of the LORD,
like the land of Egypt, in the direction of Zoar.

Genesis 13:10

For the LORD comforts Zion;
   he comforts all her waste places
and makes her wilderness like Eden,
   her desert like the garden of the LORD;
joy and gladness will be found in her,
   thanksgiving and the voice of song.

Isaiah 51:3

4.1 Visiting the Land

My first visit to the Promised Land was in 1982. It was not primarily to visit the state as such, or the countryside, or the tourist sites, but to give Bible lectures in a Palestinian town in Galilee. It was a town in which no Jew lived; 57% percent of the people were Christians (mostly Greek Orthodox), 40% were Muslims, and 3% were Druze (a small esoteric Abrahamic religion). For centuries, they had all lived together in peace. The Evangelical congregation where I gave my lectures consisted of former Orthodox, former Catholics, and even a few Druze people. For eleven evenings I gave my lectures, on many different biblical subjects. My reward was that one of the brothers,

Samir, together with a Catholic taxi driver—both Palestinians—took me on a trip through the country. It was a very unusual way to learn to see the Holy Land: through the eyes of two Christian Palestinians! We saw things that people in those days did not see from a Jewish bus or taxi, such as the well of Sychar (see John 4), the sanctuary on Mount Gerizim (cf. Deut. 11:29; Josh. 8:33), and in Hebron the cave of Machpelah with the tombs of the patriarchs (Gen. 23). Samir had some trouble gaining entrance for me into the latter because it was a Friday, the holy day of the Muslims—but he managed.

The highlight was Jerusalem, which we approached from the West Bank, from the North, at dusk. What a moving sight! I will never forget it. For us there was no hotel, but a guest room in the home of an Arab Christian, within the ancient Turkish city walls, where before falling asleep Samir and I read Psalm 122 together:

> I was glad when they said to me,
>   "Let us go to the house of the LORD!"
> Our feet have been standing
>   within your gates, O Jerusalem!
> Jerusalem—built as a city
>   that is bound firmly together,
> to which the tribes go up,
>   the tribes of the LORD, . . .
> Pray for the peace of Jerusalem!
>   "May they be secure who love you!
> Peace be within your walls
>   and security within your towers!"

Since then, I have been back to Israel many times. I have stayed with an orthodox Jewish family, and have stayed in both Jewish and Arabic hotels. I took part with some of my Dutch students in archaeological excavations near Jerusalem. I took each of my sons separately to the Holy Land, as part of their education. Moreover, my wife and I guided several groups through this extraordinary country. We saw the towns and the countryside, the plains and the hills. We were on Mount Hermon (almost 9,200 feet above sea level) and at the Dead Sea (about 1,300 feet below sea level). We saw the desert areas with the Bedouins, and the areas that had been cultivated. These were the territories whose lush splendor made it difficult to believe that a century earlier many of these areas had been desert or swamp. We saw the Jordan Valley as Abraham and Lot had once seen it: "well watered everywhere like the garden of the LORD," like old Eden (Gen. 13:10), the "thick woods along the Jordan," and the "green pasture land" (Jer. 49:19; 50:44 GNT). We saw one flourishing kibbutz after another. We saw the vines, the fig trees, the pomegranates, and the olive trees—important matters, to which we will return in §4.5.

4.2 Israel and Egypt

We also visited Egypt on a few occasions. We saw the Nile, the pyramids, and the Sphinx. And we learned the differences between Egypt and Israel, not only from a tourist point of view, but also from a theological standpoint. If I may put it in Moses' words to Israel, the main difference is this:

> [T]he land that you are entering to take possession of it is not like the land of Egypt, from which you have come, where you sowed your seed and irrigated it [lit., watered it with your feet] like a garden of vegetables. But the land that you are going over to possess is a land of hills and valleys, which drinks water by the rain from heaven, a land that the LORD your God cares for. The eyes of the LORD your God are always upon it, from the beginning of the year to the end of the year [i.e., throughout the agricultural seasons] (Deut. 11:10–12).

A highly interesting difference! The land of Egypt may be lush, too, but its wealth is dependent on the fortunes of the river Nile (dominated by the old "dragon," Ezek. 29:3), as well as on human effort: the use of the foot pump to irrigate the land. This is cumbersome, and yields only limited results. Egypt may *look* like an Eden, but it is always a man-watered Eden, if not a dragon-made Eden. It is a hoax, a false imitation, not the real thing. (Of course, I speak of Egypt in the spiritual, figurative sense.)

How different is the land of Israel! It "drinks water from the *rain of heaven*" (NASB). The water comes to the land, not from any dragon or any man-made labor, but from God himself:

> You [i.e., God] visit the earth [better: the land[1]] and water it;
>> you greatly enrich it;
> the river of God is full of water;
>> you provide their grain,
>> for so you have prepared it.
> You water its furrows abundantly,
>> settling its ridges,
> softening it with showers,
>> and blessing its growth.
> You crown the year with your bounty;
>> your wagon tracks overflow with abundance.
> The pastures of the wilderness overflow,
>> the hills gird themselves with joy,
> the meadows clothe themselves with flocks,
>> the valleys deck themselves with grain,
>> they shout and sing together for joy (Ps. 65:9–13).

The other side of this portrait shows that, when "the anger of the LORD will be kindled against you, and he will shut up the heavens, so that there will be no rain," then "the land will yield no fruit, and you will perish quickly off the good land that the LORD is giving you" (Deut. 11:17). If God withholds the "rain of heaven," Israel is worse off than Egypt (cf. the days of Elijah, James 5:17–18). Any Eden can be a genuine Eden only under the rich blessing of God, or rather, through the personal *presence* of God. Without this, there is nothing—even less than in Egypt, where some beauty still proceeds from the dragon and human effort (if I speak cynically for a moment).

There are more differences: Egypt is mostly a flat country, but Israel is a land of hills and mountains. As a consequence, it is "a land of brooks of water, of fountains and springs, flowing out in the valleys and hills" (Deut. 8:7), adding to the amount of water that the land needs in order that it flourish. Above all, the "eyes of the LORD your God are always upon it, from the beginning of the year to the end of the year" (11:12). In the end, this is the decisive factor. This

---
1 Recall the two meanings of Heb. *'erets* (§2.4).

is what makes Eden *Eden*. One day the new name of Jerusalem will be: *yhwh Shammah*, "The LORD Is There" (Ezek. 48:35). What was the first Eden without the LORD walking there? What was Noah's new world without the LORD smelling the sweet aroma of Noah's sacrifice (Gen. 8:21)? What was the tabernacle without God's promise that he would dwell there? What is the Holy Land without God having made his abode there (Exod. 15:13, 17)? And what will the new heavens and the new earth be without this promise: "Behold, the dwelling place [lit., tent] of God is with man. He will dwell with them, and they will be his people, and God himself will be with them as their God" (Rev. 21:3)?

4.3 Seven Parallelisms

The land God promised to Abraham and his offspring was undoubtedly intended to be a new Eden. In §2.6, I pointed to seven parallels between Adam, Noah and Israel; I summarize this here, with some important additions concerning Israel.

First, in all three cases there was special election: Israel was chosen from all the nations (Deut. 7:6–7). Israel is "the people whom [the LORD] has chosen as his heritage" (Ps. 33:12). In chapter 2 we heard of the angelic princes, each of whom has his own territory (country, empire). In Deuteronomy 32:8–9 we read,

> When the Most High gave to the nations their inheritance, when he divided mankind, he fixed the borders [or, territories] of the peoples according to the number of the sons of God[2] [the angelic princes, each one receiving its own territory]. But the LORD's portion is his people, Jacob his allotted heritage.

Land and nation of Israel are his personal treasured property—and this has never changed in redemptive history, even though, at dark times, the archangel Michael functioned as the angelic prince of Israel (Dan. 10:21).

Second, in all three cases we hear about the *tehom*, the "deep" (or "abyss"). At the exodus from Egypt, after Israel's passage through

---

[2] Thus a Dead Sea Scroll and the Septuagint; traditional translations follow the Masoretic text: "sons of Israel."

the Red Sea, the people sing: "At the blast of your nostrils the waters piled up; / the floods stood up in a heap; / the *tehomot* congealed in the heart of the sea" (Exod. 15:8). The *tehomot* are the chaos powers, dark abyssal monsters, which always attempt to hinder God's work. They tried to destroy the original creation, they were happy to be used as instruments in creating the great Flood, and they would have loved the waters of the Red Sea to have swallowed the Israelites, just as they swallowed the Egyptians. But they are under God's control: if he wishes to lead his people to a new "Eden," no Satanic power can prevent this: "You divided the sea by your might; / you broke the heads of the sea monsters [or, dragons, Heb. *tannim*] on the waters. / You crushed the heads of Leviathan; / you gave him as food for the creatures of the wilderness" (Ps. 74:13–14). "Your way was through the sea, / your path through the great waters; / yet your footprints were unseen. / You led your people like a flock / by the hand of Moses and Aaron" (77:19–20).

Third, in all three cases the story begins with dry land emerging from the waters; for the passage through the Red Sea, see Exodus 14:16, 21, 29; 15:19. The waters have to retreat, the dry land is for God's people. Centuries later, the prophet Isaiah points out how the dark powers tried to hinder Israel:

> Awake, awake, put on strength,
> > O arm of the LORD;
> awake, as in days of old,
> > the generations of long ago [viz., the time of the Exodus].
> Was it not you who cut Rahab [the angelic prince of Egypt[3]] in pieces,
> > who pierced the dragon [*tannin*]?
> Was it not you who dried up the sea,
> > the waters of the great deep,
> who made the depths of the sea a way
> > for the redeemed to pass over?
> And the ransomed of the LORD shall return
> > and come to Zion with singing;
> everlasting joy shall be upon their heads;

---

3 See Ps. 87:4; 89:10; Isa. 30:7.

they shall obtain gladness and joy,
and sorrow and sighing shall flee away (Isa. 51:9–11).

Fourth and fifth, in all three cases the people involved were immediately placed under God's commandments (Gen. 1:28; 2:16–17; 8:17; 9:1–17). This was true especially for Israel (Exod. 19–20), to whom God gave his Torah. The Hebrew word *torah* literally means "instruction" or "teaching,"[4] like a father or mother gives instruction to a child (Prov. 1:8; 3:1; 4:2; 6:20, 23; 7:2, where in every verse we find the Hebrew word *torah*). The Torah is not just a "yoke" to be pressed on shoulders (cf. Acts 15:10), but a clear compass, a kind and wise guideline, to bring God's people safely to its goal. For the wicked, the Torah was a "ministry of death" (2 Cor. 3:7), but for the faithful, the Torah was their "very life" (Deut. 32:47). If Israel had followed the Torah, it would not have needed forty years to reach the Promised Land; the distance between Horeb and Kadesh-barnea was only an "eleven days' journey" (Deut. 1:2). If Israel had followed the Torah, the Promised Land would have become the "Eden" intended a long time ago, whereas now the faithful among the nation have to wait until the Messianic age.

Sixth, in all three cases God is preparing an Eden, in spite of all the hindrances and counter-powers (see Gen. 1 and 9). Israel's exodus brought the people eventually to the Promised Land, another new Eden, resembling the "garden of the LORD" (Gen. 13:10), a land of delight:

> For the LORD your God is bringing you into a good land, a land of brooks of water, of fountains and springs, flowing out in the valleys and hills, a land of wheat and barley, of vines and fig trees and pomegranates, a land of olive trees and honey, a land in which you will eat bread without scarcity, in which you will lack nothing, a land whose stones are iron, and out of whose hills you can dig copper. And you shall eat and be full, and you shall bless the LORD your God for the good land he has given you (Deut. 8:7–10).

The final result will be reached only in the Messianic kingdom:

---
4   The Hebrew word *torah* comes from the root *y-r-h*, "to teach, instruct."

"For the L%%ORD%% comforts Zion; he comforts all her waste places and makes her wilderness like Eden, her desert like the garden of the L%%ORD%%; joy and gladness will be found in her, thanksgiving and the voice of song" (Isa. 51:3).

Seventh, in all three cases the people involved very soon fell into grave sin (Gen. 3 and 9). Israel fell even before Moses had returned from Mount Sinai: "[T]hey rose up early the next day and offered burnt offerings and brought peace offerings [to the golden calf]. And the people sat down to eat and drink and rose up to play" (Exod. 32:6). There is something pathetic about God's wonderful counsel to usher in Eden: the first humans fell right way, namely, by eating. Noah followed shortly after the Flood, namely, by drinking. Israel fell even before it had received the entire Torah, namely, by eating and drinking before the idols.

We may continue this line (even if eating and drinking are not always prominent). The priesthood failed already in the first generation after Aaron because his eldest sons brought "strange fire" (Lev. 10:1–3). Royalty failed immediately in the very first king that Israel had, that is, through Saul's disobedience (1 Sam. 15). The church had its first disaster already in Acts 5, when Ananias and Sapphira fell into the sin of deceit. And so on. Even the Reformation failed at an early stage in the sense that the Reformers could not agree on fundamental subjects. With respect to eating and drinking, one sad thing is that the Reformers soon developed basic differences of opinion concerning the Lord's Supper.

Indeed, God must be very merciful toward, and patient with, his people, during every age of redemptive history: "The L%%ORD%%! The L%%ORD%%! A God who is compassionate and merciful, very patient,[5] full of great loyalty and faithfulness" (Exod. 34:6 CEB). God is not tired of trying over and over again (which, of course, is a very human way of describing God's dealings). After Adam's fall, he made a new beginning with Noah, and after Noah's failure, God settled for the election of an entire nation, to be placed in a land that in many ways would resemble Eden. The twelve spies had already found out about this:

> [T]hey came to the Valley of Eshcol and cut down from there a

---

5   The literal meaning is "slow to anger" (see ASV, CJB).

branch with a single cluster of grapes, and they carried it on a pole between two of them; they also brought some pomegranates and figs. That place was called the Valley of Eshcol [i.e., cluster] because of the cluster that the people of Israel cut down from there (Num. 13:23–24).

However, ten of the twelve spies fell nonetheless, as a consequence of their unbelief.

4.4 The Planting and the Voice

Let me add some more parallelisms here, this time specifically between, on the one hand, creation and the first Eden, and on the other hand, the exodus and the Promised Land.

Let me begin with God's *planting* work. He "planted" the Garden of Eden (Gen. 2:8); similarly, he "planted" Israel: the chosen nation was the "vine brought out of Egypt; you [i.e., the LORD] drove out the nations and *planted* it. You cleared the ground for it; it took deep root and filled the land" (Ps. 80:8–9; cf. Hos. 10:1, "Israel is a luxuriant vine that yields its fruit"). "You will bring them in and *plant* them on your own mountain" (Exod. 15:17). Israel is compared to both a vine and a vineyard: Israel was a "vineyard on a very fertile hill. . . . For the vineyard of the LORD of hosts is the house of Israel, and the men of Judah are his pleasant planting," of which the LORD expected good "grapes" (Isa. 5:1–2, 7).

Then there was the *qol yhwh*, literally the "voice of the LORD," sometimes in the broader sense of "sound." Adam and Eve "heard the *qol yhwh*," the "voice" (or "sound") of the LORD in the cool of the day (Gen. 3:8). It was a threatening sound because they had sinned, and they were conscious of the possible consequences. The LORD's voice could signify peril, but also showed that God was still interested in them, and searched for them: "[T]he LORD God called to the man and said to him, 'Where are you?' And he said, 'I heard the sound [lit., voice] of you in the garden, and I was afraid, because I was naked, and I hid myself'" (vv. 9–10). The voice of the LORD calls upon humanity in order either to save or, if there is no willingness, to judge.

This was the voice that was heard once more on Mount Sinai. It was a voice like a hand stretched out: "I am the LORD your God, who brought you out of the land of Egypt, out of the house of slavery" (Exod. 20:2). Yet, the people were afraid of it—as were Adam and Eve—and said, "[W]hy should we die? For this great fire will consume us. If we hear the voice of the LORD [*qol YHWH*] our God any more, we shall die" (Deut. 5:25); "you desired of the LORD your God at Horeb on the day of the assembly, when you said, 'Let me not hear again the voice of the LORD [*qol YHWH*] my God or see this great fire any more, lest I die'" (18:16). The *qol YHWH* promises and threatens; it may guide you to Eden if you are compliant, and it may drive you out of Eden, or prevent you from getting there, if you "kick against the goads" (cf. Acts 26:14).

Indeed, Israel failed the same way the first humans had failed: "[L]ike Adam[6] they transgressed the covenant; there they dealt faithlessly with me" (Hos. 6:7). Adam and Eve were forced to leave their Eden and to go into exile, and will reenter Eden only at the end of times. The people of Israel were also forced to leave their Eden and to go into exile; their full restoration will not be before Messiah has come with the clouds of heaven. In the same book of Hosea, God says,

> I will heal their apostasy; I will love them freely, for my anger has turned from them. I will be like the dew to Israel; he shall blossom like the lily; he shall take root like the trees of Lebanon; his shoots shall spread out; his beauty shall be like the olive, and his fragrance like Lebanon. They shall return and dwell beneath my shadow; they shall flourish like the grain; they shall blossom like the vine; their fame shall be like the wine of Lebanon (14:4–7).

4.5 The Sabbath Rest

The wonderful significance of the passage last mentioned is that Israel *itself* will be like a kind of Eden: *the people* will blossom, *they* will take root, *their* shoots will spread out. It is like in the Song of Solomon chapter 4: Israel itself is not only a "he" but a "she," the beloved bride, who in person will be the "garden locked," and the "orchard of pomegranates" (vv. 12–13). Israel will be the new Eden, and it will dwell in a new Eden.

For the nation this will be the last sabbatical rest. The first full day

---

6   See chapter 2, note 13.

that Adam, and thus humanity, experienced in world history was the seventh day:

> And God saw everything that he had made, and behold, it was very good. And there was evening and there was morning, the sixth day. Thus the heavens and the earth were finished, and all the host of them. And on the seventh day God finished his work that he had done, and he rested on the seventh day from all his work that he had done. So God blessed the seventh day and made it holy, because on it God rested from all his work that he had done in creation (Gen. 1:31–2:3).

The writer of Hebrews sees a direct parallel with the future:

> [W]e who have believed enter that rest, as he has said, "As I swore in my wrath, 'They shall not enter my rest,'" [Ps. 95:11] although his works were finished from the foundation of the world. For he has somewhere spoken of the seventh day in this way: "And God rested on the seventh day from all his works" [Gen. 2:2]. And again in this passage he said, "They shall not enter my rest." Since therefore it remains for some to enter it, and those who formerly received the good news failed to enter because of disobedience, again he appoints a certain day, "Today," saying through David so long afterward, in the words already quoted, "Today, if you hear his voice, do not harden your hearts" [Ps. 95:7–8]. For if Joshua had given them rest, God would not have spoken of another day later on. So then, there remains a Sabbath rest for the people of God, for whoever has entered God's rest has also rested from his works as God did from his (4:3–10).

To be sure, this "Sabbath rest" remaining for the people of God does *not* refer to a renewed keeping of the Sabbath, as has been suggested. It is *not* a reference to the "rest" for the believer's soul, nor to the rest of "heaven" as the place where believers are thought to go when they pass away, as has been suggested as well (see chapter 7). It is a reference to the same subject the letter to the Hebrews so often refers to: the "[Messianic] world to come" (2:5), the "[Messianic] age to come" (6:5), the "[Messianic] city that is to come" (13:14). The "Sabbath rest" refers to the seventh and last "day seven" of redemptive history. The work of creation ended with the Sabbath, and the work of re-creation will end in the same way. The week of creation culminated in the first Eden; redemptive history will culminate in the new and ultimate Eden.[7]

This is expressed in a magnificent way in Psalm 92, which is explicitly called "A Song for the Sabbath":[8]

> The righteous flourish like the palm tree
>   and grow like a cedar in Lebanon.
> They are planted in the house of the LORD;
>   they flourish in the courts of our God.
> They still bear fruit in old age;
>   they are ever full of sap and green,
> to declare that the LORD is upright;
>   he is my rock, and there is no unrighteousness in him (vv. 12–15).

Here, the Sabbath implies an "Eden" of palm trees and cedars, planted at no lesser place than the "house of the LORD." But these trees are not for the enjoyment of believers—believers *themselves* are these Edenic trees.

4.6 A Land of Trees

The latter quotation (§4.5) brings us directly to the trees of Eden. The first Eden contained not only the tree of life and the tree of knowledge: "[O]ut of the ground the LORD God made to spring up *every tree that is pleasant to the sight and good for food*. The tree of life was in the midst of the garden, and the tree of the knowledge of good and evil" (Gen. 2:9; cf. v. 16; 3:6). Eden was truly a park, an orchard, not

---

7   Augustine, in his *De Civitate Dei* ("The City of God"), compared redemptive history with the seven days of creation, the seventh day referring, in his view, to the eternal state.

8   Some people seem to think that, because in most English translations such superscripts are not part of the numbered text, they are not part of the inspired text—which is a mistake.

just with ornamental trees, but with trees that had these two characteristics: "pleasant to look at" and "good for food." These are trees that bring both enjoyment and nourishment.

In the fields of Moab, Moses prepared the people for similar beauties that they would enjoy in the Promised Land:

> [T]he LORD your God is bringing you into a good land, a land of brooks of water, of fountains and springs, flowing out in the valleys and hills, a land of wheat and barley, of *vines and fig trees and pomegranates*, a land of *olive trees* and honey, a land in which you will eat bread without scarcity, in which you will lack nothing, a land whose stones are iron, and out of whose hills you can dig copper. And you shall eat and be full, and you shall bless the LORD your God for the good land he has given you (Deut. 8:7–10).

We have here seven plant products. Two are of an agricultural nature: the wheat and the barley. One is of an apidological[9] nature: bees are animals, but the honey is taken from flowers. And four are of a dendrological[10] nature: vines, fig trees, pomegranates, and olive trees.

> [T]he land that you are going over to possess is a land of hills and valleys, which drinks water by the rain from heaven, a land that the LORD your God cares for. The eyes of the LORD your God are always upon it, from the beginning of the year to the end of the year. And if you will indeed obey my commandments that I command you today, to love the LORD your God, and to serve him with all your heart and with all your soul, he will give the rain for your land in its season, the early rain and the later rain, that you may gather in your grain and your wine and your oil. And he will give grass in your fields for your livestock, and you shall eat and be full (Deut. 11:11–15).

In addition to the four trees mentioned above—vines, fig trees, pomegranates, and olive trees—we hear elsewhere about the oak, the poplar, and the terebinth (Hos. 4:13), the cedar, the acacia, the

---

9 Apidology is the science of bees.
10 Dendrology is the science of trees.

myrtle, the cypress, the plane, and the pine (Isa. 41:19). We may assume that the pistachio, the almond (Gen. 43:11), and the willow (Lev. 23:40) were common in Israel as well. But most of the trees mentioned do not fulfill the second condition: some of them may be "pleasant to look at," but they are not "good for food." This apart from the pistachio nuts and the almonds, of course, but they were not part of the people's everyday menu; they were luxuries.

Actually, there is a remarkable passage in Ezekiel, in which the trees in the "garden of God," also called the "trees of Eden," compete with another "tree," namely, the powerful Assyria or Egypt (Ezek. 31:8–9, 15–18; see Appendix 1). Among the trees of this "Eden," we find the cedar, the fir tree, and the plane tree, which are explicitly described as belonging to "all the trees of Eden, that were in the garden of God." This is remarkable because these trees again may be "pleasant to look at," but they are not "good for food." This is no wonder: these are Eden-trees of a very peculiar nature, as we will see in Appendix 1.

4.7 Milk and Honey

I will come back to the trees (§4.8), but first I wish to draw attention to another characteristic of this new Eden: it is "a land flowing with milk and honey" (Exod. 3:8, 17; 13:5; 33:3; Lev. 20:24).[11] "[Y]ou gave them this land, which you swore to their fathers to give them, a land flowing with milk and honey" (Jer. 32:22). It is the most common description of the Promised Land, underlining the goodness and blessedness that the LORD had bestowed upon it. Interestingly, this is not a botanical but basically a zoological description. The cows and the goats of the land produce the milk (even if they synthesize it from the grass they eat), and the bees of the land produce the honey (even if they collect it from flowers).

Cows, sheep, and goats constitute together the cattle of the Jewish farmer in Israel. One of the most common dairy products was curds, made of cow's milk, and God gave these to his people with a generous hand: he

---

11 "Milk and honey" is the title of a movie, a musical, a novel, a distillery in Israel, a poetry collection, a pop group, and of many pop songs; apparently, the description appeals to the imagination.

made him [i.e., Israel] ride on the high places of the land, and he ate the produce of the field, and he suckled him with *honey* out of the rock, and oil out of the flinty rock. *Curds* from the herd [i.e., the cows], and *milk* from the flock [i.e., the sheep and goats], with fat of lambs, rams of Bashan and goats, with the very finest of the wheat— and you drank foaming wine made from the blood of the grape. But Jeshurun [i.e., Israel] grew fat, and kicked; you grew fat, stout, and sleek; then he forsook God who made him and scoffed at the Rock of his salvation (Deut. 32:13–15).

This quotation would almost give the impression that Israel suffered from the *abundance* (an overdose) of God's good blessings. It is similar with the honey: "If you have found honey, eat only enough for you, lest you have your fill of it and vomit it. . . . It is not good to eat much honey" (Prov. 25:16, 27). "One who is full loathes honey" (27:7). It is the same as with the good manna that God gave to his people for almost forty years; yet, in the end they said, "[W]e loathe this worthless food" (Num. 21:5). This does not say anything about the quality of the food as such; it says something only about people who can be tired of God's wonderful blessings. The spiritually weak can begin to loathe the land of milk and honey because it is simply *too good*.

Bees are mentioned in the Bible several times in a negative sense (Deut. 1:44; Ps. 118:12), but once in a positive sense:

> After some days he [i.e., Samson] returned to take her [i.e., his bride]. And he turned aside to see the carcass of the lion [that he had killed], and behold, there was a swarm of bees in the body of the lion, and honey. He scraped it out into his hands and went on, eating as he went. . . . And he said to them [i.e., the Philistines], "Out of the eater came something to eat. Out of the strong came something sweet" (Judg. 14:8–9, 14).

In the end, Samson's battle with a fearsome enemy, namely, the lion, had produced sweetness, namely, the honey. Honey is nourishing, and it produces clarity of mind as well: honey gives brightness to the eyes, as the story of Jonathan tells us (1 Sam. 14:27, 29).

If the young lover in the Song of Solomon describes his beloved as a "garden locked," as an "orchard," in short, as a paradise, he says just before this, "Your lips drip nectar, my bride; honey and milk are under your tongue" (Song 4:11–13). The blessings of *this* paradise are basically the same as those of any Eden: it is a land flowing with milk and honey: "I came to my garden, my sister, my bride, I gathered my myrrh with my spice, I ate my *honeycomb* with my *honey*, I drank my wine with my *milk*" (5:1).

4.8 Four Main Trees

In §4.6, I mentioned many trees in the Promised Land, but no doubt the first four mentioned—vines, fig trees, pomegranates, and olive trees—are by far the most important ones, and the ones most commonly mentioned in the Bible. I find four different spiritual "fruits" in the New Testament, to be produced by believers, so that I venture to say that the four trees and the four fruits wondrously fit together. I say this in anticipation of what I will say about the church as another "Eden" of God (see chapter 6).

First, the *vine*. As we saw (§2.7), wine—the fruit of the vine—is what "cheers God and men" (Judg. 9:13); wine is given "to gladden the heart of man" (Ps. 104:15). Among the "fruit of the Spirit," joy is the second one mentioned, after love (Gal. 5:22). When Jesus encourages his followers to produce much fruit of the vine, he finishes with saying: "These things I have spoken to you, that my joy may be in you, and that your joy may be full" (John 15:11). Joy is a truly Edenic fruit: "For the kingdom of God is . . . a matter . . . of righteousness and peace and joy in the Holy Spirit" (Rom. 14:17). Indeed, joy is a special aspect of the Messianic kingdom: "[T]he ransomed of the LORD shall return and come to Zion with singing; everlasting joy shall be upon their heads; they shall obtain gladness and joy, and sorrow and sighing shall flee away" (Isa. 35:10; 51:11). "Instead of your shame there shall be a double portion; instead of dishonor they shall rejoice in their lot; therefore in their land they shall possess a double portion; they shall have everlasting joy" (61:7).

Second, the *fig tree*. In Jeremiah 24 I find a key its spiritual meaning, where the righteous in Israel are compared to good figs, viewed in the light of the Messianic kingdom:

> Like these good figs, so I will regard as good the exiles from Judah, whom I have sent away from this place to the land of the Chaldeans. I will set my eyes on them for good, and I will bring them back to this land. I will build them up, and not tear them down; I will plant them, and not pluck them up. I will give them a heart to know that I am the LORD, and they shall be my people and I will be their God, for they shall return to me with their whole heart (vv. 5–7).

Thus, I link the fig tree with what we find three times in the New Testament about the "fruit of righteousness":[12] ". . . filled with the fruit of righteousness that comes through Jesus Christ, to the glory and praise of God" (Phil. 1:11). "For the moment all discipline seems painful rather than pleasant, but later it yields the peaceful fruit of righteousness to those who have been trained by it" (Hebr. 12:11). "[T]he wisdom that is from above is first pure, then peaceable, gentle, willing to yield, full of mercy and good fruits, without partiality and without hypocrisy. Now the fruit of righteousness is sown in peace by those who make peace" (James 3:17–18 NKJV). To be precise, the "fruit of righteousness" involves the righteousness in Christian behavior as worked by the Holy Spirit, just as the water from the soil and the sun at the sky work the figs on the fig tree.

Third, the *pomegranate*. As the fruit of the sanctuary *par excellence* (see §3.9), I compare the pomegranate with the "fruit unto holiness (or sanctification)":

> [W]hen you were slaves of sin, you were free in regard to righteousness. But what fruit were you getting at that time from the things of which you are now ashamed? For the end of those things is death. But now that you have been set free from sin and have become slaves of God, the fruit you get leads to sanctification and its end, eternal life. For the wages of sin is death, but the free gift

---

12 This forms a contrast with the loincloths made of fig leaves with which the first humans covered their nakedness (Gen. 3:7), and which speak of their self-righteousness.

of God is eternal life in Christ Jesus our Lord (Rom. 6:20–23).

Notice that the goal lies in the future again: "... its end, eternal life," which cannot be severed from the Messianic kingdom: in the Synoptic Gospels, "inheriting" the kingdom (Matt. 25:34) is identical with "inheriting" eternal life (19:29 par.).

Fourth, the *olive tree*. The fruit of this tree is the olive, and the oil obtained from the olives was used to anoint kings (1 Sam. 10:1; 16:13), priests (Exod. 28:41; 29:21), and prophets (1 Kings 19:16; Isa. 61:1–3). Thus, anointing with oil in the Old Testament finds its parallel in the anointing with the Holy Spirit in the New Testament: "God anointed Jesus of Nazareth with the Holy Spirit and with power. He went about doing good and healing all who were oppressed by the devil, for God was with him" (Acts 10:38). "[I]t is God who establishes us with you in Christ, and has anointed us, and who has also put his seal on us and given us his Spirit in our hearts as a guarantee" (2 Cor. 1:21–22). Therefore, I cannot doubt that the fruit of the olive tree speaks of the fruit of the Spirit, which is "love, joy, peace, patience, kindness, goodness, faithfulness, gentleness, self-control; against such things there is no law" (Gal. 5:22-23). In 1 John 2:20 and 27, the apostle speaks of being anointed *by* the Holy One (God/Christ), but apparently this is again an anointing *with* the Holy Spirit.

Even in the Old Testaments we find hints of this connection between the anointing and the Holy Spirit: "Then Samuel took the horn of oil and anointed him in the midst of his brothers. And the Spirit of the LORD rushed upon David from that day forward" (1 Sam. 16:13). "The Spirit of the Lord GOD is upon me, because the LORD has anointed me" (Isa. 61:1).

Some references to the "age to come" are appropriate here, namely, those that compare the Spirit with water poured out on the thirsty ground, and thus underline the picture of a garden, a park, or an orchard: "[One day] the Spirit is poured upon us from on high, and the wilderness becomes a fruitful field, and the fruitful field is deemed a forest. Then justice will dwell in the wilderness, and righteousness abide in the fruitful field" (Isa. 32:15–16). "I will pour water on the thirsty land, and streams on the dry ground; I will pour my Spirit upon your offspring, and my blessing on your descendants" (44:3).

4.9 In Exile

Just as Adam was placed in the Garden of Eden, an orchard of trees, Israel was placed in the new Eden, the Promised Land, a new park of trees. And just as Adam fell into sin, and had to be driven out of Eden, Israel fell into sin, and had to be driven out of the Promised Land. Adam's exile is the mother of all exiles, so to speak. In a sense, his exile lasts until the eternal state, the new heavens and the new earth, when sin and death will have been removed from the cosmos (John 1:29; Rev. 20:14). And Israel's exile was not fully reversed when Israel returned from Babylon, because there was no new descent of the *Shekhinah* on the so-called Second Temple. Moreover, they were still slaves of the ruling world power (Neh. 9:36). Therefore, Israel's exile lasts in fact until the moment of Ezekiel 43:

> Then he led me to the gate, the gate facing east. And behold, the glory of the God of Israel was coming from the east. . . .[13] As the glory of the LORD entered the temple by the gate facing east, the Spirit lifted me up and brought me into the inner court; and behold, the glory of the LORD filled the temple. . . . Son of man, this is the place of my throne and the place of the soles of my feet, where I will dwell in the midst of the people of Israel forever (vv. 1–7).

Then, Israel will be set free from all the powers in the world.

A true exile in the spiritual sense consists of being *driven* out of the Holy Land. It is not a voluntary (and temporary) leaving, for instance because there is famine in the land (Gen. 12:10; Ruth 1:1–2). Or what is worse, a voluntary (and permanent) leaving because one is not pleased with the Land. Jacob *had to* leave the Land (Gen. 27–28), but Esau, who was an unholy man (Heb. 12:16), *wished* to leave the Land (28:9), and moved to the land of Seir, never to return (32:3; 36:8–9). In other words, some are driven out of the Land because of their sins, but they can repent and in due time return. Others leave the Land at their own initiative because of their wickedness, and never wish to return. Some *lose* Eden, others *despise* Eden; the former often receive it back—by way of repentance and faith—the latter do

---

13 Notice this direction, and compare §3.1.

not even *wish* to receive it back. The former may have great difficulty coming back; Jacob was hindered by his father-in-law (Gen. 31), by his brother Esau (Esau 32–33), and by the angel who wrestled with him—whether this was a good or a bad angel.[14] But he did come back, whereas Esau returned to his own land, that of Seir (Exod. 34).

We may put it this way: eventually, the people who will inherit the ultimate Eden will be those who *desire* to inherit it. And those who will not inherit it will be those who did not *want* to. In the end, there are only these options, as I said before: it is either a garden or a lake: it is either the eternal Garden of God, or the "lake that burns with fire and sulfur" (Rev. 21:8). C. S. Lewis wrote somewhere that hell will be closed on the inside, not the outside. That is, it will be horrible inside, but for the wicked it would be more horrible in the Garden, where all will be for the honor of God and all will constantly praise his name.

"Choose this day whom you will serve" (Josh. 24:15). Those who will be in the Garden will have been chosen by God, but they themselves have also chosen to serve the LORD. Those who will be in the lake will be there because they *chose* to be there. Perhaps not consciously—but at least they consciously rejected God. The lake of fire is the everlasting exile—however, not a compulsory exile but a voluntary one, if I may put it this way. Inside the Garden will be the Jacobs, who may wander away from it but ultimately return. Inside the lake will be the Esaus, who voluntarily turned their backs to the Promised Land, never to return.

"How often would I have gathered your children together as a hen gathers her brood under her wings, and *you were not willing!*" (Luke 13:34). This is the lovely picture of the hen and its young; in contrast with this, we hear of other birds: the unclean birds living in the great Babylon (Rev. 18:2), and the birds that are gorged with the flesh of Christ's enemies (Rev. 19:21). Or, to use that other picture, in the Garden will be the Lamb, in the lake will be the dragon.

---

14 Regarding this matter, see Ouweneel (2019, chapter 4).

5
The Garden of Joseph

And Joseph took the body,
  and wrapped it in a clean linen shroud
and laid it in his own new tomb,
  which he had cut in the rock.

Matthew 27:59–60

Now in the place where he was crucified there was a garden,
and in the garden a new tomb
  in which no one had yet been laid.

John 19:41

Jesus said to her, "Woman, why are you weeping?
  Whom are you seeking?"
Supposing him to be the gardener, she said to him,
  "Sir, if you have carried him away,
  tell me where you have laid him,
  and I will take him away."

John 20:15

5.1 Two Gardens

If you ask Christians who have visited Jerusalem what part of the city impressed them most, they may very well point to Gethsemane or The Garden Tomb, or both. Not certain buildings, streets, squares, walls, churches, or towers, but two gardens! I can understand these people—I have visited these places myself many times. I must add, however, that both also bring their own disappointment. As for Gethsemane, it is not entirely clear at all where one should look. The place the great majority of visitors go to is the garden next to the Roman Catholic Church of All Nations—to find that the most important place in it, the rock where Jesus supposedly prayed (Matt. 26:36-46), is enclosed within this church, whereas the olive trees are outside. Within the building, you lose all sense of a garden. Other guides will take you to the Tomb of the Virgin Mary as supposedly being within the ancient garden of Gethsemane. The Greek Orthodox will take you to their own location, more to the east. And the Russian Orthodox will take you to the orchard next to the Church of Mary Magdalene.

Do not be confused or embarrassed; it is like this with many places in the Holy Land. We can only be thankful that the Protestants do not have their own Gethsemane on the Mount of Olives!

It is only in John's Gospel that Gethsemane is called a "garden"; Matthew (26:36) and Mark (14:32) just call it a "place." John tells us: "Jesus ... went out with his disciples across the brook Kidron, where there was a garden, which he and his disciples entered" (18:1; cf. v. 26). Because the garden is on the Mount of Olives, tradition depicts Gethsemane as a garden with olive trees; some of the trees near the Church of All Nations are so old that the guides assure us that Jesus must have seen some of these trees when they were still very young. Because the new tomb in the garden is said to be Joseph's tomb, it has been generally accepted that the garden was Joseph's garden.

With the Garden Tomb, that other favorite place in Jerusalem, it is a very different story. It is a tomb in Jerusalem hewn from the rock, a little north of the Turkish city walls. It was discovered in 1867. In 1883, the place was visited by British Major General Charles Gordon, who examined it and began to strongly defend the view that *this* was the tomb of Jesus. One of his arguments was that the hill very nearby, called Skull Hill, looked the same as what the Bible described as Golgotha, a word derived from an Aramaic word for "skull" (cf. Matt. 27:33; Mark 15:22). Indeed, Skull Hill has some vague resemblance to a human skull. Masses of Christians, especially Protestants, have accepted Gordon's hypothesis, but the experts have rejected it. Roman Catholic and Orthodox believers have always done the same; to them, there is no doubt that the real tomb of Jesus is within the

The Garden of Joseph

Church of the Holy Sepulchre, in the Christian quarter within ancient Jerusalem.

I fear that the latter are right. The great problem, though, is that the Church of the Holy Sepulchre least resembles a garden. To the naïve, uninformed pilgrim this Church is shocking, not only because every square inch is the object of dispute among various denominations, but also because of all the gold and silver, and all the candles, decorating the places of Jesus' cross and tomb. Christians have formed a picture of these places in their minds from their early youth, but they fail to look *through* the gold and the silver. I myself was so confused that, after having climbed the stairs of Golgotha, I asked a nun: "Is *this* the place of the cross?" She looked sternly at me, and asked: "Are you a Christian?" In other words, how could you ask such a stupid question!

The picture that many Christians have carried within them since their youth is no mistake at all. On the contrary, what does John's Gospel tell us about the place where Jesus died and was buried? "Now in the place where he [i.e., Jesus] was crucified there was a garden, and in the garden a new tomb in which no one had yet been laid. So because of the Jewish day of Preparation, since the tomb was close at hand, they laid Jesus there" (19:41–42). Notice, first, that the garden was very near to the cross, exactly as we find it in the Church of the Holy Sepulchre. For the rest, forget every memory that you have in your mind about a hill and a garden.

After Jesus' resurrection we read of his encounter with Mary Magdalene:

> Jesus said to her, "Woman, why are you weeping? Whom are you seeking?" Supposing him to be the gardener, she said to him, "Sir, if you have carried him away, tell me where you have laid him, and I will take him away." Jesus said to her, "Mary." She turned and said to him in Aramaic, "Rabboni!" (which means Teacher) (John 20:15).

Apparently, we are still in the same garden where Jesus had been buried; otherwise it can hardly be explained how Mary could think he was the gardener. Notice how close these places were: the place of the cross, the place of the tomb, and the place of this appearance of the risen Lord. The latter two were in the same garden, and the first one, the place of the cross, was very nearby. And over the entire area, the Crusaders built their church.

5.2 A Third "Garden"?

I described two gardens: Gethsemane and the garden of the Garden Tomb. But there is a third garden—of which not the slightest sign is left. Everything associated with a garden has been replaced by stones, and by gold, silver, and jewels, something that might disappoint contemporary visitors. Chances are very high (one Jewish specialist told me: 99%) that whatever is left of the Garden of Joseph of Arimathea is to be found in the Church of the Holy Sepulchre.

In order to comfort the disappointed visitor, let me say that, according to a cherished tradition, this is the place associated not only with the death of Christ, but also with the death of . . . Adam. Visitors who descend to the Church's lower levels will find on the ground floor, directly beneath the Golgotha chapel, the so-called Chapel of Adam. Notice the position: the Golgotha chapel is directly above the Chapel of Adam, which means that the cross of Jesus was directly above the place where, according to tradition, Adam's skull had been buried. One version declares that the blood of Christ ran down the cross and seeped through the rocks to cover the skull of Adam, thus bringing atonement upon him in a very literal way.

I love such legends, not because they are historically true but because they often contain deep spiritual insights. One source of the legend is the (Arab Christian) *Kitab al-Magall* ("The Book of the Rolls"). It tells us that Shem and Melchizedek traveled to the resting place of Noah's Ark, retrieved the body of Adam from it,[1] and were led by an angel to a place called "Golgotha": a skull-shaped hill at the center of the earth [!]:[2]

---

1 A strange detail! What did the body of Adam do in Noah's Ark?
2 http://www.sacred-texts.com/chr/aa/aa2.htm; see also "The Conflict of Adam and Eve with Satan," a sixth-century Christian work, and from the same century, the Cave of Treasures, as well the Nazm al-Jauhar ("Row of Jewels") by the Melkite Patriarch Eutychius of Alexandria (c. 900).

> ... Then Shem called Melchizedek by night, and bore with him the body of Adam secretly. They went out, the angel going before them, till he brought them to the place with the utmost speed. He said to them, "Set him down, for this is the center of the earth." And they put him down from their hands. When he came to the ground, the earth was cleft for him as a door, and the body was let down into it, and they put him in it. When the body rested in its place, the earth returned and covered it over. The place was called *Gumgumah*, "of a skull," because in it was placed the skull of the father of mankind, and *Gulgulah*, because it was conspicuous in the earth.

Again, the real significance of such a story is the spiritual insight it contains: awareness of the profound connection between the first Adam and Jesus, the last Adam, and I may add, between the Garden of Adam and the Garden of Joseph, in which was Jesus was buried and arose. And if we think of the women involved, we realize that Eve was the protagonist in the former garden, and Mary Magdalene was the protagonist in the latter garden. This is a subject that we must discuss briefly, later in the chapter (§5.4).

5.3 The Cherubim
But before discussing Eve and Mary, let me say something about the cherubim:

> Mary stood weeping outside the tomb, and as she wept she stooped to look into the tomb. And she saw two angels in white, sitting where the body of Jesus had lain, one at the head and one at the feet. They said to her, "Woman, why are you weeping?" She said to them, "They have taken away my Lord, and I do not know where they have laid him" (John 20:11–13).

Luke speaks of "two *men*," and Matthew speaks of only one "angel." These differences do not concern us right now, although liberal theologians often use them to cast doubt on the historicity of the entire story. My point is rather that John's two angels cannot but remind us of the cherubim of Genesis 3: God "drove out the man [and his wife], and at the east of the garden of Eden he placed the cherubim and a flaming sword that turned every way to guard the way to the tree of life" (v. 24).

The conspicuous difference here catches the eye. The cherubim of Genesis 3 are there to keep people *out*. The angels at the tomb are there to invite people *in*, to see for themselves that the tomb is empty. In Matthew 28:5–6, the angel says, "Do not be afraid, for I know that you seek Jesus who was crucified. He is not here, for he has risen, as he said. Come, *see the place where he lay*" (cf. Mark 16:6). The *Stay out!* of Genesis 3 is just as remarkable as this *Come in!* of the Gospels. The reasons for these calls are clear: in Genesis 3, the first humans had to stay out of Eden because sin and death had entered the garden. In the story of Jesus' resurrection, the humans of the new Eden were allowed into the very place where sin and death had been overcome. Death closes the way to Eden, resurrection opens it. The first Adam had to go out, the last Adam takes us in.

People have reminded us here of what farmers do in some countries, where they are afraid of raging field fires. Under strict supervision, such farmers burn certain strips of land around their houses and possessions, so that the field fires can do no damage there. I have closely observed this in South Africa, many years ago. The fire cannot touch these burned down places anymore *because they had already been burned.* In other words, the only place on earth where those who repent will be safe is the tomb of Jesus *because it is the only place where God's judgment has already done its work.* God's judgment cannot touch a place where it already was. The first Eden was ruined through sin and death. But at the tomb of Jesus, angels invite the believers to enter because *there*, and there alone, sin and death have been conquered. The cherubim in Genesis prevented any access to the tree of life. The angels in the Gospels *offer* access to a new Eden because the Prince of Life has overcome death.

This is one of the peculiar aspects of Christian baptism: "Do you not know that all of us who have been baptized into Christ Jesus were baptized into his death? We were buried therefore with him by baptism into death, in order that, just as Christ was raised from the dead by the glory of the Father, we too might walk in newness of life" (Rom.

6:3-4). Being baptized represents being buried with Christ in his tomb. As Christ's earthly life ended on the cross and in the tomb, in baptism people are joined with Christ in this death and burial. They are figuratively buried into the only safe place in the world where God's judgment cannot reach them anymore because it raged there already. Beyond the tomb of Christ these young Christians walk in newness of life as followers of the risen Christ. Thus, baptism has an Edenic aspect, just as we will discover in connection with the Lord's Supper (§§6.6 and 6.7).

5.4 Eve and the Two Marys[3]

In the Garden of Joseph Jesus meets the earliest witnesses of his resurrection: first, Mary Magdalene, afterward, the other Mary (Matt. 28:1) and Salome (Mark 16:1). These were all women! Eve brought the forbidden fruit to Adam, and he ate of it. In this way, she dragged him along to utter misery. Mary Magdalene brought the news of the risen Lord to the disciples, thus leading them on the way to salvation and joy. Eve led the first Adam to death, Mary, through the last Adam, led others to life.

The two most important women of the New Testament, at least certainly in the light of what Christian tradition has made of them, were both called Mary. The one was the mother of Jesus, the other was Mary Magdalene. Both came from Galilee: the former from the town of Nazareth, the latter from the town of Magdala, hence her name. Both women belonged to those who were standing near the cross (John 19:25). Both were addressed by Jesus with the honorary title *gynai*, which means as much as "lady" (John 2:4; 19:26; 20:15). The one Mary was the first witness of Jesus' birth, the other Mary was the first witness of Jesus' resurrection.

Tradition tells us that the most important distinction between the two Marys is that each represents an opposite aspect of femininity:[4] mother Mary is the perfectly blameless virgin, Mary Magdalene is the converted prostitute (if we may believe tradition on this point).[5] The

---

3   See Ouweneel (1998, §3.5).
4   Cf. Trudgill (1976), title: *Madonnas and Magdalenes*.
5   Regarding Mary Magdalene, see extensively, Warner (1990, 265-278); see also Ouweneel (1998, §3.5). The origin of the tradition arose when

Virgin Mary was thought to correspond with the pre-Fall sinless virgin Eve; Mary Magdalene was thought to represent the post-Fall sinful Eve, whose sin is traditionally viewed as closely related to sexual lust.[6] If mother Mary is the virgin of virgins, Mary Magdalene was called by Hrabanus Maurus (ninth century)[7] the "apostle to the apostles" (Lat. *apostolorum apostola*) that is, the woman who brought a good message to those who were called to go out and preach Jesus' good message.[8]

If Eve was the wife of the first Adam, the Virgin Mary was viewed not only as the mother of Jesus but also as his mystical bride, and as such the prototype of the church. But Mary Magdalene also received her special place in redemptive history. She reminds us of the Eve who was converted after her fall. In this sense, she too has been viewed as a second Eve. The first similarity may be negative: the *sad* fallen Eve hid herself among the trees, and in the Garden of Joseph, the *sad* Mary Magdalene wander about not knowing what to do, either. But then: just as the paradisal condition of the first Eden was annulled by the failure of the woman as priestess, the new paradisal condition is ushered in by a new Eve. As Dutch theologian Frank de Graaff put it, Mary Magdalene "expects that he [i.e., Jesus] will lead her back to the original paradisal state, in which her feminine being may again mediate with the divine world. . . . Jesus returns to Mary [Magdalene] her paradisal, feminine relationship with the divine world."[9] The latter is related to the fact that it was not Adam but Eve who was able to

---

Mary Magdalene was identified as the sinful and repentant woman of Luke 7:36–50.

6   See Ouweneel (1998, chapter 3).

7   He was presumed to be the poet of the well-known hymn *Veni, Creator Spiritus*, "Come, Holy Spirit."

8   Medieval painters (e.g., the Grimani Breviary, Fra Angelico) sometimes depicted Mary with her Child within a *hortus conclusus*, the "locked garden" of Song 4:12, thus referring this verse to her. The "locked garden" was understood to point to her immaculate conception and her perpetual virginity, or even specifically to her undefiled womb. Even today, Mary is sometimes referred as "Our Lady of the [Enclosed] Garden." This is one of the most exceptional interpretations of Eden: Mary's womb was the paradise of Song 4!

9   De Graaff (1982, 42, 46).

converse with the world of the serpent (dragon), and thus with the supernatural world as a whole.

In the Garden of Eden, God revealed himself in his forgiving grace to Adam and Eve—in the Garden of Joseph, the last Adam, alive and risen, revealed himself to Mary. God came with life, with salvation, with new hope to Adam and Eve. Jesus did the same to Mary Magdalene, and afterward to the other women. One Eden was lost, a new Eden opened.

Notice the connection between the various questions: to Adam, "Where are you?" (Gen. 3:9), and to Eve, "What is this that you[10] have done?" (v. 13). And then to Mary, "Woman, why are you weeping? Whom are you seeking?" (John 20:15; cf. v. 13). These are elementary questions: Where? What? Why? Who? In all three cases—Adam, Eve, Mary—they are intended to confront the person with his or her condition: Do you realize in what situation you have landed? Do you see what is going on within you and around you? In the end, such a confrontation is with *oneself*: Where am I? What have I done? *Who am I?* No person can enter the new Eden, that is, no person can meet the Lord, without first having met oneself. The prodigal son had to first come to himself before he could come to his father (Luke 15:17, 20).

5.5 The Second Eve

Mary Magdalene was the first to encounter the risen Lord. A second Eve meets the last Adam! She encountered him who was going to ascend to his and our Father, and was called upon to testify of this to his "brothers and sisters":

> Jesus said to her, "Don't hold on to me, for I haven't yet gone up to my Father. Go to my brothers and sisters and tell them, 'I'm going up to my Father and your Father, to my God and your God.'" Mary Magdalene left and announced to the disciples, "I've seen the Lord." Then she told them what he said to her (John 20:17–18 CEB).

To summarize the similarities and contrasts: the first Adam belonged to the first Eden, the last Adam appears in a new Eden, even

---

10 The "you" in both questions is singular, and thus very personal.

a literal garden like the first one. Adam was the (literal) gardener of the first Eden, Jesus was the (figurative) gardener of the new Eden (in a sense that went much deeper than Mary Magdalene could know and extended far beyond the Garden of Joseph). There were trees in the former Eden, but above all it contained the tree of life. There were also (literal) trees in the latter Eden—but above all, the latter one contained the tree on which Jesus was crucified and died: "The God of our fathers raised Jesus, whom you killed by hanging him on a tree," said Peter to the Jewish leaders (Acts 5:30). "They put him to death by hanging him on a tree" (10:39). "And when they had carried out all that was written of him, they took him down from the tree and laid him in a tomb" (13:29).

Traditionally, expositors have seen in the tree of life either Jesus himself, or the cross of Jesus. The former explanation seems to me more likely, but the Orthodox Church thinks of the cross.[11] As the Dutch poet Hieronymus van Alphen (d. 1803) put it in a well-known Dutch hymn:

Wij schuldig, door God uitgedreven,
    wij bleven ver van Eden staan.
Maar 't kruis werd ons de boom van 't leven;
    die wees de Vader zelf ons aan.[12]

The first Eden was where the first Adam and Eve spiritually died (Gen. 2:17)—but after their conversion, Eve (which means "Life" or "Life-giving") was named the "mother of all living" (3:20). Her offspring would be a spiritual people, opposed to the serpent's offspring (v. 15). The new Eden was where the last Adam returned from death, who as the risen One brought life to Mary Magdalene and so many others. Her spiritual offspring were the brothers and sisters to whom she brought the message of the risen Christ. There was a new beginning in the first Eden after the Fall. There is a new beginning in the new Eden after, and through, the resurrection of Christ—and a wom-

---

11 See Ouweneel (2018, chapter 7).

12 "We, guilty, driven out by God, / we remained far from Eden. / But the cross became to us the tree of life, / pointed out to us by the Father himself."

an took a prominent place on both occasions.

Notice the role of the names in this. In fact, Eve received her name only after her fall and her conversion. Adam gave her this name, seeing in faith the living ones who were to come forth from her. By contrast, Jesus did not *give* Mary her name, but *called* her by this name: "Mary!" (John 20:16). This was enough for her to recognize who he was. It reminds us of what he himself had said of the Good Shepherd: "The sheep hear his voice, and he calls his own sheep by name and leads them out" (10:3). Before these events, Eve was simply the "woman" (Gen. 2:22-23; 3:1-6, 12-16), and this is also the first thing Jesus said the Mary: "Woman" (John 20:13, 15). After the great turn, the former woman became "Eve," and the latter woman became "Mary," so to speak. Unfortunately, we do not know for sure what "Mary" means (there are more than sixty explanations!), but at least we know the meaning of "Magdalene": woman from Magdala, that is, "tower." She is like a monument of the new Eden, erected in the Garden of Joseph.

5.6 The Seven Tents

Allow me to travel back from the Garden of Joseph a bit more than thirty years earlier, to the time of Jesus' birth. In previous chapters, we have dealt with gardens and sanctuaries, matters that sometimes clearly coincided. After having spoken extensively of the tabernacle in chapter 3, it is now time to draw attention to the fact that God seems to link his presence to *seven* successive *tents* (Heb. *ohel*, Gk. *skēnē*), which are also seven sanctuaries because God's dwelling-places are sacred by definition. Here is a summary.

The first tent was the tabernacle in the wilderness (see chapter 3), traveling with the people of Israel, and later pitched in the Promised Land, first at Shiloh (1 Sam. 4:3-4), later at Gibeon (1 Chron. 16:39; 21:29). Its function ceased when God replaced it with the temple of Solomon (cf. Ps. 78:60, 67-69).

The second tent was the one King David pitched near the "city of David" (on Mount Moriah?[13]) in order to place the ark of the covenant

---

13 Mount Moriah (cf. 2 Chron. 3:1) and Mount Zion are confusing terms, which often must be identical (see, e.g., Ps. 76:2; 132:13; 135:21; Isa. 8:18); but Zion can also refer to the hill of the "City of David," and to-

in it: "[T]hey brought in the ark of the LORD and set it in its place, inside the tent that David had pitched for it. And David offered burnt offerings and peace offerings before the LORD" (2 Sam. 6:17; cf. 7:2) (not to be confused with the tabernacle, which at that moment stood in Gibeon; see previous point). In my view, when David spoke of his desire to stay in the "house of the LORD," in order "to gaze upon the beauty of the LORD" (Ps. 27:4; cf. 26:8, "the habitation of your house"; see also 5:7; 23:6), he was thinking of this tent.

The third tent is the body of Jesus Christ, an important subject to which I will return in §5.7.

The fourth tent is the body of each New Testament believer, which is sometimes called a "tent" (2 Cor. 5:1–4; 2 Pet. 1:13–14), and which is a temple in which the Holy Spirit dwells (1 Cor. 6:19).

The fifth tent will be the Jerusalem of the Messianic kingdom, which is described as "an untroubled habitation, an immovable tent, whose stakes will never be plucked up, nor will any of its cords be broken" (Isa. 33:20), where the *Shekhinah* will dwell in the temple of Ezekiel (Ezek. 40–44).

The sixth tent, spoken of in Amos 9:11 as the "booth [Heb. *sukkah*; Septuagint: *skēnē*] of David that is fallen," refers to the dynasty of David, as it will be restored in the Messianic kingdom (cf. the application in Acts 15:16); that is, the Holy Spirit will rest upon the Messiah (Acts 10:38).

The seventh tent is the tent (or tabernacle) in which God will dwell among the people in the new heavens and on the new earth (Rev. 21:3).

5.7 Christ and the *Shekhinah*

God, or the *Shekhinah*, dwelt in Eden, in the tabernacle, in the First Temple—and he dwelt in Christ. Jesus' body was the new and true temple, in which the Holy Spirit dwelt. The wording is very important here: "And the Word became flesh and dwelt among us" (John 1:14a). Literally, the Word "tabernacled" (*eskēnōsen*, from *skēnē*, "tent, tabernacle"); as other renderings have it: "tabernacled (fixed His tent of flesh, lived awhile) among us" (AMPC; cf. EXB; OJB: "made his sukkah [tent, booth, hut], his Mishkan [Tabernacle] among us"). That is,

day Zion is the name of the hill southwest of old Jerusalem.

his human flesh was a tabernacle in which the *Shekhinah*—read: the Holy Spirit—dwelt (cf. Luke 3:21–22; 4:1, 14; John 1:33), as it had formerly dwelt on the ark in the tabernacle and in the temple (cf., e.g., Num. 7:89; Ps. 80:1). Jesus' body was God's true temple on earth as long as he lived here.

Verse 14 continues: "... and we have seen his glory, glory as of the only Son from the Father, full of grace and truth." In my terms: his disciples caught glimpses of the *Shekhinah*, as the latter was manifested in Jesus' sayings and actions. By the power of the Holy Spirit, Jesus' own followers—and only they—could perceive his divine glory, directly through the veil of his humanity: "That which ... we have heard, which we have seen with our eyes, which we looked upon and have touched with our hands, concerning the word of life—..." (1 John 1:1). They were like the priests in the tabernacle, who were permitted to see some of the glory on the inside, whereas the rest of the nation saw only the not-so-beautiful outside of the tabernacle. The outer coverings of the tabernacle (Exod. 26:14) were as unimpressive as Jesus: he had "no beauty that we should desire him" (Isa. 53:2). In both cases, there was a plain vessel with a magnificent inside.

Beautiful or not, Jesus' body was God's true temple, and Herod's temple was not—no matter how magnificent *this* temple was ("what wonderful stones and what wonderful buildings!" Mark 13:1; "adorned with noble stones," Luke 21:5). This marvelous temple was an empty shell, so to speak: there was no ark (cf. Jer. 3:16), and there was no *Shekhinah*. Since this was so, we can understand that as he stood next to this building, Jesus could truly say: "'Destroy *this* temple, and in three days I will raise it up.' The Jews then said, 'It has taken forty-six years to build this temple, and will you raise it up in three days?' But he was speaking about the temple of his body" (John 2:19–21). Jesus was saying that his body, and not Herod's temple, was the real dwelling-place of the *Shekhinah* at that moment. His enemies would destroy this "temple" by crucifying him; but Jesus himself would "raise" the temple of his own body in three days. And when *this* happened, and after his ascension, his beauty was undeniable: "brighter than the sun" (Acts 26:13); "his face was like the sun shining in full strength" (Rev. 1:16).[14]

---

14 The only time that this happened during Jesus' ministry was on the

During Christ's life on earth, namely, from the time of his baptism by John the Baptist, the *Shekhinah* rested upon him, or as one could also say, dwelt in him. In other words, if someone would have asked where "Eden" was in those days, the answer could only have been: in the person of Jesus Christ. The temple of Herod was a splendid vessel but, as I said, it had an empty inside. The temple of Jesus' body was perhaps an unattractive vessel, but it had a glorious inside. It reminds us of Song 4:12-15, where the beloved is compared to a magnificent inside, but the garden is "locked": no intruder can look into it. The onlooker saw only the (not necessarily attractive) exterior wall—the beloved saw the interior splendor. Or to use another picture, Jesus' glory was like a burning torch, but hidden in a jar of clay (cf. Judg. 7:16, and see Paul's application of it in 2 Cor. 4:7). After the jar had been smashed to pieces, the brilliant light shone abroad (cf. Judg. 7:19-20).

5.8 Christ As the Tree of Life[15]

In addition to Genesis 2:9 and 3:22-24, where we hear of the tree of life in the literal sense, we read in Proverbs about the tree of life, namely, in the sense of divine wisdom, which gives life to those who receive it and live by it. Indeed, wisdom "is a tree of life to those who lay hold of her" (3:18). "The fruit of the righteous is a tree of life, and whoever captures souls is wise" (11:30). "Hope deferred makes the heart sick, but a desire fulfilled is a tree of life" (13:12). "A gentle tongue is a tree of life" (15:14). Here, the tree of life is a figure related to wisdom, to righteous acting, to desires that are fulfilled, and to gentleness. In short: true wisdom leads to the true Edenic life, as God always intended it for humans (cf. 1 Tim. 6:19, ". . . thus storing up treasure for themselves as a good foundation for the future, so that they may take hold of that which is truly life"). Leading such a life of godliness, as a truly godly person, is equivalent to eating of the tree of life. It is the type of godliness that manifested itself in the first place, and above all other people, in the person of Jesus Christ; he was, and is, the true Wisdom of God (1 Cor. 24; Col. 2:3). Living through him is living by the fruits of the tree of life.

Mount of Transfiguration: "[H]is face shone like the sun" (Matt. 17:2).

15 See Ouweneel (2018, chapter 7).

John Calvin underscored the sacramental significance of the tree of life, thus indirectly linking it with Jesus:

> The term sacrament . . . includes, generally, all the signs which God ever commanded men to use, that he might make them sure and confident of the truth of his promises. These he was pleased sometimes to place in natural objects—sometimes to exhibit in miracles. Of the former class we have an example, in his giving the tree of life to Adam and Eve, as an earnest of immortality, that they might feel confident of the promise as often as they ate of the fruit.[16]

Thus God himself is the actual giver of life; the tree is just the sacramental symbol of life,[17] just as—we may add—*literal* bread and wine can be sacramental symbols of the body and blood of Jesus. If the bread speaks of Jesus' body, and the wine of Jesus' blood, the tree speaks of Jesus' life.

In the Bible, especially in John's Gospel and John's first letter, eternal life is not only a quantitative notion (everlasting existence) but, more importantly, also a qualitative notion: it is the "true life" of 1 Timothy 6:19, which is the life with God. This life is even God himself, more specifically, God the Son: "the true God and eternal life" (1 John 5:20).[18] Thus, in the book of Revelation, too, eternal life is not just a matter of everlasting existence but a matter of the *bliss* of this life with God (think, for instance, of the "water of life," Rev. 21:6; 22:1, 17). As Dutch theologian Berend J. Oosterhoff put it,

> Through the Fall, Man lost not just immortality. He lost Paradise as well, he lost peace and happiness, he lost fellowship with God. In one word, he lost life in the full sense of the word. The life that God, through the tree of life, offered to Man, was the true, spiritual

---

16 Calvin, *Institutes* 4.14.18 (http://www.ccel.org/ccel/calvin/institutes.vi.xv.html?highlight=tree%20of%20 life#highlight); cf. Leupold (1942, 120–21).

17 Hamilton (1990, 163).

18 Cf. Visscher (1928, 153–54) with regard to the tree of life.

life in his fellowship.[19]

And German theologian Wolfhart Pannenberg said, "Since sin is turning from God, sinners separate themselves not only from the commanding will of God but also from the source of their own lives."[20]

King David says, "[W]ith you [i.e., the Lord] is the *fountain of life*" (Ps. 36:9; cf. Prov. 14:27, "The fear of the LORD is a *fountain of life*"). And the LORD himself says in the book of Jeremiah, "[M]y people have committed two evils: they have forsaken me, the *fountain of living waters*, and hewed out cisterns for themselves, broken cisterns that can hold no water" (2:13). And the prophet says, "O LORD, the hope of Israel, all who forsake you shall be put to shame; those who turn away from you shall be written in the earth, for they have forsaken the LORD, the *fountain of living water*" (17:13). In Revelation 22:1-2 the image of the freshly flowing water is connected with that of the tree of life, which will exist together in the New Jerusalem.

Of course, the problem in any such exegesis concerning the tree of life is the fact that one cannot possibly receive *spiritual* life through eating of a *literal* tree. We are helped in solving this problem through the emphasis on the sacramental significance of the tree. Water as such cannot regenerate; but God can grant the life of rebirth through that of which water is an image (John 3:5; cf. 15:3; Eph. 5:26). Oil as such cannot heal; but God can grant healing through that of which oil is an image (cf. Mark 6:13; James 5:14–15). In other words, the tree of life was just as literal as the water of baptism, the bread and wine of the Lord's Supper, and the oil of the ministry of healing[21]—but God is the actual Giver of life (both physically and spiritually), of strength and comfort, and of healing.[22]

Thus, the story that the tree of life was telling, so to speak, was that life in fellowship with God is reserved for humans if they remain in the way of obedience. If they fall into sin, the way to God's life is cut off for them. In Adam's case, this was literally illustrated in his being

---

19 Oosterhoff (1972, 130).
20 Pannenberg (1994, 266; cf. 267).
21 Notice how in James 5:14-15 it is not the oil that is said to heal, but the elders' prayer, which appeals to God's power.
22 Pannenberg (1994, 112).

driven out of the Garden of Eden. This brings us to the heart of soteriology: only through a work of redemption can the door to the true life be opened again: whoever believes in the Son of God, "has [i.e., possesses] "eternal life" (John 3:15–16; cf. v. 36; 5:24; 6:40, 47). It is the same with Israel: having been driven from the Promised Land, which to them should have been another Eden, only through repentance and conversion will they find true life again in that same Land: "They shall come and sing aloud on the height of Zion, and they shall be radiant over the goodness of the LORD, over the grain, the wine, and the oil, and over the young of the flock and the herd; their life shall be like a watered garden, and they shall languish no more" (Jer. 31:12). A new Eden will be opened for them like a "watered garden": a place of new life and new joy.

We find this figurative, soteriological sense of the tree of life also in Revelation 2:7 and 22:2. I love to think here of Christ himself, for he is our life (Col. 3:4); in him is life, and he grants life (John 1:4; 5:26; 1 John 1:1–2; 5:11–13). The tree of life in the middle of the Garden was a hint to, and a promise of, something (or Someone) better and greater than all the good with which God had surrounded Adam and Eve. In this tree, that is, in Christ, was the "promise of eternal life" (1 John 2:25), that is, before sin entered, and even "before the ages began" (Titus 1:2; cf. 2 Cor. 1:20). This is the life that came to earth in the person of Jesus Christ; it is the life that passed through death, and that rose from the tomb in the Garden of Joseph.

What was lost in Eden, when the first humans were chased from the tree of life, began to blossom again in Joseph's Garden, where the tree gave its first fruits to Mary Magdalene, and through her to his brothers and sisters. The highest aim in Christianity is not forgiveness. Forgiveness is a means, not a goal. Through forgiveness, the door is opened to that domain characterized by true divine life, and in which Christ himself is the source and fountain of life; we will come back to this important subject in chapter 6.

The true divine life that is in Christ and is granted to believers will come to full fruition only in the world to come:

> I will greatly rejoice in the LORD; for he has clothed me with the garments of salvation; he has covered me with the robe of righ-

teousness, as a bridegroom decks himself like a priest with a beautiful headdress, and as a bride adorns herself with her jewels. For as the earth brings forth its sprouts, and as a garden causes what is sown in it to sprout up, so the Lord God will cause righteousness and praise to sprout up before all the nations (Isa. 61:10–11).

6
Church Life

They shall come and sing aloud on the height of Zion,
　and they shall be radiant over the goodness of the Lord,
over the grain, the wine, and the oil,
　and over the young of the flock and the herd;
their life shall be like a watered garden,
　and they shall languish no more.

Jeremiah 31:12

6.1 Cathedrals and Church Huts

If we ask what Eden we might find on earth today, it helps to think not so much of the garden aspect of Eden but rather of its sanctuary aspect. What sacred places do Christians have? Only one. They have no earthly sanctuaries, they have no sacred cities, neither Rome for the Catholics, nor Wittenberg for the Lutherans, Geneva for the Reformed, or Westminster for the Anglicans.[1] Protestants, except high church Protestants perhaps, do not even *call* their church buildings "sacred" or "holy."

Yet, I do understand that Roman Catholics and Greek and Russian Orthodox call their church buildings "sacred." Indeed, the splendor of those buildings seems to reflect some heavenly Eden. I must admit that I love being in such buildings because of their sheer beauty. I think I have visited more than seventy churches in Rome alone, first and foremost of course the four major basilicas, the St. Peter's, the St.

---

[1] Even Jerusalem is in the strict sense not a "holy city" as long as the *Shekhinah* has not returned to it (cf. Ezek. 43:1–23; see also 48:35).

Paul's Outside the Walls, the Santa Maria Maggiore, and the St. John Lateran. I have visited the main church of the Eastern world (since the 15th century a mosque): the Aya Sophia in Istanbul. I have visited the Cathedral of Christ the Savior and the Saint Basil Cathedral and many other churches in Moscow. I have visited the Westminster Abbey in London, the Notre Dame in Paris (now so badly damaged), the Berlin Cathedral in Berlin, the St. Stephen's Cathedral in Vienna, and St. Patrick's Cathedral in New York. What a splendor! What a foretaste of heaven, some would say.

Imagine what it meant to live in a medieval European city, enclosed by city walls, and in the middle the huge cathedral. Imagine the many little houses, often not more that hovels in poor, pitiful slum areas. Image all the dirt, the dust, and the (animal and human) droppings. Imagine the unbearable stench of the open sewers, of all the unwashed bodies, of all the rotting materials. Imagine now to step out of this miserable mess and intolerable junk into the cathedral. It is like stepping from hell into heaven, from a decaying world into Eden. Everything is beautiful here: the gold, the silver, the jewels, the statues, the altars, the ornaments, the ceilings, the pillars. Think of the marvelous colors, think of the bright sunlight coming through the stained glass. No stench but the sweet smell of the incense. No poverty, only riches. No dirt, only cleanness. No unpleasant noises, but the most wonderful music. The people of the city loved to be here. No day passed without them having been in the church, perhaps to attend mass but also to do their business, to have their conversations, to escape from their hell to have some moments of heaven. What could resemble Eden more than such churches?

I have been in the Sagrada Família Basilica (the Basilica of the Holy Family) in Barcelona, whose construction began in 1882. The church was consecrated in 2010, but will not be finished until 2025 (after 143 years of building). The great master architect Antoni Gaudi (d. 1926) was the designer of it. His design seems to capture features of Eden. In one of the porticos is the tree of life. You will hardly find any straight lines in the church because the entire place should resemble a forest, all the pillars looking like trees. Anyone seeking an imitation of Eden here on earth should not look for beautiful parks, but come to the Sagrada Família.

And yet, every Protestant knows that there are no sacred places on earth, not in Barcelona, not in Rome or Moscow, not even in Jerusalem. Protestants, too, appreciate good architecture, but they do not consecrate their buildings. To put it more strongly, every place will do as a location where the saints can gather. During the persecutions in the seventeenth and eighteenth centuries, the French Huguenots had their open-air meetings in the forests, where they could secretly hear God's Word. In certain French Protestant regions, the custom was retained long after the Huguenots had received their religious liberty. I remember having preached myself once in the open air at Roumezoux, in the mountains, on August 15 (Assumption of Mary), which is a holiday in France. And speaking of France, I remember the dirtiest and poorest church building that I ever preached in, located in a little village somewhere in the Cévennes, the low mountains of South-East France. We had to step through dirt and manure, between the chickens and the geese, to reach the little, unsightly place. What sweet brothers and sisters, happy with their little chapel, although even that word seemed too nice!

Or I remember that other poor little building, in the middle of a huge squatters' camp near Klerksdorp in South Africa. One walked between the poorest shacks and the hovels of wooden boards and sink plates to the little chapel. I have preached there several times. It was a holy place, not because it resembled Eden, not because the wood and the bricks were sacred in any sense, but because of the *people* there: "[Y]ou are a chosen race, a royal priesthood, a holy nation, a people for his own possession, that you may proclaim the excellencies of him who called you out of darkness into his marvelous light" (1 Pet. 2:9). I loved the dear African brothers and sisters there, meeting together to glorify God.

6.2 The Temple of God

So what *is* the Christians' "sacred place"? The answer is twofold. First, the church *as such*—not the building but the people—is a sanctuary: "Do you not know that you are God's temple and that God's Spirit dwells in you?" (1 Cor. 3:16). "[W]e are the temple of the living God; as God said, 'I will make my dwelling among them and walk among them, and I will be their God, and they shall be my people'" (2 Cor.

6:16; cf. Lev. 26:11–12). The church is "built on the foundation of the apostles and prophets, Christ Jesus himself being the cornerstone, in whom the whole structure, being joined together, grows into a holy temple in the Lord. In him you also are being built together into a dwelling place for God by the Spirit" (Eph. 2:20–22).

The second part of the answer is this. The church may be the temple of God today, but if all its members stay at home, there is little that can be *seen* of it. The church does not *manifest* itself as a temple. Therefore, believers must *come together*. Only then does Jesus' promise become true: "[W]here two or three are gathered in my name, there am I among them" (Matt. 18:20). Believers must be *gathered*, and when they do so, it must be *in his name*. Then, as he promised, he will be among them (more literally, in their midst).

Here we must mention the *Shekhinah* again. Just as the *Shekhinah* first filled the tabernacle (Exod. 40:34), afterward the temple of Solomon (1 Kings 8:10–11; 2 Chron. 5:13–14), and will fill the eschatological temple of Ezekiel (Ezek. 43:1–5; cf. 10:3–4), so today it fills the temple of God, that is, the church. We can make a direct comparison between Acts 2 and Exodus 20, 1 Kings 8 and Ezekiel 43. As on earlier occasions, there were visible signs at the outpouring of the Spirit: a "sound like a mighty rushing wind," "divided tongues as of fire," speaking "in other tongues." Thus, the Holy Spirit was sent down from heaven (cf. John 14:26; 15:26) just as the *Shekhinah* had formerly been sent down. He came to dwell in the church just as the *Shekhinah* had dwelt among God's people. Just as the cloud had filled God's house, the Holy Spirit now fills the church (cf. Acts 2:2; cf. Eph. 5:18), which is the house of God (1 Tim. 3:15; cf. 2 Tim. 2:20; 1 Pet. 4:17).

The *Shekhinah* could be observed whenever it took the form of the "pillar of the cloud," but the Holy Spirit cannot be seen; only his effects are seen. This is the great difference with earlier ages in God's redemptive history. Eden was always a *visible* thing. This visibility is what Christians have tried to retain in their magnificent church buildings. This is a very understandable and praiseworthy error—yet an error. The Eden of today is entirely a spiritual matter, and this is hard to accept for those who cling to the outward things. Christians have not lost their senses, including their sense of beauty; they still appreciate the arts, also the art of architecture in thousands of beautiful church buildings. But beauty in any spiritual-biblical sense lies on the inside: "Do not let your adorning be external—the braiding of hair and the putting on of gold jewelry, or the clothing you wear—but let your adorning be the hidden person of the heart with the imperishable beauty of a gentle and quiet spirit, which in God's sight is very precious" (1 Pet. 3:3–4).

The connection between the *Shekhinah* and the Holy Spirit (and [the Spirit of] Christ) casts a special light on Matthew 18:20. Some expositors have linked this promise by Jesus with passages in the Talmud, which go back to the post-exilic Malachi 3:16, "Then those who feared the LORD spoke with one another. The LORD paid attention and heard them, and a book of remembrance was written before him of those who feared the LORD and esteemed his name." First, we find here the "two or three" (the text literally says, "a man to his neighbor"), and second, the remembrance of the LORD's name. These are two elements that are also part of Matthew 18:20. One Talmud passage says: "[When] two sit together and there are words of Torah [spoken] between them, the *Shekhinah* abides among them," followed by the quotation from Malachi 3:16.[2] In another Talmud passage we read: "[H]ow do you know that if two are sitting and studying the Torah together the Divine Presence is with them? For it is said"—followed again by the quotation from Malachi 3:16.[3] In both passages two persons are sitting together to ponder the Torah, the Word of God, and in both cases the word from Malachi is quoted to prove that the *Shekhinah* is among them.[4]

The rabbis said that where two, remembering the LORD's name, have the Torah in their midst, the *Shekhinah* is in their midst. They knew very well that *no* pillar of the cloud would be visible; it is all spiritual, but nevertheless true reality. Jesus said (to those who may have known this rabbinic exegesis), where two or three remember my name, I will be in their midst, that is, in the Spirit, that is, the Spirit of Jesus Christ (Acts 16:7; Rom. 8:9; Gal. 4:6; Phil. 1:19).

This makes the church—not the building but the gathered saints—

---

[2] Aboth iii.2.
[3] Berakoth 6a.
[4] Edersheim (1971, 2.124).

such a *sacred* place. Where two or three (or two or three thousand) are together in Jesus' name, to celebrate his name, and where they focus on the Word of God, Jesus is personally present through the Spirit of Christ. There, people may even fall on their face before the glory of God, and confess that God is really among his people (1 Cor. 14:25). The *Shekhinah* may be so palpable—even though not visible—that those who are present may experience what is described in Acts 4:31, "And when they had prayed, the place in which they were gathered together was shaken, and they were all filled with the Holy Spirit and continued to speak the word of God with boldness." Or they experience what happened in John 20, when the risen Lord appeared in the midst of his gathered disciples: "Then the disciples were glad when they saw the Lord," and they later told Thomas: "We have seen the Lord" (John 20:20, 25).

Please note that the disciples not only saw the risen *Man* Jesus Christ but his *divine* glory was present as well in the *Shekhinah*: it was he who, as the Creator of the new creation, "breathed" on his disciples (v. 22), as God had breathed into Adam (Gen. 2:7). And it was Jesus whom Thomas confessed as "My Lord and my *God*" (v. 28). In the same way, the prophet Ezekiel fell down before the *Shekhinah* when he beheld the glory of the Lord (Ezek. 43:3–5; 44:4).

6.3 Pentecost

In Acts 2:1 we read about the Day of Pentecost dawning, literally the day of the "fiftieth" (Gk. *pentēkostē*) because of the seven weeks between *Yom habBikkurim* (the "day of the firstfruits," the presentation of the firstfruits of the barley harvest; Lev. 23:10–14) and *Shavuot* (lit. "sevens," the Feast of Weeks, or Pentecost).[5] After the destruction of Jerusalem and the temple, when Israel was dispersed among the nations, the harvest aspect of *Shavuot* lost its significance. The only element that still refers to the harvest is that the Jewish houses and synagogues are abundantly ornamented with flowers; *Shavuot* has become a real flower festival. But it is also possible that the flowers are meant as a festival ornament for the Torah, the Law that God gave Israel on Mount Sinai. This brings us to the entirely new meaning that *Shavuot* developed in Israel, a meaning that can be demonstrated as

---

5   Regarding this feast, see Ouweneel (2001, §4.2).

early as the second century, in the Diaspora, but probably in earlier centuries. It has become *zeman mattan Toratenu*, the "time of the giving of our Law," the festival of the law-giving on Sinai. It is a holiday during which Torah-loving Jews study the Torah even more intensely than usually; some spend the entire night of Pentecost studying God's Law.

The connection between *Shavuot* and the law-giving on Sinai is based on the fact that *Shavuot* is celebrated on the same day (the sixth day of the third month) as the day on which, according to the rabbis' calculation, the Law was given. However, whereas Israel at *Shavuot* thinks of the Sinaitic law-giving (Exod. 20), Christians think of the outpouring of the Holy Spirit during that festival (Acts 2). At the *first* Pentecost festival in history, Israel was born as the covenant people of God, and at the *first* Pentecost festival after Messiah's death and resurrection, the New Testament church was born. On Mount Sinai, God's relationship began with his Old Testament people, when he gave them the Torah, just as on Mount Zion his relationship with his New Testament people began, when God gave them his Holy Spirit.[6]

On both occasions, on Mount Sinai in Exodus 19–20 and on Mount Zion in Acts 2, many "voices" were heard (thus literally in both Exod. 19:16 [Heb. *qolot*] and Acts 2:4 [Gk. *glōssai*]). On Sinai, there was first a sound, that changed into a fire, which the people understood as a language; according to Philo, these are the three signs of God's presence.[7] These were the same three phenomena we find in Acts 2:2–4, 6.[8] Fire was observed both on Sinai (Exod. 19:18) and in Acts 2:3. Interestingly, the Torah, or God's Word, is compared to both fire (Jer. 23:29) and water (Eph. 5:26; cf. John 15:3), just as the Spirit is compared to both fire and water.[9] Giving the Torah is like giving the Holy Spirit, just as—on the negative side—grieving God through breaking the Torah (Ps. 78:39–41) is like grieving the Spirit (Isa. 63:20–21; cf.

---

6   Already the Venerable Bede (c. 700) pointed to this parallel; see Burgess (1997, 22–23).

7   Philo, *De Decalogo* 33.

8   Longenecker (1981, 270).

9   According to Gregory of Narek (ca. 1000), the Spirit manifested himself on Sinai through an earthquake, a strong wind, and a consuming fire; see Burgess (1989, 127).

Eph. 4:30). Under the new covenant the Spirit of the living God writes Christ in believers' hearts (2 Cor. 3:3), which is virtually the same as saying that the Torah is written in their hearts (Jer. 31:33; Heb. 8:10).

Living by the Spirit is living under the law of Christ, and no longer under legalism (Gal. 5:13–6:2). This is true freedom, for the law is the "law of freedom" (James 1:25; 2:12; cf. 2 Cor. 3:17). Just as the Torah (i.e., "instruction") led and taught God's people, the Spirit leads and teaches God's people (John 14:26; 16:13; Rom. 8:14). Just as the Torah makes alive and illuminates the eyes (Ps. 119:93; 19:9), the Spirit makes alive and illuminates the heart's eyes (2 Cor. 3:6; Eph. 1:17–18). The Torah was written "with the finger of God" (Exod. 31:18; Deut. 9:10), while Jesus acted "by the finger of God" (Luke 11:20), that is, by the Spirit of God (see the parallel passage, Matt. 12:28). True sons of God are those who keep the Torah, that is, those who are led by the Spirit (Deut. 8:5-6; Rom. 8:14). Both the Torah and the Spirit convince people of sin, of righteousness, and of judgment (cf. Rom. 3:20; 5:20; 7:7–11; Gal. 3:19 with John 16:8). Rejecting the Torah is of the same category as resisting or grieving the Holy Spirit (Acts 7:38–51; Eph. 4:30; Isa. 63:10). Through the power of the Holy Spirit, the righteousness (i.e., righteous demand) of the Torah is fulfilled in believers (Rom. 8:4).

6.4 The Hundred and Twenty

Acts 1:15 tells us about one hundred twenty believers waiting together for the coming of the Holy Spirit. They were the twelve apostles (Matthias replacing Judas; vv. 16–26), plus a number of other followers, including Mary, Jesus' mother. I suppose Mary Magdalene, Joanna, the wife of Chuza, Susanna (Luke 8:3), and Mary the wife of Clopas (John 19:25), were there as well. The house where they were staying (2:2) probably included the upper room mentioned in 1:13. Others have thought of the temple territory (cf. Luke 24:53), which would explain more easily how Peter could address such a large crowd, namely, on the temple square (cf. Acts 2, especially v. 46).

One of the Bible passages traditionally read during *Shavuot* is Ezekiel 1. If this was the case already in New Testament times, one can imagine how the disciples mentioned in Acts 2 were impressed with the words: "As I looked, behold, a *stormy wind* came out of the north, and a great cloud, with brightness around it, and *fire* flashing forth continually, and in the midst of the fire, as it were gleaming metal" (Ezek. 1:4). This was so especially because some moments later they experienced similar things: "And suddenly there came from heaven a sound like a mighty rushing *wind*, and it filled the entire house where they were sitting. And divided tongues as of *fire* appeared to them and rested on each one of them" (Acts 2:2–3).

John the Baptist had announced a baptism "in the Holy Spirit and fire" (Gk. *en pneumati hagiōi kai pyri*, lit. "in holy wind and fire"), and this seems literally the way it occurred. The fire of the Spirit was visible on them through the tongues of fire that were upon them, and audible through the spoken tongues in which they expressed themselves.[10] The church fathers viewed the speaking in tongues as a reversal of the Babylonian confusion of tongues (Gen. 11:1–9).[11] It was closely connected with prophesying (cf. 19:6) by both the men and the women among the hundred and twenty.[12] This was underscored by Peter when he quoted Joel's word: "[Y]our sons and your daughters shall prophesy" (2:17), thus confirming what the bystanders had already observed. We see the same effect occurring among the elders of Israel on whom the Holy Spirit came: the Lord "took some of the Spirit that was on him [i.e., Moses] and put it on the seventy elders. And as soon as the Spirit rested on them, they prophesied" (Num. 11:25).

According to Luke, what happened on the Day of Pentecost was the fulfillment of Jesus' word in Acts 1:5 concerning the baptism with (or rather, in) the Holy Spirit (cf. 11:16–17), even though in 2:4 he uses a different word: ". . . they were all *filled* with the Holy Spirit." Jesus was baptized with water by John, when he was anointed with the Holy Spirit, which constituted the basis for his entire ministry. Similarly, the one hundred twenty were baptized and anointed with the Holy Spirit by Jesus, an event that constituted the basis for *their*

---

10 In v. 11 the Gk. word is also *glōssa*, but in v. 6 it is *dialektos*, "language" (cf. 1:19).

11 Congar (1997, 1.44 and 48n5).

12 In the Septuagint, *apophthengesthai* ("to give utterance," v. 4; "to address," v. 14; "to speak," 26:25) is characteristic of the prophets' speaking (1 Chron. 25:1; Ezek. 13:9, 19; Micah 5:11; Zech. 10:2).

entire ministry.[13]

6.5 A New Eden

There is a deep connection between the exodus from Egypt and the founding of the church in Acts 2. In earlier chapters we saw the deep connection between the exodus from Egypt and the earlier planting of Eden, and Noah entering a new world after the Flood. These are all new beginnings, and they belong to one long Edenic series: Adam – Noah – the tabernacle – the Promised Land – the temple of Solomon – Pentecost and the church.

We also saw the connection between the Torah-giving on Mount Sinai (Exod. 20) and the Spirit-giving on Mount Zion (Acts 2). To the similarities already mentioned, I may add that Israel sang the song of Moses (Exod. 15), and that New Testament believers sing "the song of Moses, the servant of God, and the song of the Lamb" (Rev. 15:3). Israel's path through the wilderness is like the path of the church through the present world, as is explicitly taught in the New Testament by the apostle Paul (1 Cor. 10:1–11) and by Hebrews 3:7–4:11. God's warfare against Israel's spiritual adversaries (cf. Exod. 12:12; 15:3–10; Num. 33:4) is continued in the warfare of the New Testament church against the powers of darkness (2 Cor. 10:3–6; Eph. 6:12; Phil. 1:27–30; 1 Tim. 6:12).

Interestingly, the church itself is like a Garden of Eden. As there were fruit trees in Eden, we similarly read of the "fruits" produced by the believers. I have argued in §4.7 that the fruit of the vine is joy in the Spirit, the fruit of the fig tree is the "fruit of righteousness," the fruit of the pomegranate is the "fruit unto holiness," and the fruit of the olive tree is the "fruit of the Spirit," love being the primary one. The church is a garden with the wonderful flowers of joy, righteousness, holiness, and love. In addition to this botanical metaphor, Galatians 6:7–8 uses an agricultural metaphor when it speaks of reaping (cf. §6.8): "Do not be deceived: God is not mocked, for whatever one sows, that will he also reap. For the one who sows to his own flesh will from the flesh reap corruption, but *the one who sows to the Spirit will from the Spirit reap eternal life.*"

Another important element of Eden were the rivers: "A river

---

13 Longenecker (1981, 268–69).

flowed out of Eden to water the garden, and there it divided and became four rivers" (Gen. 2:10). Jesus told the people, "If anyone thirsts, let him come to me and drink. Whoever believes in me, the Scripture has said, 'Out of his heart will flow rivers of living water.' Now this he said about the Spirit, whom those who believed in him were to receive, for as yet the Spirit had not been given, because Jesus was not yet glorified" (John 7:37–39). To the church, too, the words of Song 4:12–15 can be applied: "A garden locked is my sister, my bride, a spring locked, a fountain sealed... a garden fountain, a well of living water, and flowing streams from Lebanon."

Each new phase in God's ways with his people debouches in rest: Adam lived in Eden in peace, Noah found rest in the post-Flood new world, Israel found rest in the Promised Land. The temple of Solomon was a "house of rest" (1 Chron. 28:2). Similarly, the church is a place of rest and peace (Rom. 5:1; Phil. 4:7; Col. 3:15). This is one side of the story. But just as every new phase ended in spiritual decline, thus it happened to the church, if viewed from the standpoint of human responsibility: Adam and Noah each ate of the forbidden fruit, Israel fell into apostasy, the Promised Land fell into the hands of its conquerors, and the temple of Solomon was burned down. The church did not fare any better. In 2 Timothy 2:20 the church is not called the "house of God" anymore (cf. 1 Tim. 3:15) but a "great house," a mixed place of vessels to the honor as well as vessels to the dishonor of the master. Peter says, "[I]t is time for judgment to begin at the household of God" (1 Pet. 4:17).

The general lesson is this: until the ultimate Eden is reached, every Eden will fail, and thus meet with destruction. However, let us also look at some brighter sides of the church. It is easy to emphasize the inevitable decline, but it is more edifying to stress the beautiful sides of each Eden, not least the church. Every Eden may fade and disappear, except the ultimate one, but this does not change the fact that every Eden is a beautiful picture of this ultimate Eden.

6.6 The Lord's Supper

Perhaps the most important connection between Israel's exodus and the New Testament church's beginning is the link between the Passover and the Lord's Supper. In §5.3 we found a link between Eden and baptism; let us now look at the link between Eden and the Lord's Supper.

We have seen (§1.7) that redemptive history begins in heaven, with the (supposed) picture of the Father and the Son dining together (John 1:18; cf. 13:23). Adam and Eve ate in Eden, Melchizedek came out with bread and wine for Abraham and his men (Gen. 14:18). Three "men" from the celestial world came and ate with Abraham (18:6–7). Isaac and Abimelech, and later Jacob and Laban, ate covenant meals together (26:28–31; 31:44–54; also cf. Ps. 41:9 and Obad. 1:7). These are all foreshadows of the Lord's Supper as the expression of a covenantal community, both with the Lord and with each other (1 Cor. 10:16–22; also cf. Rev. 3:20)—just like the Lord's Supper is a foreshadow of the ultimate Eden.

In the Old Testament, we find an even more remarkable example in Exodus 24:10–11. When the elders of Israel, led by Moses, saw on Mount Horeb the glory of the God of Israel, "they beheld God, and *ate and drank*" (Exod. 24:10–11). This, too, was a covenant meal confirming the covenant that just had been made (vv. 3–8). There is no genuine contemplation of God apart from the covenantal relationship with God, that is, without fellowship with God, and this fellowship—a typical Edenic feature—is expressed in no clearer and simpler way than through a meal (also cf. Deut. 12:6–7, 17–18; 14:23–28; 27:7; 1 Sam. 16:1–5; 1 Chron. 29:22; Isa. 25:6; Matt. 8:11; Luke 15:23, 29; Acts 2:46–47; Rev. 19:9).

Beautiful examples are found in that marvelous Edenic book, the Song of Solomon. The fellowship of the king and his beloved is often expressed through the picture of a meal: "While the king was at his table, my perfume spread its fragrance" (1:12 NIV). "He brought me to the banqueting house, and his banner over me was love" (2:4). "I came to my garden [cf. 4:12, 16], my sister, my bride, I gathered my myrrh with my spice, I ate my honeycomb with my honey, I drank my wine with my milk" (5:1).

Some New Testament examples must be added here. Note the seven times mentioned in Luke's Gospel when Jesus ate with people (5:29; 7:36–49; 9:17; 11:37; 14:15; 22:14; 24:43). After his resurrection, Jesus ate with his own disciples (Luke 24:43; Acts 10:41; also 1:4 in certain renderings). One of the first things we hear of the

Spirit-filled believers is that they ate together (2:42, 46). One of the first things that the renewed Saul of Tarsus did was to eat (9:9, 19). Peter brought the gospel to a Roman company, but also ate with them (11:3). The converted jailer at Philippi made a meal for Paul and Silas and his own family in the middle of the night (16:34). Paul participated in the meal of the church at Troas (20:7, 11), and he ate with the people on board during the shipwreck (27:21, 33–38). Eating and drinking is a very Edenic matter, as we saw in §1.7.

6.7 Passover and the Lord's Supper
The Lord's Supper is the Christianized version of the Jewish Passover. Celebrating the Passover (*Pesach*), the Jews commemorate their deliverance from Egyptian slavery, as well as their undertaking of their journey to the new Eden. When Christians celebrate the Lord's Supper, they commemorate *their* deliverance from the slavery of sin and death through *their* Passover Lamb (1 Cor. 5:7), as well as their continuing journey to *their* new Eden: "For as often as you eat this bread and drink the cup, you proclaim the Lord's death *until he comes*" (1 Cor. 11:26).

This eschatological dimension is illustrated by the fact that the Passover meal contains four cups of wine, two taken before the meal and two after it. Each of them is traditionally associated with one of God's four promises in Exodus 6:6–7, "I will bring you out . . . I will deliver you . . . I will redeem . . . I will take you to be my people." Two of these cups are referred to in Luke 22:17 and 20, where Jesus gives them a more profound meaning. The cup of verse 17 must be the first or the second of the four, since the breaking of the bread (v. 19) comes right after the second cup. The cup of verse 20 must be the third, and is therefore called the "cup of salvation" (cf. Ps. 116:13), or the "cup of blessing," or "of thanksgiving" (cf. 1 Cor. 10:16).[14] Jesus used this cup to introduce the new covenant (Luke 22:20; Matt. 26:28), which one day will introduce the new Eden.

It is interesting that, according to Jewish scholar David Daube, Jesus also alludes to the fourth and last cup in the sense that he refrained from drinking of it: "I tell you I will not drink again of this

---

14 Others think of the fourth cup of Pesach; see the discussion in Thiselton (2000, 759–60).

fruit of the vine until that day when I drink it new with you in my Father's kingdom" (Matt. 26:29).[15] If Daube is right, Jesus deliberately postponed the last part of the liturgy until the arrival of the actual, ultimate kingdom of God. *Then* the fourth cup will be drunk, so to speak: "On this mountain [i.e., Zion] the LORD of hosts will make for all peoples a feast of rich food, a feast of well-aged wine, of rich food full of marrow, of aged wine well refined" (Isa. 25:6).

Both the Passover and the Lord's Supper are not only meals of commemoration but also meals of longing, in particular the longing for the Messiah and his kingdom.[16] Therefore, we find this important line in the traditional Passover liturgy: *Leshanah haba'ah birushalayyim*, "Next year in Jerusalem." This means next year let this festival be under the blessed rule of the Messiah. Here and now we are still eating in affliction, but soon we will be eating in Eden. Therefore, for centuries the Jews read Psalm 118, especially the eschatological verses 22–26. In an analogous way, the Lord's Supper is not only a looking back, but also a looking forward: a feast of longing for the coming Lord. We eat and drink "until he comes" (1 Cor. 11:26), that is, until he, together with all his people, will drink of the fruit of the vine in his Father's kingdom (Matt. 26:29).

6.8 Eden and Eternal Life

In this context, we must add a few words on eternal life. The expression "eternal (or, everlasting) life" is found in the Old Testament only two times, and, as I believe, both times with an eschatological meaning. This is very clear in Daniel 12:1–3,

> [T]here shall be a time of trouble, such as never has been since there was a nation till that time. But at that time your people shall be delivered, everyone whose name shall be found written in the book. And many of those who sleep in the dust of the earth shall awake, some to *everlasting life*, and some to shame and everlasting contempt. And those who are wise shall shine like the brightness of the sky above; and those who turn many to righteousness, like the stars forever and ever.

---

15 Daube (1956, 330–31).
16 Vander Zee (2004, 150).

The eschatological meaning of Psalm 133 may be less clear to many:

Behold, how good and pleasant it is
> when brothers dwell in unity!

It is like the precious oil on the head,
> running down on the beard,

on the beard of Aaron,
> running down on the collar of his robes!

It is like the dew of Hermon,
> which falls on the mountains of Zion!

For there the LORD has commanded the blessing,
> *life forevermore.*

Notice the article before the word "blessing": everlasting life is called *the* blessing that the LORD has commanded (v. 3), suggesting that this everlasting life is the blessing *par excellence* in the Messianic kingdom.

There is here a remarkable similarity to the New Testament: the believers have been blessed with "every spiritual blessing in the heavenly places" (Eph. 1:3). I would not know how, in the Pauline terminology, eternal life could be described more adequately than in this way. In various letters, Paul describes eternal life as a future possession (Rom. 2:7; 5:21; 6:22–23; Gal. 6:8; 1 Tim. 1:16; 6:12; Titus 1:2; 3:7). But in Ephesians 2:6, the believers *have been* seated in the heavenly places, in Christ, just as they *have been* blessed with every spiritual blessing in the heavenly places. It is a present spiritual reality; it is Eden *here and now.*

Allow me to bring in a little typology here, as believers are encouraged to do (see Gal. 4:21–31, especially v. 21; also cf. Rom. 15:4; 1 Cor. 10:11). Inheriting eternal life (cf. Matt. 19:29; 20:29; Mark 10:17; Luke 10:25; 18:18; Titus 3:7) is like receiving an inheritance in the Promised Land, that is, in the Messianic kingdom (Matt. 25:34; 1 Cor. 6:9; Gal. 5:21; Eph. 5:5), beyond Jordan, the river of death. Believers inherit eternal life as having been made one with Christ in his resurrection and glorification. The Holy Land is not at all a picture of heaven in the sense of some "hereafter" (see the next chapter). How could it be otherwise: in the Holy Land Israel had to *fight* to conquer their inheritance, just as today there is still spiritual warfare in the "heavenly places" (Eph. 6:12). Canaan is not heaven; rather I see it as an image of what Paul in Ephesians refers to as the "heavenly places," a sphere in which believers are viewed as being there already now, where they enjoy "every spiritual blessing," and also engage in spiritual warfare against the dark powers (the "Canaanites," cursed descendants of Ham [§2.7]). It is the sphere of eternal life, of divine fellowship, of perfect joy (1 John 1:1–4).

Thus, crossing the Jordan river (Josh. 3) is indeed a type of death—but *not* a type of physical death, bringing the believer into heaven (see the next chapter). Rather, I (with many others) see it as a type of the practical realization in the believers' souls of having died with Christ, having been raised with him, and being seated in him in the heavenly places.

Notice here the typical and typological agrarian language that the New Testament uses. It is in the Promised Land that believers "sow to the Spirit" in order to "reap eternal life" (Gal. 6:8). In that Land they have their "fruit resulting in sanctification—and the final result is eternal life" (Rom. 6:22 EHV). As Jesus said, "Already the one who reaps is receiving wages and gathering fruit for eternal life, so that sower and reaper may rejoice together" (John 4:36). Believers "share in the inheritance of the saints in light. He has delivered us from the domain of darkness and transferred us to the kingdom of his beloved Son" (Col. 1:12–13). They share in an "inheritance that is imperishable, undefiled, and unfading, kept in heaven for you" (1 Pet. 1:4)—"heaven" not in the sense of some "hereafter," but in the sense of the place from where the divine gifts descend.

Gentile believers, together with Jewish believers, are "fellow heirs, members of the same body, and partakers of the promise in Christ Jesus through the gospel" (Eph. 3:6). This promise involves in a very special way "eternal life, which God, who never lies, promised before the ages began" (Titus 1:2; cf. 2 Tim. 1:1); "this is the promise that he made to us—eternal life" (1 John 2:25). Paul speaks of "the Holy Spirit, whom he [i.e., God] poured out on us richly through Jesus Christ our Savior, so that being justified by his grace we might become heirs according to the hope of eternal life" (Titus 3:5–7).

6.9 Conquering the Land

Through Christ's incarnation, death, resurrection, and glorification, as well as the believers' union with him in this position, the eternal promise of "eternal life" has now become a spiritual reality. In this way, the life of rebirth has become the believers' part in an Edenic fullness, riches and abundance as never before possible (cf. John 10:10). And even now there is a dimension that has not entirely been fulfilled; it will be fulfilled only in the eternal bliss of the Father's house (John 14:1–3; see §7.8).

These spiritual blessings in the "heavenly places" must be appropriated by believers, by each of them personally. To carry the typological language a little further: the Land must be conquered. In principle, all believers have been blessed with these spiritual blessings; in practice, many know only little of them. God told the Israelites through Joshua, just before they entered the land, "Every place that the sole of your foot will tread upon I have given to you, just as I promised to Moses" (Josh. 1:3). *In principle* you possess it all; *in practice* you possess only that where your feet have walked. *In principle* you had it already when God promised it to Moses; *in practice* you will have to conquer it for yourself.

Three groups of God's people never practically possessed the Edenic blessings of the land:

(a) Those who had died in the wilderness (cf. 1 Cor. 10:5); they had been liberated from Egypt, but all the time they remained spiritually impoverished. They set off to the new Eden, but never reached it because of their own unfaithfulness.

(b) Those who were satisfied with living in the land East of Jordan: the Reubenites, the Gadites, and the half-tribe of Manasseh (Num. 32). They assisted in conquering the Promised Land (Josh. 4), but did not care about living there. Their lands were the first to be conquered by the Assyrians (2 Kings 15:29).

(c) Those who failed to secure the *entire* land that God had promised them (Judg. 1); large parts were left to the enemies, the Canaanites, and the Philistines in particular.

Notice that the Egyptians tried to prevent that Israel from *reaching* their Eden; the Philistines tried to prevent Israel from possessing *all* of Eden; and the Assyrians and the Babylonians tried to remove Israel *out* of "Eden" (as the serpent did in Gen. 3). There are always enough enemies around to rob us of our Edenic blessings, and these enemies often easily find a kind of Fifth Column within us: our own sinful flesh.

In principle, it is spiritually the same today. There are those who are happy with their wilderness journey or with the "land beyond Jordan," so to speak (by which they mean the hereafter); that is, they are happy with their liberation from Egypt, but never arrive at the full possession and enjoyment of their spiritual blessings in the heavenly places. They have never put any spiritual effort into securing these blessings, that is, making them spiritually their own. They are either *unaware* of these blessings (because of deficient teaching), or they are spiritually *too lazy* to put any effort into the matter. Consciously or unconsciously they seem to believe that spiritual babies will get to heaven as well as spiritual adults, so why take so much trouble?

Securing these blessings means that such appropriation takes time and effort, perhaps even money (buying good study books). It means especially spiritual warfare against the evil powers, because the latter will do everything to keep Christians as spiritually poor as possible: "But I, brothers, could not address you as spiritual people, but as people of the flesh, as infants in Christ. I fed you with milk, not solid food, for you were not ready for it. And even now you are not yet ready" (1 Cor. 3:1–2). "For though by this time you ought to be teachers, you need someone to teach you again the basic principles of the oracles of God. You need milk, not solid food" (Heb. 5:12).

I could briefly summarize these matters as follows: regeneration and justification are sufficient to lead you safely through the wilderness (cf. Heb. 3–4). But our Eden entails all the blessings of what for us is the Promised Land. Securing them makes a Christian a truly rich person (cf. Rom. 9:23; 10:12; 11:33; Eph. 1:18; 2:7; 3:8, 16; Col. 1:27; 2:2). As long as you are still in the wilderness, you have at least been set free from Egypt's slavery; and at least you are on the right track. But on earth you will always remain a spiritually impoverished Christian. Securing all the spiritual blessings in the heavenly places, that is, securing the Eden that has been destined for *you*, will make you a spiritually rich Christian.

7
The Hereafter

[The criminal] said,
"Jesus, remember me when you come into your kingdom."
And [Jesus] said to him,
"Truly, I say to you, today you will be with me in paradise."
                                            Luke 23:42–43

7.1 "Going to Heaven"

During my extended visit to Florence, many years ago, I found multiple traces of that great Italian, Dante Alighieri (d. 1321), the writer of the famous *La Divina Commedia* ("The Divine Comedy"). I visited his house there (the *Casa di Dante*), I admired the famous octagonal baptistry, where Dante was baptized in 1265, I saw the library (the *Biblioteca Riccardiana*), where the manuscript of his *Divina Commedia* is kept, and I visited the *Santa Croce* church, where we find a monument commemorating the great poet, who is buried elsewhere.

Of course, as a Dutchman I know the city of Zwolle, where Thomas à Kempis (d. 1471), the writer of the famous *De imitatione Christi* ("The Imitation of Christ"), spent so many years as a monk, and where he also passed away. An amazing man of an amazing book. He was a pupil of Geert Grote in Deventer, who was the man of the "Modern Devotion," and spent some early years in this city, where I myself lived as a young boy. The bones of Thomas have been moved from one church to the other, but since 2006 they have been kept in the Basilica of the Assumption of Mary, a medieval church in the center of the city. He was born in the German town of Kempen, not far from the Dutch border.

To mention a third great man, I have been near Bedford in England, but unfortunately never had the opportunity of looking for traces of John Bunyan (d. 1688), the author of the famous *The Pilgrim's Progress*. Otherwise, I certainly would have visited the John Bunyan Museum. And in London I should have visited Bunhill Fields, which contains the graves not only of Bunyan, but also of Susanna Wesley, the mother of John and Charles Wesley.

The three works mentioned written by these great writers have exerted an influence among Christians that can hardly be overestimated. They belong to the best-selling Christian works of all time, appearing in numerous translations; I would suggest that they belong to the basic reading of every educated Christian.

One may wonder what an Italian poet and philosopher, a canon of German descent, and an English Reformed Baptist preacher could possibly have in common. Perhaps several points could be mentioned but I limit myself to this one: their three principal and thoroughly Christian works have this in common, that they all ignore the second coming of Christ (almost) entirely. Instead, they present an eschatology where at death the believer goes to heaven (that is to say, according to Dante, through the middle station of purgatory), and the unbeliever goes to hell. Dante has described hell (*inferno*) most extensively. These are the only two destinations: either to the bliss of heaven (through the fire of purgatory) or to the fire of hell. One wonders what function is served in this model by Christ's second coming and by human resurrection.

When describing a believer's death, Thomas à Kempis applies Bible verses to this event that in reality point to the second coming of Christ, such as Luke 12:40 ("You also must be ready, for the Son of Man is coming at an hour you do not expect"). Or he argues that believers must be prepared for death since "here we have no lasting city" (Heb. 13:14)—a verse that refers to the Messianic kingdom. He appears to think that the believer's death and Christ's second coming merge entirely.

With Thomas' reference to the "city" we encounter several biblical metaphors for a city, descriptions including "the city that has foundations" (Heb. 11:10; cf. v. 16), the "city of the living God, the heavenly Jerusalem" (12:22), the "city of my God, the new Jerusalem, which comes down from my God out of heaven" (Rev. 3:12), and the "holy city, new Jerusalem, coming down out of heaven from God" (21:2; cf. v. 10; 22:19). There is an ancient Christian tradition—Catholic, Orthodox, Protestant—that does not link these metaphors with the Messianic kingdom, or with the new heavens and the new earth, but with *heaven in the sense of the hereafter*, that is, *the intermediate state between death and resurrection*. This erroneous approach was an ancient Catholic tradition, which was readily adopted by the great majority of Protestant theologians.

John Bunyan elaborated the city metaphor in his great work, in which he describes the life of a Christian who, as a pilgrim, is on the way—not to the Messianic kingdom, which arrives at Christ's second coming, but—to the "celestial city," which is the hereafter. Bunyan supplied us with a marvelous description of heaven-as-the-hereafter, but had no place for the resurrection and Christ's second return. As a good Christian he would certainly have *believed* these things, but they served no practical function in his description of the Christian's final destination. Just as with Thomas à Kempis, Bunyan merged the believer's death and Christ's return: at the moment the Christian enters the celestial city he is transfigured (cf. 1 Cor. 15:51). When the Christian enters heaven, he is immediately invited to the marriage supper of the Lamb (Rev. 19:6–9). The celestial city is described in terms derived from the New Jerusalem (streets of gold) and many other metaphors in Revelation, none of which refers to the intermediate state.

From the Middle Ages, this has been the eschatology of many Christians, both Catholic and Protestant: when the believer dies, the believer goes to heaven, and that's it. If one asks what then remains of the significance of the bodily resurrection and Christ's second coming, there often is no clear answer. These events will be at the "last day" (John 6:39–40, 44, 54; 11:24; 12:48), which is the last day of world history, and is therefore still far away. But these matters serve no function in one's personal earthly life. This eschatological shift is clearly illustrated in the way many Christians understand the term "kingdom of heaven," namely, as the place where believers go when they die; in short: heaven. When Luther wrote about the kingdom of heaven (Ger. *Himmelreich*), he was clearly thinking of heaven-as-the-hereafter. And since then, many poets have written about the kingdom of heaven (Dutch *hemelrijk*) as this future celestial reality. Recently, a beloved pastor in the Netherlands, terminally ill, wrote while on his deathbed that he was looking forward to soon entering the kingdom of heaven.

I am convinced that the "kingdom of heaven"—an expression found only in Matthew's Gospel—or the "heavenly kingdom" of 2 Timothy 4:18, is a kingdom that Christ will establish in glory *on earth*, when he returns and heaven rules over the earth (cf. Daniel's word to king Nebuchadnezzar: "... that you may know that Heaven rules" [Dan. 4:26]).

Some of the authors who, in our own times, have furthered most strongly the faith in "going to heaven when you die" are Randy Alcorn with his book *Heaven*, and Elyse Fitzpatrick with her book *Home*.[1] The great difference with Dante, à Kempis, and Bunyan is that they do pay great attention to the return of Christ and the future of the believers after this event. The great similarity with these three is that they describe the place where believers go to when they die as "heaven"—as thousands have done before them. The books of both Alcorn and Fitzpatrick have sold sold many copies, but that does not make their views about the hereafter any better than that of Dante, à Kempis and Bunyan. They all fell into the same age-old error: the notion of "going to heaven when you die."

Notice the difference: many Christians believe they will enter Eden when they die, whereas the New Testament proclaims entrance to an Eden *only* when Christ returns.

7.2 The Jewish *Gan Eden*

The traditional Christian expectation is that, when believers die, they go to heaven, (or to paradise), and when unbelievers die, they go to hell. I have little doubt that this Christian view also influenced the rabbinic views on the hereafter. The rabbis believe that at death, godly Jews go to the *Gan Eden*, the Garden of Eden, that is, the heavenly paradise, the celestial counterpart of the earthly Eden of Genesis 2–3. Sometimes we encounter here the same phenomenon as among

---

1   Alcorn (2004); Fitzpatrick (2016).

Christians who confuse paradise (the hereafter) with the Messianic kingdom. That is to say, the rabbis have sometimes referred to *Gan Eden* as the *Olam habbah*, the "world to come" (cf. Heb. 2:5), which in fact is the Messianic kingdom. The great Jewish expositor Nachmanides referred to *Gan Eden* as the *Olam haNeshamot*, "the world of the souls," namely, the departed souls of the righteous.[2]

Rabbinic literature connects an incredible number of legends with *Gan Eden*. One of these is about Rabbi Joshua ben Levi (third century), who reportedly met often with Elijah (who had never died!) before the gates of paradise, where he also saw the Messiah sitting.[3] Rabbi Joshua obtained permission from the angel of death to visit paradise before he had actually died, in order to inspect the place that had been assigned to him. The rabbis did not hesitate to supply their followers with extensive reports about, for instance, the various chambers of paradise, destined for various groups of righteous or penitent people. The third chamber is the best of all; here stands the tree of life, five hundred "years" high.

Let me quote here one of the many smaller *midrashim*, the *Midrash Konen*:

> The tree of life is like a ladder on which the souls of the righteous may ascend and descend. In a conclave above are seated the patriarchs, the ten martyrs, and those who sacrificed their lives for the cause of his Sacred Name. These souls descend daily to the *Gan Eden*, to join their families and tribes, where they lounge on soft seats studded with jewels. Everyone, according to his excellence, is received in audience to praise and thank the Ever-living God; and all enjoy the brilliant light of the *Shekhinah*. The flaming sword, changing from intense heat to icy cold and from ice to glowing coals, guards the entrance against living mortals. The size of the sword is ten "years." The souls on entering paradise are bathed in the 248 rivulets of balsam and attar.[4]

---

2   For references, see the Jewish Encyclopedia under "Paradise" (http://jewishencyclopedia.com/articles/11900-paradise).
3   Talmud: Sanhedrin 98a.
4   Jewish Encyclopedia, s.v. "Paradise."

Most amazing is the description of the fifth chamber:

> The fifth chamber is built of precious stones, gold, and silver, surrounded by myrrh and aloes. In front of the chamber runs the river Gihon [cf. Gen. 2:13], on whose banks are planted shrubs affording perfume and aromatic incense. There are couches of gold and silver and fine drapery. This chamber is inhabited by the *Messiah of David*, Elijah, and the *Messiah of Ephraim*.[5] In the center are a canopy made of the cedars of Lebanon, in the style of the tabernacle, with posts and vessels of silver; and a settee of Lebanon wood with pillars of silver and a seat of gold, the covering thereof of purple. Within rests the *Messiah, son of David*, "a man of sorrows and acquainted with grief" (Isa. 53:3), suffering, and waiting to release Israel from the Exile. Elijah comforts and encourages him to be patient. Every Monday and Thursday, and Sabbath and on holy days the Patriarchs, Moses, Aaron, and others, call on the Messiah and condole with him, in the hope of the fast-approaching end.

Let the reader identify and reflect upon what (mixed) feelings this description stirs in him or her. In this Jewish writing, especially the reference to Isaiah 53 is highly remarkable because it shows that in certain Jewish traditions the awareness that this chapter refers to the suffering Messiah was definitely present.

7.3 New Insights

To return to Christian theology: fortunately, many theologians have pointed out that "going to heaven" is not at all the actual expectation of New Testament believers. If we hear about "expecting" and about "waiting for" in the eschatological sense in God's Word, it rather involves the second coming of Christ and the resurrection of the believers (e.g., Matt. 24:44, 50; Luke 12:36, 40, 46; Rom. 8:19–25; 1 Cor. 1:7; Phil. 3:20; 1 Thess. 1:10; Titus 2:13; Heb. 9:28; 10:13; 2 Pet. 3:12–14).

---

5   Jewish tradition distinguishes between Messiah ben Joseph and Messiah ben David, the former characterized more as the suffering Messiah, and the latter as the triumphing Messiah.

I can hardly imagine a subject about which the Bible and orthodox Christians present more divergent views than this one. The New Testament *never* says that at death the believer "goes to heaven." By now, all Christians who search the Scriptures could and should know better, if not through the New Testament itself, then through many writings that have cast light on the matter. Greg Beale speaks of the "eschatological concept" of New Testament theology, that is, it is not the hereafter but the new creation that is the center of New Testament thinking.[6] In my terminology, the ultimate Eden is not at all associated with the hereafter but rather with the new heavens and the new earth (Rev. 19-22). It refers not to any bliss *before* the resurrection but to the great bliss *after* the resurrection. John the Baptist (Matt. 3:1-2), Jesus himself (Mark 1:14-15; Acts 1:3), the twelve (Matt. 28:18-20; 2 Pet. 1 and 3), and the apostle Paul (Acts 9:20, 22; 20:25; 28:23, 31) did not preach the hereafter—they preached the kingdom of God in the sense of the Messianic kingdom and of the "times of refreshing" that would "come from the presence of the Lord," when he would "send the Christ appointed for you, Jesus, whom heaven must receive until the time for restoring all the things about which God spoke by the mouth of his holy prophets long ago" (Acts 3:20-21).

To some it may come as a surprise to discover how little the New Testament explicitly speaks about the hereafter at all. Paul's "desire to depart and be with Christ, for that is far better" (Phil. 1:23) cannot be just a description of the hereafter but must extend to eternity, with the emphasis on Christ's coming, because *this* is what he actually *expected* according to the same letter (3:20-21). Compare what he says elsewhere: "For the Lord himself will descend from heaven. . . . And the dead in Christ will rise first. Then we who are alive, who are left, will be caught up together with them in the clouds to meet the Lord in the air, and *so we will always be with the Lord*" (1 Thess. 4:16-17). That is, to Paul, "being with Christ" finds its culmination in what lies not before the resurrection but thereafter.

When Jesus says, "In my Father's house are many rooms. . . . And if I go and prepare a place for you, *I will come again* and will take you to myself, that where I am you may be also" (John 14:2-3), he is not referring to the hereafter at all—as many Christians think—but to

---

6   G. K. Beale in Brower and Elliott (1997, 11-44).

his second coming (see §7.8). And when Paul says, "[W]e know that if the tent that is our earthly home is destroyed, we have a building from God, a house not made with hands, eternal in the heavens" (2 Cor. 5:1), he is clearly referring to the resurrection body.[7]

The *only* seeming exceptions are Jesus' metaphorical description in Luke 16:19–31 (the rich man and Lazarus) and 23:43, "today you will be with me in paradise" (see §7.7). But at this point I would ask how the *bodiless* condition of any person could ever be described as "eternal bliss," or could be thought of as the believer's final destination. Only those who adhere to some Greek soul–body dualism, which considers the soul more valuable than the body and death to be a "deliverance" from the body—an ancient Greek heresy—could think that dying leads to the highest and final Christian destination. The deepest truth is that many Christians actually believe in some "transmigration" of the soul at physical death, and basically and half-consciously do not know what to think of, and how to handle, the resurrection of the body.[8] Far too many Christians disconnect their resurrection body from their present body by refusing to acknowledge the (purified) continuity between this world and the world to come. The apostle Paul knew better; he did not speak about some redemption *from* the body, but the ultimate redemption *of* the body, and calls *this* our true sonship: the believer with his glorified body (Rom. 8:23).

What Christians *look forward to* is not some heavenly hereafter, in which they will be divested of the body, but they are "waiting for and hastening the coming of the day of God, because of which the heavens will be set on fire and dissolved, and the heavenly bodies will melt as they burn! But according to his promise we are waiting for new heavens and a new earth in which righteousness dwells" (2 Pet. 3:12–14). Paul's "hope" was the "resurrection of both the just and the unjust," in accordance with Jewish expectation (Acts 24:15).

7.4 Old Testament Hints

One who believes in some blessed hereafter will easily find that teaching in passages that do not speak of it at all. Let me give some

---

7   See, e.g., Berkouwer (1972, 56–57).
8   Cf. Heidelberg Catechism Q&A 57: at resurrection, my body is "reunited with my soul."

well-known examples. One is Genesis 5:24, about Enoch, "God took him [away to be home with Him]" (AMP). The text says only "took him," from which no conclusions about any hereafter could be possibly drawn. Hebrews 11:5 also says "took him" (NKJV), but the KJV (and other versions) has the quite misleading phrase "translated him."[9] Here, erroneous prejudices have governed the rendering of the text. In any case, Enoch's case is special because the latter verse tells that he did not die; so it is hard to see the possible relevance of his story for Christians who do die.

Second Kings 2:1–11 does not help us either, because Elijah, too, "went up by a whirlwind into heaven" (v. 11) without dying. Imagine how easy it is to read here that heaven is some blessed abode for the departed. However, going up "into heaven" commonly does not mean anything more than going up toward the sky, as is the case so often in the Old Testament (cf. Gen. 28:12; Exod. 9:22–23; 10:21–22; Deut. 4:19; 32:40).

Or consider Ecclesiastes 12:5, 7: "[M]an is going to his eternal home.... [T]he dust [of his body] returns to the earth as it was, and the spirit returns to God who gave it." Again, some have thought of the hereafter here, and the phrase "his eternal home" as referring to heaven, an idea far removed beyond the author's thinking. The text may be saying nothing more than that a person's breath returns to him who gave it, as many versions render it (CEV, GNT; cf. Gen. 2:7). The "eternal home" is nothing more than *Sheol*, which in the Old Testament is sometimes rendered as Hades (the "realm of the dead," or "of death"[10]), but in fact can be rendered virtually always as the "grave."[11] "Eternal" means either "very long," or "for always," because the resurrection lies outside the author's (self-chosen) scope; that is, for the greater part of the book he has chosen to look no further than at what is "under the sun," that is, belongs to the empirical world.

Think of Psalm 73:24, "You guide me with your counsel, and af-

---

9   These are examples of eisegesis, which entails reading into the text things foreign to Scripture and found only in certain traditions.

10 The term certainly does not mean "hell," as the KJV and others render it.

11 Some rare exceptions are Isa. 14:9 and Ezek. 32:21, where *Sheol* has the meaning of Hades as the realm of the dead.

terward you will receive me to glory." Some have called this the clearest reference to the hereafter in the Old Testament. The CSB renders "take me up," where the "up" is totally unwarranted by the Hebrew text (cf. "take me" in the NIV and others). Expositors are unsure; but the English theologian John Gill (d. 1771) understood here the believer's being received "into a kingdom and glory, or a glorious kingdom; and into glorious company, the company of Father, Son, and Spirit, angels and glorified saints, where glorious things will be seen, and a glory enjoyed both in soul *and body* to all eternity," that is, emphatically *after* the resurrection.

Gill also points to another, more literal rendering of verse 24b, "after glory [Heb. *achar kavod*] you will receive me." In another sense than Gill argues, I would suggest that "after glory" could mean, "after the glorious appearance of the Messiah," you will receive me into his kingdom. At any rate, the text does not speak of "taking *up*," but either of "taking away" (through death; cf. Isa. 53:8), or of "accepting (or receiving)," namely—in my view—into the glory of the coming Messianic kingdom.

7.5 "Eternal Tents" and Abraham's "Bosom"

It is interesting to see that in the entire Bible only two passages seem to refer unequivocally to a blessed intermediate state for believers. Both passages are found in the Gospel of Luke. Shortly before the account[12] of the rich man and Lazarus (Luke 16:19–31), Jesus concludes the parable of the dishonest manager this way: "[M]ake friends for yourselves by means of unrighteous wealth, so that when it fails they [i.e., the friends] may receive you into the eternal dwellings [lit., tents, tabernacles]" (v. 9). Here again, the word "eternal" points far beyond the intermediate state; it refers to the believer's eternal home with the Father, which will be enjoyed eternally, also, or in particular, *after* the resurrection (cf. §7.8).

This is important because the immediately following episode of the rich man and Lazarus also takes place in eternity, *after* the resurrection. When a person "falls asleep" (cf. Matt. 27:52; 1 Cor. 11:30;

---

12 It is not called a "parable," and could hardly be called so because a real biblical person is mentioned in it (Abraham), and the protagonist is also called by a name (Lazarus).

15:6, 18, 20, 51; 1 Thess. 4:13–15), he wakes up either in bliss or in pain. I am not leaving out the possibility that the intermediate state is included in this story, but it is rather the "*eternal* tents" that are mentioned here. Actually, many have argued that we must be careful about deriving an eschatology of any kind from this story.[13] The point of the account is not to describe the hereafter but to show us the destiny of the selfish rich man, who did *not* make friends with Mammon (as many render v. 9). The only certain conclusion that can be drawn from the story is that the righteous and the wicked will land forever in a different destination: bliss for the former, and misery for the latter, as well as the conscious experience of this. This must be maintained no matter how metaphorical all the details ("eyes," "bosom," "finger," "tongue," "flame," "chasm") may be.

The expression "Abraham's bosom" (v. 22 NKJV) immediately calls to mind two passages in John's Gospel: 1:18 and 13:23. It evokes again the idea of a meal as an expression of fellowship and bliss,[14] just as in 13:28–29,

> In [hell] there will be weeping and gnashing of teeth, when you see Abraham and Isaac and Jacob and all the prophets in the kingdom of God but you yourselves cast out. And people will come from east and west, and from north and south, and recline at table in the kingdom of God.

The contrast is remarkable: in 16:21, the rich man is at table, and Lazarus, who is outside his gates, has nothing; in verses 22–23, we find the reverse: Lazarus is at table, and the rich man, who is this time the person "outside the gates," has nothing. It reminds us of the pseudepigraphical *Testament of Abraham* 20, which says, "Take ... my friend[15] Abraham into paradise, where are the tabernacles [cf. Luke 16:9!] of my righteous ones, and the abodes of my saints Isaac and Jacob in his bosom [!], where there is no trouble, nor grief, nor sighing,

---

13 Zahn (1913, ad loc.); Geldenhuys (1983, 429); Liefeld (1984, 991).
14 Greijdanus (1941, 85); Liefeld (1984, 992); Green (1997, 607).
15 See 2 Chron. 20:7; Isa. 41:8; James 2:23; cf. Gen. 18:17.

but peace and rejoicing and life unending."[16] For this metaphor of reclining at table and eating, see further §1.7 above.

7.6 Edenic Features

Again, we encounter here the typically Edenic metaphor of bliss in the form of eating and drinking. Wherever the "eternal tents" of verse 9 may be localized, they are places of delight. Another Edenic feature is comfort (v. 25; cf. Rev. 7:17; 21:4). Both elements, eating and comfort, are found in Isaiah 25:6–8,

> On this mountain the LORD of hosts will make for all peoples a feast of rich food, a feast of well-aged wine, of rich food full of marrow, of aged wine well refined. And he will swallow up on this mountain the covering that is cast over all peoples, the veil that is spread over all nations. He will swallow up death forever; and the LORD God will wipe away tears from all faces, and the reproach of his people he will take away from all the earth, for the LORD has spoken.

Some have felt that the story cannot be taken literally because this would lead to an anachronism, namely, that the rich man would be tortured before the judgment before the great white throne and before the judgment of the lake of fire have occurred (Rev. 20:11–15).[17] I prefer the opposite conclusion, namely, that the *main* significance of the story is not the intermediate state at all, but the "eternal tents" of the righteous and the "eternal fire" for the wicked (cf. Matt. 18:8; 25:41; Jude 1:7). As someone has put it: just as the heavenly bliss is experienced only fully *after* the resurrection, so too the fulness of the horror of hell will be experienced only *after* the resurrection.[18] Or as another has said, Luke 16 does not specifically localize the destinies of the rich man and Lazarus within the course of time, that is, does not deal with the question what will be before, and what after, the day of judgment, because the sufferings of the wicked will be terrible

---

16 www.newadvent.org/fathers/1007.htm.

17 Liefeld (1984, 991, 993).

18 Heyns (1988, 399).

anyway.[19]

It may be pointed out here that the story of the rich man and Lazarus is not about the unbeliever versus the believer, but about the wicked versus the righteous. It is the same in Revelation 2:7, where it is not simply the believer but the conqueror (or overcomer) who will receive a share in Paradise. This is not the same: in all the letters of Revelation 2–3 the conquerors are those church members who are not just believers but believers who overcome the specific perils that threaten each church separately.

This is the general picture in the New Testament: God

> will render to each one *according to his works*: to those who by patience in well-doing seek for glory and honor and immortality, he will give eternal life; but for those who are self-seeking and do not obey the truth, but obey unrighteousness, there will be wrath and fury. There will be tribulation and distress for every human being who does evil, the Jew first and also the Greek, but glory and honor and peace for everyone who *does good*, the Jew first and also the Greek (Rom. 2:6–10).

> "For we must all appear before the judgment seat of Christ, so that each one may receive what is due for *what he has done in the body*, whether good or evil" (2 Cor. 5:10; cf. Rom. 14:10).

> And I saw the dead, great and small, standing before the throne, and books were opened. Then another book was opened, which is the book of life. And the dead were judged by what was written in the books, *according to what they had done*. And the sea gave up the dead who were in it, Death and Hades gave up the dead who were in them, and they were judged, each one of them, *according to what they had done* (Rev. 20:12–13).

Of course, faith does play an essential role, but then a faith "working through love" (Gal. 5:6). As a Jew, the rich man was perhaps very religious, but there was no love in his religion (cf. the Pharisee in the parable of Luke 18:9–14). He should have listened to the apostle

---

19 Greijdanus (1941, 86).

James, if he had known him: "Religion that is pure and undefiled before God the Father is this: *to visit orphans and widows* [and all other people in misery] *in their affliction*, and to keep oneself unstained from the world" (1:27). "For judgment is without mercy to *one who has shown no mercy*. Mercy triumphs over judgment. What good is it, my brothers, if someone says he has faith but does not have works? Can that faith save him?" And then we find, so to speak, the clearest picture of the loveless rich man:

> If a brother or sister is poorly clothed and lacking in daily food, and one of you says to them, "Go in peace, be warmed and filled," without giving them the things needed for the body, what good is that? So also faith by itself, if it does not have works, is dead. . . . You see that a person is justified by works and not by faith alone (James 2:13–17, 24).

The rich man was perhaps religious, but not godly; Lazarus was poor but godly, as his name indicated: *El-Azar*, "God helps," "God is my help," His name was the description of his faith, his trust in God.

7.7 "With Me In Paradise"

Many Christians have seen in Luke 23:43 the clearest possible reference to the intermediate state (between death and resurrection) for the believer. Yet, I venture to say that the passage has often been so misunderstood that the latter conclusion can hardly be viewed as warranted. It begins with misunderstanding the prayer of the criminal: "Jesus, remember me when you come into your kingdom [other manuscripts, in your kingly glory]." What does this mean? Is the criminal speaking of Jesus entering into the "kingdom of heaven" taken in the sense of "heaven"? Not at all. His question was entirely in accordance with the Old Testament expectation of the Messianic kingdom. The Old Testament Jew was hardly occupied with any intermediate state; he looked forward to the coming of the Messianic kingdom. The miracle that occurred in the criminal on the cross was that the Holy Spirit had opened his eyes to see that *Jesus* was this Messiah. He understood that Jesus would pass *through* death, and would one day reappear:[20] "Remember me when you come as King" (CJB, GNT), or "when you begin ruling as king" (ERV).

This is the prayer of the criminal: Jesus, when you return and begin ruling as a King, do not forget me. Let me rise from the dead as well—just like you—and grant me my share in the Messianic kingdom. His prayer had basically the same content as what the King himself will say one day: "Then the King will say to those on his right [i.e., the righteous], 'Come, you who are blessed by my Father, *inherit the kingdom* prepared for you from the foundation of the world'" (Matt. 25:34). As we will see in the next and last chapter, the Messianic kingdom is the ultimate Eden, the ultimate Paradise. This is what Revelation 2:7 and 22:1–2 clearly indicate: Paradise lies beyond the resurrection. The criminal could have prayed: Jesus, remember me when you come into Eden or Paradise, that is, the Messianic kingdom.

Jesus' answer is noteworthy (if I read it correctly). He says as it were, You will indeed have a share in my kingdom to come, that is, in the ultimate Eden, in the eternal Paradise. Moreover, in some sense, even today you will have a foretaste of it, in some way or another (which is not further explained). Interestingly, the apocryphal *History of Joseph* (i.e., Joseph of Arimathea) suggests that what Jesus promised here is *not* the portion granted to all believers who die; only the criminal would be with Jesus in Paradise.[21] Apparently, the unknown writer was a little embarrassed with Jesus' answer, as, I feel, we all should be. Ultimate Paradise is so clearly a notion connected with the Messianic kingdom and the new heavens and new earth, that it would be quite amazing if we would have to accept that Jesus was suddenly, and exceptionally, giving here a description of the intermediate state as such. The righteous do not "go to Paradise" when they die because Paradise is a state after the resurrection. But in some way or another, the righteous who have passed away are with Christ already now, and this very fact is a foretaste of Paradise; it is paradisal in nature.

The emphasis is not on the question where the departed believers are, but *with whom* they are. They are "with Christ" (Phil. 1:23). This reality will enjoy a far greater fulness at the resurrection than before the resurrection, but already now our beloved who have passed away

---

20 Luce (1933, ad loc.).

21 www.pseudepigrapha.com/apocrypha_nt/narjoe.htm.

are with Jesus, abiding in his shadow (cf. Ps. 91:1), and that is "best of all" (GNV). Do not ask for any more details, because tradition will probably whisper into your ears all kinds of details that in fact belong to the world to come and the age to come. Please notice that, in the Bible, places as such never have glory, and never are holy. Only the Triune God has glory, only he is intrinsically holy. Wondering what "glorious *place*" believers are heading for is an act that is mistaken from the outset.[22] The glory or holiness of a place is determined by the presence of God, or the Son of God. What the Lord basically told the criminal is this: You ask me not to forget you. But I won't have a chance to forget you, for as of today you will be forever with me, in my presence, in the hollow of my hands. And where I am is Eden, is Paradise. Although in the fullest sense, Eden or Paradise is for the world to come, you will be *with me*, and that in itself is already a glimpse of the Eden to come.

As the Swiss theologian Frédéric Godet (d. 1900) wrote, "[I]t is not in heaven that one finds God, but in God one finds heaven."[23] It is an error to think of Paradise as a place of delight *apart from Christ*. As he is in his person the tree of life, in a sense we could even say that in his person he is Paradise. Paradise is magnificent because God, or the Son of God, is there. But perhaps it is even more correct to say that, wherever God is , or wherever the Son of God is, there is Paradise. The point is not that the departing believer is going to a certain magnificent place; his prayer is rather, "In *your* hands I commit my spirit [my breath, my very life, *myself*]" (Ps. 31:5), just as Jesus prayed (Luke 23:46).

7.8 The Father's House

There are several passages that refer to Jesus' second coming and the establishment of the Messianic kingdom, but which are traditionally applied by many Christians to the intermediate state. These are just a few examples:

(a) Many Old Testament passages that describe the blessings of

---

[22] It reminds us of the Muslim "Paradise," which contains many pleasures and delights, but Allah is not mentioned at all (Quran, Sura 76:12–22).

[23] Godet (1879), on John 14:1–3.

the Messianic kingdom are applied by many to the supposed blessings of the hereafter; I will give examples of them in the next and last chapter.

(b) Eternal life is often understood as the life in heaven in the sense of the intermediate state. In Christian obituaries, we often read that So-and-so has passed away "in hope of eternal life" (Titus 1:2), that is, hopeful that he or she has entered the blessed life of the hereafter. In reality, "eternal life" is a relationship with God, fellowship with God (John 17:3; 1 John 1:1–4).

(c) In 2 Corinthians 5:1–2 we read, "[W]e know that if the tent that is our earthly home is destroyed, we have a building from God, a house not made with hands, eternal in the heavens. For in this tent we groan, longing to put on our heavenly dwelling." This is often understood to mean that, when the believers leaves the earthly body, he enters heaven as the "building from God," the "house not made with hands, eternal in the heavens." In my view, the text makes perfectly clear that Paul is speaking about the resurrection body as opposed to "this tent" (v. 4), which was the mortal body he still had when writing these words.

(d) The New Jerusalem in Revelation 21 is often regarded as heaven, the blessed place where the departed believers are thought to be. Many songs and poems tell us about the "streets of gold" on which the departed are walking (v. 21). The truth is that the New Jerusalem is not heaven at all (in any meaning) but, as we are explicitly told, the bride, the wife of the Lamb (v. 9).

(e) In John 14:2–3, Jesus says, "In my Father's house are many rooms. If it were not so, would I have told you that I go to prepare a place for you? And if I go and prepare a place for you, I will come again and will take you to myself, that where I am you may be also." In other Christian obituaries, we read that So-and-so has been taken up into the Father's house—whereas the text makes clear that believers will go to the Father's house when, and only when, Jesus comes in person to take them to himself into the house of his Father all believers collectively (cf. 1 Cor. 15:51–54; Phil. 3:20–21; 1 Thess. 4:13–17). The Father's house is not the abode of bodiless believers, but of glorified believers with glorified bodies.

Jesus is here perhaps comparing himself to a servant who is sent forth to prepare lodging for the guests,[24] more or less in the sense of the girl of Song 8:2, "I would lead you and bring you [as a guest] into the house of my mother." Perhaps Jesus was also thinking of 1 Chronicles 17:9 by way of comparison: "I will appoint a place for my people Israel and will plant them, that they may dwell in their own place and be disturbed no more" (cf. for the latter phrase, John 14:1, "Let not your hearts be troubled").

Notice the phrase *and will plant them*—could the Father's house be called an Eden, where Jesus' followers are viewed as flourishing plants? At any rate, the Father's house is undoubtedly a *sanctuary*. This is because there must be a connection with John 2:16, where Jesus says in the temple of Herod, "[D]o not make my Father's house [i.e., the temple] a house of trade." In spite of a small difference (Gk. *oikos* in 2:16 and *oikia* in 14:2), it is almost inconceivable that such a connection would be lacking.[25] As soon as we accept such a link, we must suppose that in 14:2 Jesus is referring to the heavenly temple (cf. Rev. 3:12; 7:15; 11:19; 14:15, 17; 15:5–6, 8; 16:1, 17), of which the earthly temple in John 2:16 is a material reflection.

This assumption sheds light directly on the expression "many rooms (abodes)." In the temple of Solomon there were "chambers (rooms)" (1 Chron. 9:26, 33; 23:28; 28:11–12), which in the temple of Ezekiel 40–44 can be recognized even more clearly as priestly abodes (41:6–11; 42:1–14). The Greek word for "room" used in John 14:2, *monē*, began to mean "monastery" in later Greek; consider also the cognate word "monk." The priestly chambers will be like monk cells in a monastery, linked together, places of privacy *and* of heavenly fellowship. If I understand the Old Testament passages correctly, there will be no corridors from which the cells can be reached one by one. No, to go to a certain room one will have to pass through many other rooms. Privacy will not be absolute; fellowship and friendship will have the priority. In the next and last chapter, we will discuss

---

24 Dods (1979, 822).
25 See Grant (1897, 576); Gaebelein (1980, 266).

these wonderful abodes further.

7.9 The Third Heaven

At the end of this chapter, as a kind of appendix, I wish to say a few things about 2 Corinthians 12:2–4,

> I know a man in Christ [read, Paul] who fourteen years ago was caught up to the third heaven—whether in the body or out of the body I do not know, God knows. And I know that this man was caught up into paradise—whether in the body or out of the body I do not know, God knows—and he heard things that cannot be told, which man may not utter.

What does "paradise" mean here? The problem is that we do not know anything more about what the apostle Paul understands by "paradise" here than what the text tells us. Expositors have often understood this to refer to the hereafter (the departed believers in heaven), but the text says nothing of the kind; that interpretation has arisen only because of the traditional prejudices concerning the hereafter.

The "third heaven" is usually understood to refer to what lies beyond the first heaven (the sky with its clouds) and the second heaven (the firmament with the stars). Or perhaps these are counted as one: the sky with clouds and stars, and in this case, the second heaven could be something like the "heavenly places" in Ephesians (1:3, 20; 2:6; 3:10; 6:12). Or perhaps the "third heaven" is what in the Old Testament is sometimes called the "heaven of heavens" (Deut.10:14; 1 Kings 8:27; 2 Chron. 2:6; 6:18; Neh. 9:6; Ps. 68:33; 148:4). But even then the exact meaning of the expression within the context of 2 Corinthians 12 remains uncertain.

A more literal translation of verse 4 says, "he heard inexpressible words [Gk. *rhēmata*], which it is not lawful for a man to utter." So Paul heard "words" in this paradise, about which he tells us two things: it is not *possible* to express (formulate) these words, and it is not *permitted* to express them. But who is uttering, or who are uttering, these words? Expositors are vague on these things, and understandably so. But if these words *cannot* and *may not* be repeated, perhaps they came from God himself. And this might mean that the "third heaven" refers to God's own dwelling-place (although even "the heaven and heaven of heavens cannot contain him," 2 Chron. 2:6 KJV). God is the One who "sits in the heavens" (Ps. 2:4); his "throne is in heaven" (11:4; cf. 103:19; Isa. 66:1; Matt. 5:34; Acts 7:49; Heb. 8:1; Rev. 4:2). Consider this statement as well: "The heavens are the LORD's heavens, but the earth he has given to the children of man" (Ps. 115:16).

And paradise? Perhaps here it is nothing more than a description of the Edenic character of God's dwelling-place. As such, the meaning might not be too much different from the celestial Eden that we have encountered in Ezekiel 28 (see §§2.2 and 2.3 above). This heavenly Eden is older and more magnificent than the earthly garden of Genesis 2–3. The apostle was caught up into this place—whether in the body or out of the body—to catch there a glimpse of things and words so magnificent that he could not express them. But these are no doubt the things that one day *will* be revealed in the "world to come."

8
The Ultimate Eden

He who has an ear,
let him hear what the Spirit says to the churches.
To the one who conquers
I will grant to eat of the tree of life,
which is in the paradise of God.
Revelation 2:7

Then the angel showed me the river of the water of life,
bright as crystal,
flowing from the throne of God and of the Lamb
through the middle of the street of the city;
also, on either side of the river,
the tree of life with its twelve kinds of fruit,
yielding its fruit each month.
The leaves of the tree were for the healing of the nations.
Revelation 22:1–2

. . . it is for you that paradise is opened,
the tree of life is planted,
the age to come is prepared,
plenty is provided,
a city is built,
rest is appointed,
goodness is established
and wisdom perfected beforehand.
4 Esdras 8:52 (apocryphal)

8.1 A Simple Grave

The main city in which I grew up was Apeldoorn, a city in the Dutch province of Gelderland where I still preach eight times a year. In earlier centuries, Apeldoorn was a tiny, inconspicuous village. But it had two great advantages. It lay at the crossroads of the road heading east from Amersfoort to Deventer, and the road going south from Zwolle to Arnhem. This is why it had an unusually large number of inns. Often, the bishop of Utrecht passed by on his way to the province of Overijsel, part of his bishopric. The other advantage of Apeldoorn was that near the village stood the castle of stadholder William III, prince of Orange and later also king of Great Britain. A larger palace was built there, where several Dutch kings as well as Queen Wilhelmina resided (see §2.1). As a consequence, Apeldoorn underwent rapid growth, so that, today, it is not a village anymore but a city of 150,000 inhabitants.

As Apeldoorn was growing, a new cemetery was needed, a little distance from the old center, at the road called the Soerenseweg (the Way to the village of [Hoog-]Soeren). It was constructed during the closing years of the nineteenth century, in the midst of the forest. Today the cemetery features many trees, with little winding lanes in a beautiful romantic landscape. It is an oasis of silence, rest and harmony, and every time I come there I have Edenic feelings.

By the end of the nineteenth century, many wealthy people had come to reside in Apeldoorn, a town attractive because of its magnificent surroundings and its ideal location. Members of well-known noble families came to be buried at the Soerenseweg, along with local politicians, court functionaries, military officers, pastors, and artists. But when I visit the cemetery, I pass the graves of these notable people, and I look at the inscriptions on their gravestone, but they are not the reason why I come there. I come to visit the grave of my parents (who, by the way, were not so wealthy and not so notable). My mom passed away in 2001, and my dad in 2009. They have a beautiful stone on their gravesite with these words, chosen by my father from 1 Thessalonians 4:17, "Forever with the Lord." This was the essence of their lives, the great thing they looked for: to be forever with him who had died for them, and had risen again for them. They did not think very much (I believe) about "how it would be in heaven," and things like that; it was the desire of their heart to be forever *with the Lord*, before and especially after the resurrection (1 Thess. 4 explicitly speaks of *post*-resurrection blessings).

Once in a while, I come to Apeldoorn to spend some time at the grave of my parents in those wonderful Edenic surroundings. Some may wonder why I do this. They might even say, "Your parents are not here," thus falsely applying Mark 16:6, where this is said of an *empty* tomb: "He is not here." My parents, not just their "remains," *are* in that grave. This is a false Greek idea: the *soul* has left, and only what "remains" is buried. Such people overlook what John 19 clearly tells us: his friends laid *Jesus* in the tomb, not just his "remains' (v. 42). When I am at the grave of my parents, I know that *they* are there—although I also know that, in some way or another, they are "with the Lord." They are in his presence, and that is far better than anything they experienced on earth (cf. Phil. 1:23). I meditate a little on these mysterious things every time I visit their grave. I do not know exactly how I must understand these things. I know they did not understand this either. But they knew—as I do—that they would be "forever with the Lord." What mattered most to them was not the *how* and *where* and *when*, but the *who*. I look around the beautiful cemetery and I get a glimpse of Eden. I look at the gravestone again, and again I realize: this is what Eden is all about—being forever with the Lord.

8.2 Springtime

I was only twenty-seven when I gave a series of lectures on the Song of Solomon in a lovely fishing village in the Netherlands. With some pride, I told the audience that orthodox Jewish men were not allowed to read the book before they were thirty, apparently because of its erotic contents. I spoke of the typological and eschatological significance of this wonderful little love song; afterward, my lectures were printed in a book.[1] One of the many magnificent passages is this, in which the young lover calls to his beloved girl:

> Arise, my love, my beautiful one, and come away, for behold, the winter is past; the rain is over and gone. The flowers appear on

---

1 Ouweneel (1973, ad loc.).

the earth, the time of singing has come, and the voice of the turtledove is heard in our land. The fig tree ripens its figs, and the vines are in blossom; they give forth fragrance. Arise, my love, my beautiful one, and come away (2:10–13).

I am sure I hear the voice of the Messiah here, resounding in our time to Israel, even though today there is still little spiritual response among the nation. It is Israel's spiritual spring, and has been since the nineteenth century, but certainly from the second half of the twentieth century. And this spring will debouch in a wonderful summer, that is, the Messianic kingdom of peace and righteousness. This is the summer about which Jesus spoke, the summer that begins with the trees producing their leaves, Israel first, but also the neighboring countries: "From the fig tree learn its lesson: as soon as its branch becomes tender and puts out its leaves, you know that summer is near" (Matt. 24:32). I am sure this is what we experience today: summer is approaching! The ultimate Eden is near! One sign of this is the founding of the state of Israel (1948), but at least as important is this other sign: when East Jerusalem was captured (1967), there were virtually no Messianic (i.e., Jesus-believing) Jews in Israel, whereas today there are many thousands of them.

Summer is the time about which Isaiah speaks, the time of the most opulent growth of plants and trees, Eden at its best: "I will put in the wilderness the cedar, the acacia, the myrtle, and the olive. I will set in the desert the cypress, the plane and the pine together, that they may see and know, may consider and understand together, that the hand of the Lord has done this, the Holy One of Israel has created it" (Isa. 41:19–20). "For the LORD comforts Zion; he comforts all her waste places and makes her wilderness *like Eden*, her desert like the *garden of the LORD*; joy and gladness will be found in her, thanksgiving and the voice of song" (51:3).

[Y]ou shall go out in joy and be led forth in peace; the mountains and the hills before you shall break forth into singing, and all the trees of the field shall clap their hands. Instead of the thorn shall come up the cypress; instead of the brier shall come up the myrtle; and it shall make a name for the LORD, an everlasting sign that shall not be cut off (55:12–13).

Thus says the Lord GOD: "On the day that I cleanse you from all your iniquities, I will cause the cities to be inhabited, and the waste places shall be rebuilt. And the land that was desolate shall be tilled, instead of being the desolation that it was in the sight of all who passed by. And they will say, 'This land that was desolate has become like the garden of Eden, and the waste and desolate and ruined cities are now fortified and inhabited'" (Ezek. 36:33–35).

Or consider this portrait from the world of the birds. The young man in Song 2 told his beloved about the turtledove that had reappeared in the land, as a sure sign of summer. The migrating birds are returning! God says, "[T]he stork in the heavens knows her times, and the turtledove, swallow, and crane keep the time of their coming" (Jer. 8:7), that is, the proper time of their return during spring.

Very near where my wife and I are living there is high, man-made stork nest to offer shelter and safety to a pair of storks. In the winter, the nest is empty. What a joy, in springtime, when we see the storks that have returned to this nest! The trees begin to sprout, the flowers begin to blossom, and the storks return. Summer is close! A friend of mine lives in a farmhouse, and announces to us every spring via the internet when the barn swallows have returned from the far south, to occupy the nests in his barn. They are the joy of every nature lover: all those signs (about which city people know so little) that summer is approaching. This is what we are experiencing today in the spiritual world: summer is near.

The realization of Eden as well as the loss of Eden is like going from one season to the other. Israel's present spring was preceded by a long winter, which in fact began already with the destruction of the First Temple in 586 BC. The return from Babylon and the construction of the Second Temple did not fundamentally change this, because the celestial fire and the *Shekhinah* did not descend upon it at this temple's consecration (cf. Ezra 6; Hag. 2). It remained cold and dark, so to speak. The flowers were gone, stork and swallow had left the country. The trees were bare, the nests were empty. Psalm 84:3

says, "Even the sparrow finds a home, and the swallow a nest for herself, where she may lay her young, at your altars, O LORD of hosts, my King and my God." This can only be the temple in spring and summer time. But in the Second Temple, spiritually speaking, there were no such signs of spring and summer.

Perhaps it is very significant—to those who are sensitive to such midrashic hints in the New Testament—that the only season mentioned in Jesus' days was winter, described in such a dry way: "It was winter" (John 10:22). No Eden can flourish in winter. Notice in this context a remarkable statement by Jeremiah: "The harvest is past, the summer is ended, and we are not [yet] saved" (8:20). The summer is over, and also autumn.² Jeremiah saw winter approaching, and saw no springtime looming. He could not know how terribly long this winter was going to last. And winter means: no Eden. For centuries, the faithful could ask (in spiritual language): Where are the flowers and the migrating birds? Why are they away for so long?

8.3 Seven Seasons

Extending the metaphor just presented, I could survey the history of Eden in terms of seven seasons.

First season: Israel's oppression in Egypt was the long, cold, dark, depressing winter with which Israel's existence as a nation began: "[T]hey ruthlessly made the people of Israel work as slaves and made their lives bitter with hard service, in mortar and brick, and in all kinds of work in the field. In all their work they ruthlessly made them work as slaves" (Exod. 1:13–14).

Second season: Israel's redemption from Egypt heralded the spring; these were Israel's "days of betrothal," which, just as in Song 2, correspond with the blossoming springtime: "I remember the devotion of your youth, your love as a bride, how you followed me in the wilderness, in a land not sown" (Jer. 2:2).

Third season: the period of the kingship of David and Solomon was like a summer in Israel, a summer that, typologically and prophetically, corresponds with the summer of the Messianic kingdom. One of its Edenic characteristics was the emphasis on eating and drinking:

---

2   The Dutch word for autumn, *herfst*, is etymologically related to the English word *harvest*.

Judah and Israel were as many as the sand by the sea. They ate and drank and were happy. Solomon ruled over all the kingdoms from the Euphrates to the land of the Philistines and to the border of Egypt [cf. the promise of Gen. 15:18]. They brought tribute and served Solomon all the days of his life. Solomon's provision for one day was thirty cors[3] of fine flour and sixty cors of meal, ten fat oxen, and twenty pasture-fed cattle, a hundred sheep, besides deer, gazelles, roebucks, and fattened fowl. For he had dominion over all the region west of the Euphrates from Tiphsah to Gaza, over all the kings west of the Euphrates. And he had peace on all sides around him. And Judah and Israel lived in safety, from Dan even to Beersheba, every man under his vine and under his fig tree, all the days of Solomon (1 Kings 4:20–25).

Notice the latter expression, "under his vine and under his fig tree," which is a truly Edenic expression (Micah 4:4; Zech. 3:10).

Fourth season: the horrible aftermath of the David monarchy constituted the autumn that Jeremiah experienced (see §8.2), the prophet who saw the harsh winter approaching for Israel Read this as well: "I weep with the weeping of Jazer for the vine of Sibmah; I drench you with my tears, O Heshbon and Elealeh; for over your summer fruit and your harvest the shout has ceased" (Isa. 16:9; cf. Jer. 48:32, two remarkably similar passages).

Fifth season: the long exile from 586 BC to AD 1948, interrupted by the Second Temple period in which Israel lived without the *Shekhinah*, has been Israel's winter. "It was winter" (John 10:22). There was one long cry during these thousands of years: "Come, gentle spring, ethereal mildness, come," as we hear it so marvelously in the opening choir of Joseph Haydn's oratorio *The Seasons*.

Sixth season: today we experience Israel's spring, which can still have its cold spells, like the cold days of March (in the moderate regions of the northern hemisphere), yet moves steadily toward the summer. That will be the time when the bride of the Messiah is going to respond to his voice, which lovingly appeals to them, as we found

---

3   A cor was about six bushels or a bit more than fifty-eight gallons (220 liters).

it in Song 2: "... The flowers appear on the earth, the time of singing has come, and the voice of the turtledove is heard in our land. The fig tree ripens its figs, and the vines are in blossom."

Seventh season: the Messianic kingdom will be Israel's summer; then for a thousand (literal or figurative) years Israel's jubilant voice will be heard: "My beloved is mine, and I am his" (Song 2:16). I repeat: without the summer there can be no Eden. The realization of the ultimate Eden will figuratively be when summer comes to the land. Summer *can* be a negative picture: "For day and night your hand was heavy upon me; my strength was dried up as by the heat of summer" (Ps. 32:4). But usually it is a very positive picture: "From the fig tree learn its lesson: as soon as its branch becomes tender and puts out its leaves, you know that summer is near" (Mark 13:28).

8.4 Edenic Dwellings

In chapter 7, I compared the Father's house in John 14 to the temple as a place of priestly worship. If this is the correct approach, we must indeed view the "many abodes" in John 14:2–3 as priestly abodes, which were part of the earthly temple but apparently also of the heavenly temple. In the Father's house, there are many abodes for the heavenly priests who, under the guidance of God's Son, will forever perform their temple service of spiritual sacrifices (cf. 1 Pet. 2:5; Rev. 22:3). This also explains the phrase "preparing a place" more clearly:

> Thus it was necessary for the copies of the heavenly things [i.e., the earthly sanctuary] to be purified with these rites [i.e., the Old Testament sacrifices], but the heavenly things themselves with better sacrifices than these. For Christ has entered, not into holy places made with hands, which are copies of the true things, but into heaven itself, now to appear in the presence of God on our behalf (Heb. 9:23–24).

That is, the blood of Christ cleanses not only God's *people* from their sins, but also the way into the heavenly sanctuary (cf. 10:19–22). Divine purification is not only cleansing people *from* sin and uncleanness, but also consecrating them *to* priestly service.

These are indeed two different things; cleansing from sins does not automatically imply free access to God in the heavenly sanctuary. Jesus not only bore the sins of his people but he also prepared for them a place in the Father's house, the heavenly temple, where they will eternally carry out their temple service of spiritual sacrifices: "[T]he hour is coming, and is now here, when the true worshipers will worship the Father in spirit and truth, for the Father is seeking such people to worship him" (John 4:23). Believers are "a spiritual house, to be a holy priesthood, to offer spiritual sacrifices acceptable to God through Jesus Christ" (1 Pet. 2:5). "Through him then let us continually offer up a sacrifice of praise to God, that is, the fruit of lips that acknowledge his name" (Heb. 13:15).

Revelation 22 makes a direct connection between this everlasting temple service and the new Eden:

> Then the angel showed me the river of the water of life, bright as crystal, flowing from the throne of God and of the Lamb through the middle of the street of the city [i.e., the new Jerusalem]; also, on either side of the river, the tree of life with its twelve kinds of fruit, yielding its fruit each month. The leaves of the tree were for the healing of the nations. No longer will there be anything accursed, but the throne of God and of the Lamb will be in it, and *his servants will worship him*. They will see his face, and his name will be on their foreheads. And night will be no more. They will need no light of lamp or sun, for the Lord GOD will be their light, and they will reign forever and ever (vv. 1–5).

This is what the heavenly temple will be, namely, what it always was: both an Eden and a sanctuary. A garden with the "water of life" and the "tree of life," which will be yielding its fruit for the blessing of the city's inhabitants. And it will also be a sanctuary, a place of worship for the heavenly priests, who at the same time will be kings, "reigning forever and ever": "[Y]ou have made them a kingdom and priests to our God, and they shall reign on the earth" (5:10; cf. 1:6). They are fellowshipping, worshipping together, rejoicing, and exulting. They are very active in their service, yet it will be eternal rest, perfect harmony, and joyful bliss.

8.5 A Tree and a Tent

Let me return to that marvelous promise of Revelation 2:7b, "He who has an ear, let him hear what the Spirit says to the churches. To the one who conquers I will grant to eat of the tree of life, which is in the paradise of God." Or, in the version of The Message: "Are your ears awake? Listen. Listen to the Wind Words, the Spirit blowing through the churches. I'm about to call each conqueror to dinner. I'm spreading a banquet of Tree-of-Life fruit, a supper plucked from God's orchard." The faithful in the church of Ephesus are called upon to gain the spiritual victory, so that they may eat of the tree of life. Christ himself is the true source of life, and he will forever be such for his people beyond death and tomb (cf. Rev. 22:2, 14). In Revelation, spiritual overcoming or conquering is clearly linked with the resurrection (cf. 2:26–27; 3:12, 21; especially 15:2). Thus, after their resurrection, the faithful will enjoy forever the blessings of God's Eden. Of course, this bliss will be for all believers, but here it is mentioned as a special consolation for those who, here on earth, have kept their "first love" (cf. 2:4).

The blessing for the faithful in Ephesus refers to the garden aspect of Eden, and the blessing for the faithful in Philadelphia refers to the sanctuary aspect of Eden: "The one who conquers, I will make him a pillar in the temple of my God. Never shall he go out of it, and I will write on him the name of my God, and the name of the city of my God, the new Jerusalem, which comes down from my God out of heaven, and my own new name" (Rev. 3:12).

The sanctuary aspect returns in Revelation 20:3b: "Behold, the dwelling place [or, tent, tabernacle, Gk. *skēnē*] of God is with man. He will dwell with them, and they will be his people, and God himself will be with them as their God." The Greek word *skēnē* is a very interesting term. In Hebrews 8–9 it is the term for the tabernacle of Israel in the wilderness, the tent of God, in which his *Shekhinah* dwelt. This is the first link with Eden (see chapter 3). In the book of Revelation, the first use of *skēnē* is in 7:15, which speaks of the great multitude of verse 9: ". . . they are in front of the throne of God. They serve [or, worship] him day and night in his temple. The one who sits on the throne will spread his tent [*skēnē*] over them" (GW). Again, *skēnē* reminds us here of the tabernacle in the wilderness, when the *Shekhinah* dwelt in the midst of Israel (Exod. 40:34–38). In the same way, Revelation 20:3 says that God's *Shekhinah*, his holy, glorious splendor will dwell among God's people on the new earth.

It is also possible to think in this passage of the Feast of Booths, *the* great festival of Israel, and the clearest picture of the Messianic kingdom, as well as a commemoration of Eden ("[Y]ou shall take on the first day the fruit of splendid trees, branches of palm trees and boughs of leafy trees and willows of the brook, and you shall rejoice before the LORD your God seven days," Lev. 23:40). We can read Revelation 20:3b to teach that God will invite his people into his "tent," that is, his *sukkah* ("booth"). Eden itself will be like a large *sukkah*, adorned with the olives and the grapes of the full harvest. The booths remind the people of Israel's forty years in the wilderness, when they had to live in booths—but the olives and the grapes (which they did not have in the wilderness) speak to them of a new time, even an eternity, of wealth and bliss.

Revelation 7 seems to refer to the Feast of Booths, for the people of the great multitude have like a *lulav* (a closed frond of the date palm tree) in their hands, as the Jews do during the Feast. The gathered people whom God will invite into his *sukkah* will be "from every nation, from all tribes and peoples and languages, standing before the throne and before the Lamb, clothed in white robes, with palm branches in their hands" (v. 9).

8.6 Five Features of Eden

Let me try to describe the blessings of the ultimate Eden that will characterize the saints in the new heavens and on the new earth. I do this in terms seven features (five in this section, and two in following sections), without denying that other features might be mentioned as well.

(1) *Dwelling*. God's people will forever live in "eternal tents" (Luke 16:9) or in the "many rooms" of the Father's house (John 14:2–3). Eden will be their eternal home. The most important thing, though, is not *where* they will live, but *with whom*: "forever with the Lord" (cf. Luke 23:43; 2 Cor. 5:8; Phil. 1:23; 1 Thess. 4:17). The ultimate glory of Eden is not its magnificent rivers, plants, and trees, but the glory of the Triune God itself that will fill the place. And remember, because

the Father has become *their* Father, they will not simply lodge in Eden but *dwell* there. It is their home, just as much as for children their parents' home is *their* home. Today, the Father and the Son may come and make their home with the believers (John 14:23); in eternity, the believers will make their home with the Father and the Son.

(2) *Rest*. Eden is the place where God's people "rest from their labors" (Rev. 14:13). They will not be lazy and inactive (see the following features), yet it is a place of perfect peace and harmony: "[T]he meek shall inherit the land [or, earth] and delight themselves in abundant peace" (Ps. 37:11). "In his days shall the righteous flourish; and abundance of peace so long as the moon endureth" (72:7 KJV). There will be endless peace, yet much activity—but without effort and trouble. "So then, there remains a Sabbath rest for the people of God, for whoever has entered God's rest has also rested from his works as God did from his" (Heb. 4:9–10). This explicit link with the seventh day of the creation week implies another Edenic feature.

(3) *Enjoyment*. Eden will be the place of eternal, blissful delight (which is the meaning of the word "Eden"): "Blessed [more correctly, blissful; in everyday English: happy[4]] are the dead who die in the Lord" (Rev. 14:13). It is the place where tears, mourning and pain will be things of the past (21:4; cf. 7:17; Isa. 25:8). It is the place of comfort (Luke 16:25), of the "joy of the master" into which the faithful servants may enter (cf. Matt. 25:21, 23; see also Isa. 35:10; 51:11, "everlasting joy"). It is the place of "an eternal weight of glory beyond all comparison" (2 Cor. 4:17). Paul quotes, "What no eye has seen, nor ear heard, nor the heart of man imagined, what God has prepared for those who love him" (1 Cor. 2:9). It is the fulfillment of Psalm 34:8, "[T]aste and see that the LORD is good!" John Calvin says that the LORD "will give himself to be enjoyed by them."[5]

(4) *Shining*. In Matthew 13:43, the LORD says, "Then the righteous will shine like the sun in the kingdom of their Father" (cf. Dan. 12:3, "[T]hose who are wise shall shine like the brightness of the sky above;

---

4   This points to a traditional weakness of English Bible translations: in Greek, the word "blessed" is *eulogētos* (Heb. *barukh*; Lat. *benedictus*), but the text says *makarios*, "blissful, happy" (Heb. *ashrey*; Lat. *beatus*).

5   *Institutes* 3.25.10 (http://www.ccel.org/ccel/calvin/institutes.v.xxvi.html?highlight=enjoy#highlight).

and those who turn many to righteousness, like the stars forever and ever"). The bride of the Lamb will be "prepared as a bride adorned for her husband" (Rev. 21:2), and will have the "glory of God" (vv. 9–11). This shining is in fact nothing but the reflection of the glory of Christ: "God, who said, 'Let light shine out of darkness,' has shone in our hearts to give the light of the knowledge of the glory of God in the face of Jesus Christ" (2 Cor. 4:6; cf. 3:18). Interestingly, there is a Jewish Midrash that wishes to read in Genesis 3:21 the phrase "coats of *light*,"[6] suggesting that Adam and Eve began "shining" again after their fall. If there is truth in this interpretation, we may say that the first shining was in old Eden! Because God himself made these new clothes for Adam and Eve, the clothes were as radiant as God is himself, said the rabbis.

(5) *Contemplation*. Eden will be the place where God's people will behold the glory of God. It was the Son's will that they, as he said, may "see my glory that you have given me" (John 17:24). "For now we see in a mirror dimly, but then face to face" (1 Cor. 12:12); "we shall see him as he is" (1 John 3:2). "They will see his face, and his name will be on their foreheads" (Rev. 22:4). "Blessed are the pure in heart, for they shall see God" (Matt. 5:8). "Strive for peace with everyone, and for the holiness without which no one will see the LORD" (Heb. 12:14; cf. 1 John 3:6; 3 John 1:11).[7] In a sense, this contemplation is essentially a new Edenic feature; one could hardly imagine such a wonderful thing in old Eden, either before or after the Fall. It was great enough that they could *hear* the LORD, speaking to them, or even *hear* the sound (lit., voice) of God in the garden (Gen. 3:10). One could also argue that, even in the coming eternity, perceiving God's *inner being* will not be possible for the eyes of creatures, even renewed creatures. This is what humans have always known because God himself said, "[Y]ou cannot see my face, for man shall not see me and live" (Exod. 33:20; cf. 3:6; Judg. 6:22; 13:22; Isa. 6:5). In conclusion: there will be the *visio Dei*, "the seeing of God," but only insofar as this is possible for humans, even glorified humans.

---

6 The Hebrew has *cor*, "skin," but some rabbis have argued that this can also be read as *'or*, "light."

7 See further Exod. 24:11; Num. 12:5-8; Deut. 34:10; Ps. 24:6; 27:8; 63:2; 105:4; 2 Cor. 3:18.

8.7 The Sixth Feature of Eden

The last two features of Eden are perhaps the most characteristic, and remind us in fact of all the previous stages in Eden's history.

(6) *Reclining, eating.* The new Eden will be the place of God's great feast with his people, and of his people together (see §1.7 and other places). It is the image of enjoyment and fellowship that seems to have begun in John 1:18 (see §1.7), and that we find at many other places. In metaphorical language, there is hardly anything more Edenic than a banquet. Jesus says of his followers: "Truly, I say to you, he [i.e., Jesus himself] will dress himself for service and have them recline at table, and he will come and serve them" (Luke 12:37). "To the one who conquers I will grant to eat of the tree of life, which is in the paradise of God" (Rev. 2:7). "Blessed are those who are invited to the marriage supper of the Lamb" (19:9; cf. 2:17, "the hidden manna"). "[T]he Lamb which is in the midst of the throne shall feed them, and shall lead them unto living fountains of waters" (7:17 KJV). Jesus says that one day he "will drink again of this fruit of the vine" on "that day when I drink it new with you in my Father's kingdom" (Matt. 26:29).

Having a meal together is *the* biblical image of fellowship, and this fellowship—with the Father and the Son, and with each other—is *the* characteristic of "eternal life" (John 17:3; 1 John 1:1–4). In the person of Christ, this life descended from heaven (1 John 1:1–2; 5:20), and was granted to those who believed. The Father's house will be the proper place where they will enjoy it forever (cf. Matt. 25:46; John 4:36; 12:25; Rom. 6:22; Gal. 6:8; Jude 1:21). It is amazing to see in Luke's Gospel how often he is sitting at a meal (see §6.6), and how often meals function is his parables and stories (12:19, 37–38; 14:7–24; 15:22–27; 16:19–23). All the great Festivals on the Jewish calendar, from the Passover to the Feast of Booths, feature prominently the activity of celebration. And the central Christian sacrament is the Lord's Supper (§§6.6 and 6.7).

8.8 The Seventh Feature of Eden

(7) *Service, worship.* The seventh and last characteristic of the ultimate Eden to be mentioned here is service, liturgy, or worship: "No longer will there be anything accursed, but the throne of God and

of the Lamb will be in it [i.e., in the new Jerusalem; see vv. 1–2], and his servants will worship [or, serve] him" (Rev. 22:3). The Greek verb used here is *latreuō*, from a root that we recognize in (negative) terms such as idolatry, bibliolatry, and Mariolatry. It may be rendered as "to serve," but then in the sense of a "church service," a liturgy, worship given to God. We think here again of John 14:1–3 (see §7.7), where the Father's house is to be connected with John 2:16, referring to the temple. The "many rooms" are the chambers of the priests, who dwell there and whose principal task is to bring sacrifices of praise and thanksgiving to God.

Especially in the book of Revelation, the most Edenic book of the New Testament, praise and worship play a central role, given both by angels and by glorified saints: "[T]he twenty-four elders fall down before him who is seated on the throne and worship him who lives forever and ever. They cast their crowns before the throne, saying, 'Worthy are you, our Lord and God, to receive glory and honor and power, for you created all things, and by your will they existed and were created'" (4:10–11).

> And when he had taken the scroll, the four living creatures and the twenty-four elders fell down before the Lamb, each holding a harp, and golden bowls full of incense, which are the prayers of the saints. And they sang a new song, saying, "Worthy are you to take the scroll and to open its seals, for you were slain, and by your blood you ransomed people for God from every tribe and language and people and nation, and you have made them a kingdom and priests to our God, and they shall reign on the earth." Then I looked, and I heard around the throne and the living creatures and the elders the voice of many angels, numbering myriads of myriads and thousands of thousands, saying with a loud voice, "Worthy is the Lamb who was slain, to receive power and wealth and wisdom and might and honor and glory and blessing!" And I heard every creature in heaven and on earth and under the earth and in the sea, and all that is in them, saying, "To him who sits on the throne and to the Lamb be blessing and honor and glory and might forever and ever!" And the four living creatures said, 'Amen!' and the elders fell down and worshiped (5:8–14).

And all the angels were standing around the throne and around the elders and the four living creatures, and they fell on their faces before the throne and worshiped God, saying, "Amen! Blessing and glory and wisdom and thanksgiving and honor and power and might be to our God forever and ever! Amen." ... [T]hey are before the throne of God, and serve him day and night in his temple; and he who sits on the throne will shelter them with his presence (7:11–12, 15).

"And the twenty-four elders who sit on their thrones before God fell on their faces and worshiped God, saying, 'We give thanks to you, Lord God Almighty, who is and who was, for you have taken your great power and begun to reign'" (11:16).

After this I heard what seemed to be the loud voice of a great multitude in heaven, crying out, "Hallelujah! Salvation and glory and power belong to our God, for his judgments are true and just; for he has judged the great prostitute who corrupted the earth with her immorality, and has avenged on her the blood of his servants." Once more they cried out, "Hallelujah! The smoke from her goes up forever and ever." And the twenty-four elders and the four living creatures fell down and worshiped God who was seated on the throne, saying, "Amen. Hallelujah!" And from the throne came a voice saying, "Praise our God, all you his servants, you who fear him, small and great." Then I heard what seemed to be the voice of a great multitude, like the roar of many waters and like the sound of mighty peals of thunder, crying out,

> *Hallelujah! For the Lord our God the Almighty reigns.*
> *Let us rejoice and exult and give him the glory,*
> *for the marriage of the Lamb has come!* (19:1–7).

8.9 Explanation

One night, many years ago, I brought my youngest son to bed. He was only four at the time (by now, his own children are older than this!). He said his evening prayer, and then suddenly burst out, "Dad, actually I do not like to go to heaven." I asked him, "Why not?" "Well," he said, "I don't like singing all day, and do nothing else." Interestingly, he is our very child who, at a much later age, produced a CD with spiritual songs of his own!

Of course, I understood what the boy was trying to say. Look at the first five features of Eden mentioned above: dwelling, resting, enjoying, shining, and contemplating. That is all very nice, but also very passive. Or look at the sixth and seventh features mentioned above: eating and worshiping (which includes singing). Is that all? We understand very well that eating and singing—or playing harps, or wearing crowns, or walking on golden streets, for that matter—is figurative language. Even our reigning will be rather metaphorical: what reigning will be needed in God's new, perfect world? What exactly do all these metaphors *stand for*? It is like trying to explain to a person who was born blind what watching a beautiful sunset is like. We might use parallels: it is like listening to beautiful music with the ears, which then, as an experience, must be transferred to the eyes. It might give the blind person a vague idea, but at the same time we know very well that seeing is very different from listening.

Paul uses the following image in 1 Corinthians 15:36–44: the resurrection body relates to our present body as a wheat plant relates to a grain of wheat. But if you are familiar only with grains, what picture can you form of the full-grown plant? Hardly any. Still, you do know there is a connection: *that* plant came from *this* grain. In the same way, the ultimate Eden will come from *this* world. All Edenic landscapes come from such landscapes as we know them today, and will at the same time be infinitely more magnificent. All Edenic music comes from music as we know today, and will at the same time be infinitely more glorious. All Edenic eating and drinking will sprout from *this* eating and drinking we know today, and will at the same time be infinitely more delicious. The marriage life of the Lamb and his bride finds its primordial pattern in the joys of marriage life as we know it today, and will at the same time be infinitely more exalted.

I fear that deep in their hearts, many Christians do not look forward so eagerly to this ultimate Edenic bliss because they think primarily of all the things they will presumably no longer enjoy: no more pleasant work, no more eating and drinking, no more libraries, no more symphony orchestra concerts, no more museums, no more pleasures of wedded life, no more vacations, no more cars, no more airplanes, no more gardening and fishing, no more beaches and forests, no more sports, no more plants and animals, and so on. *I think this is all a fundamental mistake.* All these things, which are so essential to the way God made us, will be found in the ultimate Eden, *but on a different level.* Just as I will have reached, there and then, the ultimate fulfillment of my humanity, I will also have reached the ultimate fulfillment of all human enjoyment. All the blessings just mentioned will be there—otherwise I would not be human anymore—but in such an exalted way that I cannot yet form a picture of them. My ultimate humanity will relate to my present humanity as the tulip to the bulb, and the same will be true of my work, my eating and drinking, my intellectual pleasures, the music and other arts that I will enjoy, the landscapes with its beaches and forests, plants and animals. If you are familiar only with bulbs, what a surprise the tulip will be! If you are familiar with present-day eating and drinking, music and other arts, beaches and forests, what a surprise the ultimate form of these things will be!

Actually, we have known this all our lives. Not even the best food and drinks, our best intellectual achievements, the most beautiful music, poems or paintings, the best vacations and sporting achievements, could ever give us complete and lasting satisfaction. There was always an element of unfulfillment, and even disappointment, in them: Is this it? Is this life at its best, or is there more? Or are all these experiences granted by God in order to make us realize that, ultimately, we were made for another world, the ultimate Eden, in which all enjoyment *will* be perfect?[8] A world in which we will finally be *perfectly at home*?

Eden is for the persecuted and oppressed, for those who mourn and who hunger and thirst for righteousness (cf. Matt. 5:4, 6 10), for those who labor and are heavy laden (cf. 11:28). For them, Eden will be the opposite of the misery they have experienced in the present

---

8   I think that no writer has expressed this more clearly and beautifully than C. S. Lewis, especially in his *Mere Christianity*, chapter 10, and in several other writings of his, including his works of fiction (*Narnia, Perelandra*).

world, and that is wonderful. However, Eden will also be the destination for believers who have led easy and happy lives, who had the opportunity to develop their talents and to make good use of their opportunities. For them, Eden will not be a contrast, a disappointment compared to their present life, but rather a proof that even the best happiness and fulfillment in the present world are only a meagre shadow of the happiness and fulfillment to come. They will say, not as the queen of Sheba said to king Solomon—"the half was not told me" (1 Kings 10:7)—but rather, until now, I knew only the shadows, but now I know full reality. "For now we see in a mirror dimly, but then face to face. Now I know in part; then I shall know fully, even as I have been fully known" (1 Cor. 13:12).

Appendix 1
Eden in Ezekiel 31

There is one passage in the Bible that is least known, and least understood. I could not easily fit it into the previous chapters, although I referred to it once or twice. Let me therefore make a few remarks on it in this Appendix. The passage is Ezekiel 31, the entire chapter, which I quote here to some extent (relevant expressions are in italics).

> In the eleventh year, in the third month, on the first day of the month, the word of the LORD came to me: "Son of man, say to Pharaoh king of Egypt and to his multitude: 'Whom are you like in your greatness? Behold, Assyria was [or, you are like] a cedar in Lebanon, with beautiful branches and forest shade, and of towering height, its top among the clouds. The waters nourished it; the deep made it grow tall, making its rivers flow around the place of its planting, sending forth its streams to all the trees of the field. So it towered high above all the trees of the field; its boughs grew large and its branches long from abundant water in its shoots. All the birds of the heavens made their nests in its boughs; under its branches all the beasts of the field gave birth to their young, and under its shadow lived all great nations. It was beautiful in its greatness, in the length of its branches; for its roots went down to abundant waters. The cedars in the *garden of God* could not rival it, nor the fir trees equal its boughs; neither were the plane trees like its branches; no tree in the *garden of God* was its equal in beauty. I made it beautiful in the mass of its branches, and all the *trees of Eden* envied it, that were in the *garden of God*. . . .

> Thus says the Lord GOD: On the day the cedar went down to Sheol I caused mourning; I closed the deep over it, and restrained its rivers, and many waters were stopped. I clothed Lebanon in gloom for it, and all the trees of the field fainted because of it. I made the nations quake at the sound of its fall, when I cast it down to Sheol with those who go down to the pit. And all the *trees of Eden*, the choice and best of Lebanon, all that drink water, were comforted in the world below. They also went down to Sheol with it, to those who are slain by the sword; yes, those who were its arm, who lived under its shadow among the nations.
>
> Whom are you thus like in glory and in greatness among the *trees of Eden*? You shall be brought down with the *trees of Eden* to the world below. You shall lie among the uncircumcised, with those who are slain by the sword.
>
> This is Pharaoh and all his multitude, declares the Lord GOD."

Several great world powers are compared to mighty trees in the prophetic books: Nebuchadnezzar and his empire in Daniel 4, Assyria and Egypt in Ezekiel 30–31, and even the late Davidic kings in Ezekiel 17. Depending on how we read Ezekiel 31:3, this chapter either speaks of Egypt itself as a mighty tree, or it speaks of Assyria as such a tree, which is set as an example for Egypt. In the latter case, we read as the esv and many others do, following the Masoretic text; in the former case, we read as the gnt and others do, with a slight emendation of the text: "You [i.e., Egypt] are like a cedar in Lebanon." The nlt has an intermediate solution: "You [i.e., Egypt] are like mighty Assyria." For our purpose, the matter is not immediately relevant.

The tree was so powerful and impressive that the trees in Eden, the "garden of God," could not rival it: "[N]o tree in the garden of God was its equal in beauty." The text says that the trees of Eden even *envied* the mighty tree of Egypt, and this is highly remarkable. How can the trees of God's own magnificent garden envy this horrible world power, which is nothing but a demonic imitation of God's own trees? Verse 16 is still more noteworthy: because of Assyria/Egypt's fall, "all the trees of Eden, the choice and best of Lebanon, all the well-watered trees, were comforted in the underworld [or, the nether parts of the earth]." This verse makes it clear that the chapter is not at all speaking about Eden literally, neither the Eden of Genesis 1–2 nor the celestial Eden of Ezekiel 28. As Rashi said, here "Eden" is the entire world. All the world powers are like magnificent "Eden trees," but before Assyria and Egypt many of them had already collapsed. Their prince, kings, and emperors find themselves in the "underworld," *Sheol*. When the mighty "tree" of Assyria/Egypt collapses, too, its king is received in *Sheol*, and all the world leaders who had fallen before him rejoice in his decline.

This is the same picture as in Isaiah 14, where the king, or the angelic prince, of Babylon is received in *Sheol*, and is gloated over by the princes that preceded him:

> Sheol beneath is stirred up to meet you when you come; it rouses the shades to greet you, all who were leaders of the earth; it raises from their thrones all who were kings of the nations. All of them will answer and say to you: "You too have become as weak as we! You have become like us!" Your pomp is brought down to Sheol, the sound of your harps; maggots are laid as a bed beneath you, and worms are your covers (vv. 9–11; cf. Ezek. 32:21).

What I read in this chapter is that, even after the debacle of Genesis 3, Eden remains a kind of ideal. The world leaders *are* no genuine "trees of Eden," but they would like to look like them. They *are* not in the genuine Garden of God, but they would like to pretend. At best they are "Eden-like trees," in a Garden-of-God-like environment, but in reality they are quite the opposite. They belong to the false Edens of this world, and to the gardens of the false gods. Whether they are small, or as large as Assyria, Babylon, or Egypt, they all end up in *Sheol*, the nether-world, the porch of hell.

Where the biblical Eden was lost, it is no wonder that godless people have tried over and over to construct their Edenic imitations, beginning with Cain's offspring in Genesis 4 (see §2.5). Every world power or world empire throughout history has been such a false Eden. The "trees" in the smaller ones of these false "Edens" always envied the greater false "Edens." In this book (chapter 2), we have seen that the "city" is the common biblical picture of such false "Edens," from the city of Enoch to the tower of Babel, and from Babel to the great Babylon. The last one will be the "great Babylon" of Revelation 17 and 18. God's final word, however, is a picture of something that will be city and garden in one: the New Jerusalem, where the river of the water of life flows through the middle of the street of the city, with the tree of life on both sides of the river (Rev. 22:1–2).

The Lord says (vv. 18–20),

I warn everyone who hears the words of the prophecy of this book: if anyone adds to them, God will add to him the plagues described in this book, and if anyone takes away from the words of the book of this prophecy, God will take away his share in the tree of life and in the holy city, which are described in this book. He who testifies to these things says, "Surely I am coming soon." Amen. Come, Lord Jesus!

Appendix 2

Seven Trees, Seven (Anti-)Edenic Events

As we have seen many times in this book, trees play a vital role in Eden, whether in the literal or the figurative sense. This is the case in Genesis 2–3, in the tabernacle and the temple, in Ezekiel 28 and 31, and in Revelation 2:7 and 22:1–2. It may help us to look a little more closely at trees in the Bible. Earlier I discussed what I see as the spiritual meaning of the fig tree, the olive tree, the pomegranate, and the vine (§4.8). Now, we will look at seven biblical trees from a very different angle. I am referring, of course, to the remarkable fact that the Bible seems to attach peculiar value to certain humans, or even angels, sitting under a tree. I am aware of seven or eight such persons; three associated events are negative, and four or five are positive. Let me begin with the negative ones.

King Saul

My first negative example is found in 1 Samuel 22:6–8,

> Saul heard that [the hiding fugitive] David was discovered, and the men who were with him. Saul was *sitting* at Gibeah *under the tamarisk tree* on the height with his spear in his hand, and all his servants were standing about him. And Saul said to his servants who stood about him, "Hear now, people of Benjamin; will the son of Jesse give every one of you fields and vineyards, will he make you all commanders of thousands and commanders of hundreds, that all of you have conspired against me?"

Notice this mention of the tamarisk under which King Saul is sitting. Why is this tree referred to all, unless the tamarisk is in some way characteristic of Saul's position? The tamarisk is mentioned positively in Genesis 21:33, where Abraham plants a tamarisk tree in Beersheba, and there calls on the name of the Lord. The other passage is more relevant to us, and is very negative: after Saul and his sons had died on the battlefield, their bones were eventually buried under the tamarisk tree in Jabesh (1 Sam. 31:13). Perhaps the tamarisk in chapter 22 is portending Saul's ultimate miserable destiny, which was the consequence of his fighting against David, a type of the coming Messiah, the Anointed of the Lord.

Listen to what Saul prophesied to his men concerning David: God's Anointed would indeed give "fields and vines" to Israel, as it was fulfilled under his son Solomon: "Judah and Israel lived in safety, from Dan even to Beersheba, every man under his vine and under his fig tree, all the days of Solomon" (1 Kings 4:25). Saul's authority, as characterized by the tamarisk, was anti-Edenic; his great opponent, the later King David, would lead the nation into a land of fields and vines, of wheat and wine, a foretaste of Eden.

The Man of God from Judah

In 1 Kings 13 we find our second negative example. It is the remarkable story of an old prophet living in Bethel, and a younger man of God coming from Judah. The latter prophesied against the false altar that King Jeroboam had erected in Bethel; moreover, he healed the hand of the king. Thereupon, Jeroboam offered the prophet a meal (always an Edenic picture) in his palace:

> And the king said to the man of God, "Come home with me, and refresh yourself, and I will give you a reward." And the man of God said to the king, "If you give me half your house, I will not go in with you. And I will not eat bread or drink water in this place, for so was it commanded me by the word of the Lord, saying, 'You shall neither eat bread nor drink water nor return by the way that you came.'" So he went another way and did not return by the way that he came to Bethel (vv. 7–10).

The LORD had said, Do not accept any food or drink at that wicked, idolatrous place. In other words, such meals are necessarily of an anti-Edenic nature, and believers should not have anything to do with them.

But now a greater danger threatened the man of God. The old prophet in Bethel heard what had happened, and hastened to meet the younger man:

> And he went after the man of God and found him *sitting under an oak* [or, *a terebinth*]. And he said to him, "Are you the man of God who came from Judah?" And he said, "I am." Then he said to him, "Come home with me and eat bread." And he said, "I may not return with you, or go in with you, neither will I eat bread nor drink water with you in this place, or it was said to me by the word of the LORD, 'You shall neither eat bread nor drink water there, nor return by the way that you came.'" And he said to him, "I also am a prophet as you are, and an angel spoke to me by the word of the LORD, saying, 'Bring him back with you into your house that he may eat bread and drink water.'" But he lied to him. So he went back with him and ate bread in his house and drank water (vv. 14–19).

Here the oak,[1] or terebinth, as many render it, must have been a single, well-known tree near Bethel, an imposing tree with which the readers would have been familiar. The Bible mentions other conspicuous terebinth trees, like the one near Shechem (mentioned on three occasions: Gen. 35:4, 8; Josh. 24:26; Judg. 9:6), the one at Ophrah (Judg. 6:11; see below), and the one at Mount Tabor (1 Sam. 12:3).

Perhaps, the sin of the man of God began with his very sitting under that oak or terebinth tree. He should have left that idolatrous world as soon as he could, but there he sat, under the tree, probably tired, and perhaps hungry, having refused the food of the king. The temptation from the king had been easy to resist because the king was a wicked man. But the temptation from the old prophet was far

---

1 The Hebrew does indeed say, "the oak," not "an oak," suggesting a well-known tree.

more difficult to resist because he was, to some extent, a true prophet of the LORD (see vv. 20–22). Yet, the word of God had been clear: Do not eat or drink anywhere in that wicked place.

It is a very sad story because this same old prophet received a word of the LORD for the man of God, to tell him that he had become disobedient, and to announce God's judgment over him. On his way back, the man of God was indeed killed by a lion.

Eating and drinking with wicked people—and the old prophet had in fact behaved wickedly—is fundamentally an anti-Edenic activity. Eating with the old prophet was a painful example of the apostle Paul's command: "I am writing to you not to associate with anyone who bears the name of brother if he is guilty of sexual immorality or greed, or is an idolater, reviler, drunkard, or swindler [or, in the old man's case, a liar, a deceiver]—*not even to eat with such a one*" (1 Cor. 5:11). In the ultimate Eden there will a wonderful banquet—but in hell, the liars are *being* eaten by the worms (Rev. 21:8; Mark 9:48; cf. Isa. 66:24). Even if this is figurative language, it is a noteworthy illustration of the tremendous difference between eternal bliss and eternal perdition.

The Prophet Elijah

Third, we read in 1 Kings 19:4–8, that Elijah

> went a day's journey into the wilderness and came and *sat down under a broom tree*. And he asked that he might die, saying, "It is enough; now, O LORD, take away my life, for I am no better than my fathers." And he lay down and *slept under a broom tree*. And behold, an angel touched him and said to him, "Arise and eat." And he looked, and behold, there was at his head a cake baked on hot stones and a jar of water. And he ate and drank and lay down again. And the angel of the LORD came again a second time and touched him and said, "Arise and eat, for the journey is too great for you." And he arose and ate and drank, and went in the strength of that food forty days and forty nights to Horeb, the mount of God.

Other translations speak of the juniper tree. The word occurs only here, and in Job 30:4 and Psalm 120:4. It is a shrub that grows in the wadis in the desert. In Job 30:4 it, or its root, is food for the poor. In Psalm 120:4, the roots of the broom tree are said to be used for charcoal.

In particular, the broom tree is a place of shelter in the desert—a poor imitation of a truly Edenic oasis. The tree hints at Elijah's miserable condition: he had withstood the Baal priests and the entire nation (see chapter 18), and now he was fleeing from a woman. Notice his miserable prayer: "Take away my life"—and he was the only man in the Old Testament who in the end ascended to heaven without seeing death![2] He would later appear with Moses on the Mount of Transfiguration, which was a foretaste of the ultimate Eden. That mountain must have been a place of trees, otherwise Peter could never have suggested to make three "booths" (Matt. 17:4 RSV), which were to be made of tree branches (see, e.g., Neh. 8:14–15). What Peter actually suggested was a kind of Feast of Booths, as if the Messianic kingdom had already arrived, and would last forever on this very mountain. Elijah in such a booth—that would have been truly Edenic. Elijah in the desert under a broom tree, at the lowest point of his career—that was truly un-, or anti-, Edenic, even though the angel prepared a meal for him under the tree that served as a sign of God's lasting love and care for him.

The Guests of Abraham

Let us now come to the four positive examples of trees, of which Abraham and his angelic guests are the first:

> And the LORD appeared to him by the *oaks* [or, *terebinths*] of Mamre, as he sat at the door of his tent in the heat of the day. He lifted up his eyes and looked, and behold, three men were standing in front of him. When he saw them, he ran from the tent door to meet them and bowed himself to the earth and said, "O Lord,[3] if I have found favor in your sight, do not pass by your servant. Let a

---

2 Of Enoch, we read only that God "took" him (Gen. 5:24).
3 Lit., "My lord," uncapitalized, because Abraham could not yet have known who his guests were; today he would simply have said, "Sir," as many modern translations render it. Notice the singular: Abraham knew immediately who was the main figure among his three guests.

little water be brought, and wash your feet, and *rest yourselves under the tree*, while I bring a morsel of bread, that you may refresh yourselves, and after that you may pass on—since you have come to your servant." So they said, "Do as you have said." And Abraham went quickly into the tent to Sarah and said, "Quick! Three seahs [i.e., about seventy-six cups, or eighteen liters] of fine flour! Knead it, and make cakes." And Abraham ran to the herd and took a calf, tender and good, and gave it to a young man, who prepared it quickly. Then he took curds and milk and the calf that he had prepared, and set it before them. And he stood by them *under the tree* while they ate (Gen. 18:1–8).

This is a truly Edenic event—interestingly enough occurring there under that terebinth! Abraham was having a meal with three angelic figures (cf. 19:1, 15), one of whom is identified later in the chapter as the Lord (YHWH; vv. 10–33). Under a mighty terebinth, they were having cakes, meat, curds, and milk. There, the Lord gave him a renewal of his promise that Abraham would have a son, in whose offspring the Messianic promises would be fulfilled. Abraham is the prototype of those who will share in the future Eden: "I have chosen [lit., known] him, that he may command his children and his household after him to keep the way of the Lord by doing righteousness and justice, so that the Lord may bring to Abraham what he has promised him." Moreover, Abraham becomes the intercessor for all the righteous able to be found in the wicked world of Sodom and Gomorrah (vv. 22–32).

The Angel at Ophrah
Judges 6:11–14 tells us:

Now the angel of the Lord came and *sat under the terebinth* at Ophrah, which belonged to Joash the Abiezrite, while his son Gideon was beating out wheat in the winepress to hide it from the Midianites. And the angel of the Lord appeared to him and said to him, "The Lord is with you, O mighty man of valor." And Gideon said to him, "Please, my lord, if the Lord is with us, why then has all this happened to us? And where are all his wonderful deeds that our fathers recounted to us, saying, 'Did not the LORD bring us up from Egypt?' But now the LORD has forsaken us and given us into the hand of Midian." And the LORD turned to him and said, "Go in this might of yours and save Israel from the hand of Midian; do not I send you?"

Again, this terebinth at Ophrah must have been well-known (see above). This time, it is an angel sitting under the tree, who addresses the fearful Gideon in order to encourage him to defeat the Midianites. Notice how the angel of the LORD (v. 1) and the LORD (vv. 14, 16) coalesce here, as for instance also in Exodus 3:1–4. God himself comes to Gideon in the form of an angelic figure, as he had done before to Abraham (see previous example).

At the deepest level, the promises to Gideon are again of a Messianic, and thus of an Edenic character, as is clear from Isaiah 9:2–7. The prophet speaks here of the coming Messiah, the great King, who will rule in peace and righteousness over all the earth on the throne of David (vv. 6–7). In view of this kingdom, all his enemies will be "broken as on the day of Midian" (v. 4). Expositors agree that this is (very probably) a reference to Gideon's victory over Midian, as this is by far the largest and most impressive victory over Midian in the entire Old Testament.

In this way, Isaiah places Gideon's victory in a clearly Messianic perspective. The angel under the terebinth, or the LORD himself, had given a clear prediction: "I will be with you, and you shall strike the Midianites as one man" (Judg. 6:16). And Isaiah adds as it were: As he did then, in the same way the LORD will one day break all the hostile powers, and establish the Messianic kingdom of which Gideon had simply been the portent: "Then the men of Israel said to Gideon, 'Rule over us, you and your son and your grandson also, for you have saved us from the hand of Midian.' Gideon said to them, 'I will not rule over you, and my son will not rule over you; the LORD will rule over you'" (Judg. 8:22–23). I take this to mean that Gideon deliberately remained in the shadow of Messiah himself, who one day will rule over Israel and over all the earth.

The Prophetess Deborah

The judge and prophetess Deborah is the third of my positive examples: "Deborah, a prophetess, the wife of Lappidoth, was judging Israel at that time. She used to *sit under the palm* of Deborah between Ramah and Bethel in the hill country of Ephraim, and the people of Israel came up to her for judgment" (Judg. 4:4–5).

The palm tree under which Deborah was sitting was not just any palm tree: it was the "palm of Deborah," apparently a place well-known to the people, where they could find her in order to bring to her their questions and controversies. She was one of the five good prophetesses in the Bible: in addition to her, there were Miriam (Exod. 15:20), Huldah (2 Kings 22:14), the wife of Isaiah (Isa. 8:3),[4] and Anna (Luke 2:36).[5] The remarkable thing about them is that God sometimes calls female leaders to perform to function that normally belongs to the men—especially in times when masculine leadership is largely failing, as in the time of Deborah (Barak actually did nothing but follow Deborah's lead).

As we have seen in this book, the palm is the special tree of the Feast of Booths, and as such it is suggestive of the Messianic kingdom, and thus of God's ultimate Eden (§§1.4, 3.6, 3.9, 4.5, and 8.5). Deborah's palm tree is an Edenic sign in the miserable, largely anti-Edenic time of the judges, where everyone "did what was right in his own eyes" (Judg. 17:6; 21:25). Prophetesses such as Deborah point forward to a time of eschatological prophets as well as prophetesses: "And it shall come to pass afterward, that I will pour out my Spirit on all flesh; your sons and your daughters shall prophesy, your old men shall dream dreams, and your young men shall see visions" (Joel 2:28).

The Disciple Nathanael

My seventh final last example of the negative and positive persons sitting under trees is Nathanael, who was to be one of Jesus' disciples:

---

4   Perhaps, she was called a "prophetess" only because she was the wife of the prophet Isaiah.

5   In addition, two false prophetesses are mentioned: Noadiah (Neh. 6:14) and Jezebel, or a Jezebel-type of woman in the church of Thyatira (Rev. 2:20).

Jesus saw Nathanael coming toward him and said of him, "Behold, an Israelite indeed, in whom there is no deceit!" Nathanael said to him, "How do you know me?" Jesus answered him, "Before Philip called you, *when you were under the fig tree*, I saw you." Nathanael answered him, "Rabbi, you are the Son of God! You are the King of Israel!" Jesus answered him, "Because I said to you, 'I saw you *under the fig tree*,' do you believe? You will see greater things than these." And he said to him, "Truly, truly, I say to you [plural!], you will see heaven opened, and the angels of God ascending and descending on the Son of Man" (John 1:47–51).

Sitting under one's fig tree is a biblical picture of being at rest in one's own home: it was *the* fig tree of Nathanael, that is, his own tree, the one at his own house. It is the picture of 1 Kings 4:24, Micah 4:4, and Zechariah 3:10; these passages show that, here again, we are dealing with a Messianic, and thus also an Edenic, picture. Here was a righteous man, as Jesus testified about him, a man evidently looking forward to the Messiah, praying to God in the seclusion of his own yard. God *heard* him praying, and Jesus *saw* him sitting. Then Philip came and told his friend about the Messiah who had indeed come into the world. At first, Nathanael was understandably suspicious, but then Jesus told him that he *saw* him praying at his house. It is as if God himself had answered Nathanael's prayer by confronting him immediately with the Messiah.

Nathanael could only exclaim: You *must* be the One I was looking forward to: the Son of God of Psalm 2, anointed as King over Zion! Jesus confirmed this, but added that he was, so to speak, not only the Son of *God* of Psalm 2 but also the Son of *Man* of Psalm 8, to whom *all* creation is subject. And he presented to him the wonderful picture of Genesis 28:12, where Jacob saw "a ladder set up on the earth, and the top of it reached to heaven. And behold, the angels of God were ascending and descending on it!" This is a shadowy portrait of the Messianic kingdom, a picture that Jesus completed by adding what Jacob could not yet have seen: ". . . you will see heaven opened, and the angels of God ascending and descending *on the Son of Man*" (John 1:51).

The Beloved Under the Apple Tree

As a bonus, let me refer to an eighth example, namely, in the Song of Solomon: "Under the apple tree I awakened you. There your mother was in labor with you; there she who bore you was in labor" (Song 8:5). Who is speaking to whom here? The Masoretic text suggests that the beloved young lady is speaking to her lover. But the Old Syriac version reverses the meaning, and this has been accepted by several expositors because it makes the interpretation much more plausible: the loving young man is speaking to his beloved, referring to the tree under which he aroused her love (cf. 2:7). He apparently speaks of the apple tree near the house of the beloved girl, where her mother had given birth to her (cf. 1:6; 3:4; 6:9; 8:1–2).

It goes even deeper than that when we recall that the loving young lady had called her beloved *himself* an apple tree: "My lover, among other men, you are an apple tree among the wild trees in the forest!" (2:3). She had been "feeding" on him, so to speak, because he says of her that "the scent of your breath is like apples" (7:8). As Dwight L. Moody wrote in the margin of his bible: How different would the scent of her breath have been if she had fed on the onions and the garlic of Egypt (Num. 11:5)!

If the young lover is like an apple tree, the beloved young lady is like a paradise, as we have seen (§§1.3, 3.9, 4.5, 4.7, 5.7, 6.5, and 6.6): "You are paradise" (4:13 GW). We could hardly find an Old Testament book that is more Edenic than the Song of Solomon.

Appendix 3
Seven Edenic Feminine Names

Interestingly, several women in the Bible have Edenic names, so to speak; I mean, names that refer to certain trees or flowers, and thus remind us of Paradise.

Five Hebrew names
1. **Tamar.** There are three women in the Bible called Tamar. The first was Judah's daughter-in-law, who bore her father-in-law the twins Perez and Zerah (Gen. 38). The second was David's daughter Tamar, a full sister of Absalom (2 Sam. 13:1), and thus a daughter of David's wife Maacah (3:3). The third was Absalom's own daughter (14:27).

The Hebrew word *tamar* means "date palm" (*Phoenix dactylifera*); as such it is quite a common word in the Old Testament (Exod. 15:27; Lev. 23:40; Num. 33:9; Neh. 8:15; Ps. 92:12; Song 7:7–8; Joel 1:12). Especially Song 7 gives us an idea how feminine beauty can be associated with a palm tree: "Your stature is like a palm tree, and your breasts are like its clusters. I say I will climb the palm tree and lay hold of its fruit."

2. **Zemirah.** In 1 Chronicles 7:8, Zemirah is apparently a boy's name—of a person who is further unknown to us—but in practice the name was given almost exclusively to girls.

The name is derived from the Hebrew root *z-m-r*, which can mean either "to sing" or "to prune"; compare Song 2:12, where spring is "the time of singing [by the birds]" *or* "the time of pruning [the vines]" (for the latter, see NABRE, NASB, TPT, and ESV note). The name Zemirah could thus mean "song, (joyous) melody," but also "the pruned (and thus fruit-bearing) vine" (cf. "pruning" in Lev. 25:3–4).

3. **Hadassah.** Esther, the wife of the Persian King Ahasuerus (Xerxes), is well-known, especially because a Bible book was named after her. Less known is that, in addition to this Persian name, she also had a Hebrew name: Hadassah (Est. 2:7).

The name Hadassah comes from the Hebrew word *hadas*, "myrtle" (*Myrtus communis*), a tree mentioned several times in the Old Testament (Neh. 8:15), especially in an eschatological context (Isa. 41:19; 55:13; Zech. 1:8, 10, 11).

4. **Keziah.** One of the daughters of Job, born to him after his time of misery, was named Keziah, or more precisely, Q'tzi͑ah, who, along with his other newborn children, was to replace the children that had perished (Job 1:19).

The Hebrew word *q'tzi͑ah* is related to an Arabic word, which, in a somewhat corrupted form, became the English word "cassia." This is the plant *Laurus cassia*, also called *Cinnamomum cassia*. As the name suggests, some species of this genus produce cinnamon. This is why we read in Psalm 45:8 about the Messiah: "[Y]our robes are all fragrant with myrrh and aloes and cassia" (in Exod. 30:24 and Ezek. 27:19, we find different Hebrew words for "cassia").

5. **Susanna.** In the apocryphal additions to the book of Daniel, we find the well-known story of Susanna: "Now there was a man that dwelt in Babylon, and his name was Joakim: and he took a wife whose name was Susanna, the daughter of Helcias, a very beautiful woman, and one that feared God" (Dan. 13:2 DRA). We find the name Susanna also in the Gospel of Luke, chapter 8:3. About the latter Susanna nothing is told us in the Bible, except that she was a rather early, and apparently well-to-do follower of Jesus.

The name Susanna comes from the Hebrew word *shoshan*, which means "lily" (*Lilium* species, or perhaps also some related flowers; see, e.g., 2 Chron. 4:5; Hos. 14:5). Again, the association with feminine beauty comes out very clearly in the Song of Solomon. Thus, the lover says of his girl: "As a lily [*shoshannah*] among brambles, so is my love among the young women" (2:2; also cf. v. 16; 4:5; 5:13; 6:2, 3; 7:2).

Two Greek names

6. **Rhoda.** In the narrative about Peter's liberation from prison, we read that he went to the house where the believers were gathered, and the door was opened by a servant girl named Rhoda, who announced his arrival to the others (Acts 12:13–15).

The name Rhoda comes from Greek *rhodon*, "rose"; compare its Latin counterpart *Rosa*, which is also the name of the genus *Rosa*, of the *Rosaceae* family.

7. **Chloe.** Let me add one more Greek name here, mentioned by the apostle Paul, who referred to "Chloe's people," apparently a family or household in Corinth (1 Cor. 1:11), about whom we know nothing further.

The name Chloe comes from Greek *chloē*, which means "young green shoot"—a real springtime name, symbolizing youth, freshness, novelty (cf. the adjective *chlōros*, "greenish-yellow," from which the English word "chlorine" was derived; rendered "pale" [or "pale greenish"] in Rev. 6:8; "green plant" in 9:4).

All seven of these taken together—the palm, the myrtle and the cassia, the vine, the lily and the rose, and all the young green shoots—what a sweet bouquet of tastes, fragrances, and spices, especially in springtime! Here are seven ladies, forming a little Eden all by themselves! As we have seen several times, no Bible book combines Edenic colors, tastes, fragrances, and spices more extensively and beautifully with feminine traits than does the Song of Solomon.

Appendix 4
Edenic Music

These are thirty very different pieces of music, from thirty composers, from thirteen different countries. Some pieces are very long, others are very short. They evoke Edenic delights, especially in the form of "Pastorales," or countryside descriptions, or paintings of heavenly life, or a love song, or, of course, descriptions of gardens. Naturally, many other pieces could be mentioned. But in my view, those listed below are some of the finest.

1. [*Italian*] Claudio Monteverdi (1610): Vespro della Beata Virgine (Vespers for the Blessed Virgin), "Pulchra es" (Song of Solomon 6:4)

2. [*Italian*] Arcangelo Corelli (1690?): Christmas Concerto, Part 6: "Pastorale"

3. [*Italian*] Antonio Vivaldi (1716-17): Le quattro stagioni (The Four Seasons), Part 1: "La primavera" (The Spring)

4. [*German*] Johann Sebastian Bach (1734): Weihnachtsoratorium (Christmas Oratorio), Part II, opening (Pastorale)

5. [*German-English*] George Frideric Handel (1741): Messiah, Pifa movement (Pastorale)

6. [*Austrian*] Wolfgang A. Mozart (1775): opera Il re pastore (The Shepherd King), especially the pastoral parts

7. [*Austrian*] Joseph Haydn (1796-98): Die Schöpfung (The Creation), Part 3 (The Garden of Eden)

8. [*German*] Ludwig van Beethoven (1808): Symphony No. 6, "Pastorale"

9. [*Austrian*] Franz Schubert (1823): Rosamunde, especially the pastoral parts

10. [*French*] Hector Berlioz (1830): Symphonie fantastique, Part 3: "Scene on the Fields"

11. [*Hungarian*] Franz Liszt (1863–1866): Christus Oratorio, Part I.2: Pastorale

12. [*German*] Johannes Brahms (1865-68): Ein deutsches Requiem (A German Requiem), Part 4: "How lovely are thy dwellings"

13. [*Austrian*] Anton Bruckner (1874, 1888): Symphony No. 4, "Romantic"

14. [*Czech*] Bedřich Smetana (1875-80): Má Vlast (My homeland), especially "The Moldau" and "From Bohemia's woods and fields"

15. [*German*] Richard Wagner (1877-79): opera Parsifal, from Part 3: "Karfreitagszauber" (the effect of Good Friday on nature)

16. [*Czech*] Antonín Dvořák (1885-86): Svatá Ludmila (Saint Ludmila), especially the landscape descriptions

17. [*French*] Claude Debussy (1894): Prélude à l'après-midi d'un

faune (Prelude to the Afternoon of a Faun)

18. [*Finnish*] Jean Sibelius (1894): Vårsång (Spring Song)

19. [*Russian*] Pyotr I. Tchaikovsky (1892): Nutcracker Suite: "Waltz of the Flowers"

20. [*Dutch*] Alphons Diepenbrock (1897): Caelestis Urbs Jerusalem (The Heavenly City of Jerusalem)

21. [*Austrian*] Gustav Mahler (1899-1900): Symphony No. 4, Part 4: "The Heavenly Life"

22. [*Russian*] Alexander Glazunov (1902): Symphony No. 7, "Pastorale"

23. [*Russian-American*] Igor Stravinsky (1906): Pastorale (various editions)

24. [*French*] Maurice Ravel (1910, orchestral 1911): Ma mère l'Oye (Mother Goose), Part. 6: "Le jardin féerique" (The Fairy Garden)

25. [*German*] Richard Strauss (1915): Eine Alpensymphonie (An Alpine Symphony)

26. [*Spanish*] Manuel de Falla (1915): Noches en los Jardines de España (Nights in the Gardens of Spain) (orchestral version)

27. [*English*] Ralph Vaughan Williams (1922): Symphony No. 3: "A Pastoral Symphony"

28. [*American*] Aaron Copland (1944): Appalachian Spring

29. [*American*] Leonard Bernstein (1956, rev. 1989): Candide, "Make Our Garden Grow" (version for choir and orchestra)

30. [*Argentinian*] Ariel Ramírez (1964): Navidad Nuestra: "Los pastores" (The Shepherds)

Bibliography

Alcorn, R. 2004. *Heaven.* Carol Stream, IL: Tyndale Momentum.
Babylonian Talmud, The. 1948–1952. London: Soncino Press.
Berg, W. 1988. "Israels Land, der Garten Gottes: Der Garten als Bild des Heiles im Alten Testament." *Biblische Zeitung* 32.35–51.
Berkouwer, G. C. 1972. *The Return of Christ.* Studies in Dogmatics. Grand Rapids, MI: Eerdmans.
Block, D. I. 1998. *The Book of Ezekiel Chapters 25–48.* Grand Rapids, MI: Eerdmans
Brower, K. E. and M. W. Elliott, eds. 1997. *Eschatology in Bible and Theology: Evangelical Essays at the Dawn of a New Millennium.* Downers Grove, IL: InterVarsity Press.
Burgess, S. M. 1989. *The Holy Spirit: Eastern Christian Traditions.* Peabody, MA: Hendrickson.
____. 1997. *The Holy Spirit: Medieval Roman Catholic and Reformation Traditions.* Peabody, MA: Hendrickson.
Congar, Y. 1997. *I Believe in the Holy Spirit.* 3 vols. New York: Crossroad Herder.
Daube, D. 1956. *The New Testament and Rabbinic Judaism.* Peabody, MA: Hendrickson.
De Graaff, F. 1982. *Het geheim van de wereldgeschiedenis.* Kampen: Kok.
Edersheim, A. 1971 (repr.). *The Life and Times of Jesus the Messiah.* Grand Rapids, MI: Eerdmans.
Fitzpatrick, E. 2016. *Home: How Heaven and the New Earth Satisfy Our Deepest Longings.* Ada, MI: Bethany House Publishers.
Geldenhuys, N. 1983 (repr.). *Commentary on the Gospel of Luke.* New International Commentary on the New Testament. Grand

Rapids, MI: Eerdmans.
Godet, F. 1879. *Commentary on the Gospel of Luke.* Edinburgh: T. and T. Clark.
Green, J.B. 1997. *The Gospel of Luke.* New International Commentary on the New Testament. Grand Rapids, MI: Eerdmans.
Greijdanus, S. 1941. *Het evangelie naar Lucas.* Vol. 2. Kampen: J. H. Kok.
Hamilton, V.P. 1990. *The Book of Genesis Chapters 1-17.* Grand Rapids, MI: Eerdmans.
Heuvel, H. W. 1927. *Oud-Achterhoeksch Boerenleven het gehele jaar rond.* Deventer: Kluwer.
Heuvel, H. W. 2020. *Oud-Achterhoeksch Boerenleven het gehele jaar rond.* Annotated edition. Soesterberg: Aspekt.
Heyns, J. A. 1988. *Dogmatiek.* Pretoria: NG Kerkboekhandel.
Leupold, H. C. 1942. *Exposition of Genesis.* London: Evangelical Press.
Lewis, C. S. 2015 (repr.). *Mere Christianity.* London: HarperOne.
Liefeld, W. L. 1984. *Luke.* Grand Rapids, MI: Zondervan.
Longenecker, R. N. 1981. *The Acts of the Apostles.* Grand Rapids, MI: Zondervan.
Luce, H. K. 1933. *The Gospel According to St. Luke.* Cambridge: Cambridge University Press.
Morales, L. M. 2012. *The Tabernacle Pre-Figured: Cosmic Mountain Ideology in Genesis and Exodus.* Leuven: Peeters Publishers.
Morris, L. 1971. *The Gospel According to John.* New International Commentary on the New Testament. Grand Rapids, MI: Eerdmans.
Oosterhoff, B. J. 1972. *Hoe lezen wij Genesis 2 en 3? Een hermeneutische studie.* Kampen: Kok.
Ouweneel, W. J. 1973. *Het Hooglied van Salomo.* Winschoten: Uit het Woord der Waarheid.
_____. 1998. *De zevende koningin: Het eeuwig vrouwelijke en de raad van God.* Metahistorische Trilogie. Vol. 2. Heerenveen: Barnabas.
_____. 2001. *Hoogtijden voor Hem: De bijbelse feesten en hun betekenis voor Joden en christenen.* Vaassen: Medema.
_____. 2008. *De schepping van God: Ontwerp van een scheppings-, mens- en zondeleer.* Vaassen: Medema.

———. 2017. *The World Is Christ's: A Critique of Two Kingdoms Theology*. Toronto: Ezra Press.

———. 2018. *Adam, Where Are You? And Why This Matters: A Theological Evaluation of the New Evolutionist Hermeneutics*. Toronto: Ezra Press.

———. 2019. *The Ninth King: The Last of the Celestial Empires: The Triumph of Christ over the Powers*. St. Catharines, ON: Paideia Press.

Pannenberg, W. 1994. *Systematic Theology*. Vol. 2. Translated by G. W. Bromiley. Grand Rapids, MI: Eerdmans.

Thiselton, A. C. 2000. *The First Epistle to the Corinthians: A Commentary on the Greek Text*. Grand Rapids, MI: Eerdmans.

Trudgill, E. 1976. *Madonnas and Magdalens: The Origins and Development of Victorian Sexual Attitudes*. London: Heinemann.

Vander Zee, L. J. 2004. *Christ, Baptism and the Lord's Supper: Recovering the Sacraments for Evangelical Worship*. Downers Grove, IL: InterVarsity Press.

Visscher, H. 1928. *Het Paradijsprobleem*. 3rd edition. Zwolle: La Rivière and Voorhoeve.

Warner, M. 1990. *De enige onder de vrouwen: De maagd Maria: Mythe en cultus*. Amsterdam: Contact.

Zahn, T. 1913. *Das Evangelium des Lucas*. Leipzig: Deichert.

Scripture Index

Genesis 1	52, 69	Genesis 2:10	111
Genesis 1:1	5, 12, 16, 52	Genesis 2:11-14	7, 30
		Genesis 2:13	126
Genesis 1:2	32, 35, 54	Genesis 2:15	1, 12, 31, 56
Genesis 1:3	32		
Genesis 1:6-7	35	Genesis 2:16	12, 17, 35, 69, 74
Genesis 1:14	54		
Genesis 1:21	52	Genesis 2:1	10, 12, 35, 69, 92
Genesis 1:22	37		
Genesis 1:26	11	Genesis 2:22-23	93
Genesis 1:27	52	Genesis 3	27, 30, 46, 70, 88, 118, 140
Genesis 1:28	11, 12, 31, 35, 37, 55, 69		
		Genesis 3:1-6	iii, 15, 93
Genesis 1:31	31, 55, 73	Genesis 3:6	38, 74
Genesis 2	13, 30, 31, 46, 52, 140	Genesis 3:7	38, 79
		Genesis 3:8	3, 48, 57, 71
Genesis 2:1-3	73	Genesis 3:9	91
Genesis 2:2	73	Genesis 3:9-10	71
Genesis 2:7	31, 37, 106, 129	Genesis 3:10	153
		Genesis 3:10-11	38
Genesis 2:8	46, 71	Genesis 3:12-16	93
Genesis 2:8-10	1, 5, 7, 9, 13, 31	Genesis 3:13	91
		Genesis 3:15	33, 92
Genesis 2:9	74, 96	Genesis 3:9-19	12, 15

Genesis 3:20	92	Genesis 10:9	34
Genesis 3:21	37, 39, 57, 153	Genesis 10:10-12	34
		Genesis 10:21-31	40
Genesis 3:22-24	96	Genesis 11:1-9	40, 109
Genesis 3:23	12, 31, 37	Genesis 11:4	40
Genesis 3:24	15, 27, 46, 88	Genesis 11:5	41
		Genesis 11:10-27	40
Genesis 4:11	37	Genesis 12:1	35
Genesis 4:16	30	Genesis 12:3	40
Genesis 4:17	32, 40	Genesis 12:10	81
Genesis 4:23-24	34	Genesis 13:10	5, 11, 36, 63, 65, 69
Genesis 5:18-24	33		
Genesis 5:24	129	Genesis 13:10-13	42
Genesis 6:7-9	35	Genesis 14:18	112
Genesis 6:14	35	Genesis 14:18-20	34
Genesis 6:18	35	Genesis 17:1	35
Genesis 7:11	35	Genesis 18:6-7	112
Genesis 7:17	36	Genesis 18:17	131
Genesis 7:24	36	Genesis 18:21	41
Genesis 8:7	35	Genesis 23	64
Genesis 8:13-14	35	Genesis 26:28-31	112
Genesis 8:17	35, 69	Genesis 27	81
Genesis 8:20-22	39	Genesis 28	81
Genesis 8:21	67	Genesis 28:9	81
Genesis 9	69, 70	Genesis 28:12	129
Genesis 9:1	37, 40	Genesis 31	82
Genesis 9:1-17	35, 69	Genesis 31:44-54	112
Genesis 9:3	37	Genesis 32:3	81
Genesis 9:7	37	Genesis 36:8-9	81
Genesis 9:13	39	Genesis 40:22	5
Genesis 9:20	36, 37	Genesis 43:11	76
Genesis 9:22	39	Exodus 1:13-14	146
Genesis 9:23	39	Exodus 2:25	41
Genesis 9:25	37	Exodus 3:5	12, 36, 48
Genesis 9:26	37	Exodus 3:6	153
Genesis 9:26-27	40	Exodus 3:8	41, 76

Scripture Index

Exodus 3:17	76	Exodus 25:22	49, 55
Exodus 6:6-7	113	Exodus 25:31	58
Exodus 7:9-12	42	Exodus 25:31-36	45, 56
Exodus 9:22-23	129	Exodus 25:33-34	11
Exodus 10:21-22	129	Exodus 25:40	51
Exodus 12:12	110	Exodus 26:14	95
Exodus 13:5	76	Exodus 27:13	47
Exodus 14:16	35, 68	Exodus 27:20	54
Exodus 14:21	35, 68	Exodus 28:33-34	62
Exodus 14:29	35, 68	Exodus 28:41	80
Exodus 15	110	Exodus 29:21	80
Exodus 15:3-10	110	Exodus 29:42-46	49
Exodus 15:8	35, 68	Exodus 30:11	53
Exodus 15:13	48, 67	Exodus 30:17	53
Exodus 15:17	48, 67, 71	Exodus 30:22	53
Exodus 15:19	35, 68	Exodus 30:34	53
Exodus 15:20	28	Exodus 31:1	53
Exodus 15:22-27	6	Exodus 31:2-5	54
Exodus 15:27	61	Exodus 31:12	53
Exodus 19	35, 69, 107	Exodus 31:13-17	53
		Exodus 31:18	108
Exodus 19:5	36, 48, 55	Exodus 32	55
Exodus 19:16	107	Exodus 32:6	36, 70
Exodus 19:18	107	Exodus 33:3	76
Exodus 20	35, 52, 69, 104, 107, 110	Exodus 33:20	153
		Exodus 34	82
		Exodus 34:6	70
Exodus 20:2	72	Exodus 34:28	52
Exodus 20:11	53	Exodus 35:8	54
Exodus 24:10-11	112	Exodus 35:14	54
Exodus 24:11	153	Exodus 35:28	54
Exodus 25:1	53	Exodus 39:24-26	62
Exodus 25:2-9	51	Exodus 39:37	54
Exodus 25:6	54	Exodus 39:42-43	55
Exodus 25:8	60	Exodus 40:34	104
Exodus 25:18-22	27	Exodus 40:34-38	54, 151

Leviticus 3	20	Deuteronomy 4:13	52
Leviticus 3:11	20	Deuteronomy 4:19	129
Leviticus 3:16	20	Deuteronomy 5	52
Leviticus 7	20	Deuteronomy 5:25	72
Leviticus 7:30-34	20	Deuteronomy 7:6-7	35, 55, 67
Leviticus 8:13	57		
Leviticus 10:1-3	70	Deuteronomy 7:13	38
Leviticus 16	50, 58	Deuteronomy 8:5-6	108
Leviticus 20:24	76	Deuteronomy 8:7	66
Leviticus 21:17-23	58	Deuteronomy 8:7-10	36, 69, 75
Leviticus 23:2	54		
Leviticus 23:6	54	Deuteronomy 9:1	40
Leviticus 23:10-14	106	Deuteronomy 9:10	108
Leviticus 23:34	54	Deuteronomy 10:1-5	50
Leviticus 23:39	54	Deuteronomy 10:4	52
Leviticus 23:40	61, 76	Deuteronomy 10:14	139
Leviticus 25:23	48	Deuteronomy 11:11-15	75
Leviticus 26:11-12	12, 48, 57, 60, 104	Deuteronomy 11:12	66
		Deuteronomy 11:17	66
Numbers 2	47	Deuteronomy 11:10-12	65
Numbers 3:7-8	57	Deuteronomy 11:14	38
Numbers 7:89	49, 55, 95	Deuteronomy 11:24	47
Numbers 11:25	109	Deuteronomy 11:29	64
Numbers 12:5-8	153	Deuteronomy 12:6-7	112
Numbers 13:23-24	71	Deuteronomy 12:17	38, 112
Numbers 13:28	40		
Numbers 15:30	41	Deuteronomy 12:18	112
Numbers 18:12	38	Deuteronomy 14:2	55
Numbers 21:5	77	Deuteronomy 14:23	38
Numbers 28:3	54	Deuteronomy 14:23-28	112
Numbers 32	117	Deuteronomy 18:4	38
Numbers 33:4	110	Deuteronomy 18:16	72
Deuteronomy 1:2	69	Deuteronomy 26:18	55
Deuteronomy 1:28	40	Deuteronomy 27:7	112
Deuteronomy 1:44	77	Deuteronomy 28:51	38

Scripture Index

Reference	Page
Deuteronomy 32:8-9	67
Deuteronomy 32:40	129
Deuteronomy 32:47	69
Deuteronomy 32:13-15	77
Deuteronomy 33:16	12
Deuteronomy 33:27	14
Deuteronomy 34:2	47
Deuteronomy 34:3	61
Deuteronomy 34:10	153
Joshua 1:3	117
Joshua 3	116
Joshua 4	117
Joshua 8:33	64
Joshua 18:1	60
Joshua 18:8-10	60
Joshua 19:51	60
Joshua 24:15	82
Judges 1	117
Judges 6:22	153
Judges 7:16	96
Judges 7:19-20	96
Judges 9:13	38, 78
Judges 13:22	153
Judges 14:8-9	77
Judges 14:14	77
Judges 18:31	60
Ruth 1:1-2	81
1 Samuel 1:3	60
1 Samuel 1:24	60
1 Samuel 4:3	60, 93
1 Samuel 4:4	49, 55, 93
1 Samuel 10:1	80
1 Samuel 10:5	28
1 Samuel 14:27	78
1 Samuel 14:29	78
1 Samuel 15	70
1 Samuel 15:16-28	29
1 Samuel 16:1-5	112
1 Samuel 16:13	80
1 Samuel 18:6	28
2 Samuel 6:2	49
2 Samuel 6:5	28
2 Samuel 6:17	94
2 Samuel 7:2	94
2 Samuel 7:6	50
2 Samuel 7:14	60
1 Kings 4:20-25	147
1 Kings 6	60
1 Kings 6:18	56
1 Kings 6:29	11, 56
1 Kings 6:32	11
1 Kings 6:35	11
1 Kings 7:18	60
1 Kings 7:20	60
1 Kings 7:36	11, 60
1 Kings 7:42	60
1 Kings 8	104
1 Kings 8:9	50
1 Kings 8:10-11	104
1 Kings 8:27	49, 139
1 Kings 10:7	159
1 Kings 19:16	80
2 Kings 2:1-11	129
2 Kings 15:29	117
2 Kings 19:15	49, 55
2 Kings 21:18	24
2 Kings 21:26	24
1 Kings 22:19	26
2 Kings 25:4	24

Reference	Page
1 Chronicles 9:26	138
1 Chronicles 9:33	138
1 Chronicles 13:6	49
1 Chronicles 13:8	28
1 Chronicles 16:39	93
1 Chronicles 17:9	138
1 Chronicles 21:29	93
1 Chronicles 23:28	138
1 Chronicles 25:1	109
1 Chronicles 25:1-6	29
1 Chronicles 28:2	111
1 Chronicles 28:11-12	138
1 Chronicles 29:22	112
2 Chronicles 2:6	139, 140
2 Chronicles 3:1	93
2 Chronicles 3:5	61
2 Chronicles 3:15-16	61
2 Chronicles 4:11-13	61
2 Chronicles 5:11-14	30
2 Chronicles 5:13-14	104
2 Chronicles 6:18	139
2 Chronicles 20:7	131
2 Chronicles 28:15	61
Ezra 6	145
Nehemiah 2:8	6
Nehemiah 3:15	24
Nehemiah 8:15	61
Nehemiah 9:6	139
Nehemiah 9:36	81
Esther 1:5	24
Esther 7:7-8	24
Psalm 2:4	140
Psalm 2:4-6	iii
Psalm 5:7	94
Psalm 11:4	140
Psalm 19:9	108
Psalm 23:6	94
Psalm 24:6	153
Psalm 26:8	94
Psalm 27:4	94
Psalm 27:8	153
Psalm 31:5	136
Psalm 31:19	15
Psalm 32:4	148
Psalm 33:12	67
Psalm 36:9	98
Psalm 37:11	152
Psalm 40:7	14
Psalm 41:9	112
Psalm 46:4	34
Psalm 48:2	25
Psalm 63:2	153
Psalm 65:9-13	66
Psalm 68:33	139
Psalm 72:7	152
Psalm 73:24	129
Psalm 74:12	14
Psalm 74:13	42
Psalm 74:13-14	68
Psalm 76:2	93
Psalm 77:5	14
Psalm 77:11	14
Psalm 77:16	35
Psalm 77:19-20	68
Psalm 78:39-41	107
Psalm 78:54	48
Psalm 78:60	60, 93
Psalm 78:67-69	60, 93
Psalm 80:1	95
Psalm 80:1-2	47, 49, 55
Psalm 80:8-9	71

Psalm 82:1	25, 26	Proverbs 4:2	69
Psalm 84:3	145	Proverbs 5:18-19	18
Psalm 87:3	34	Proverbs 6:20	69
Psalm 87:4	68	Proverbs 6:23	69
Psalm 89:10	68	Proverbs 7:2	69
Psalm 89:12	25	Proverbs 8:22	13
Psalm 90:2-3	13	Proverbs 11:30	96
Psalm 91:1	136	Proverbs 13:12	96
Psalm 92:12-15	74	Proverbs 14:27	98
Psalm 93:2	13	Proverbs 15:14	96
Psalm 95:7-8	73	Proverbs 25:16	77
Psalm 95:11	73	Proverbs 25:27	77
Psalm 99:1	49, 55	Proverbs 27:7	77
Psalm 103:19	140	Proverbs 31:4	38
Psalm 104:2	49	Song of Solomon 1:12	112
Psalm 104:6-9	35	Song of Solomon 2:4	112
Psalm 104:15	38, 78	Song of Solomon 2:10-13	143, 144
Psalm 105:4	153		
Psalm 115:16	140	Song of Solomon 2:16	148
Psalm 116:13	113	Song of Solomon 4:11	78
Psalm 118	114	Song of Solomon 4:12	90, 112
Psalm 118:12	77	Song of Solomon 4:12-13	62, 72, 78
Psalm 118:22-26	114		
Psalm 119:93	108		
Psalm 121:5	47	Song of Solomon 4:12-15	6, 96, 111
Psalm 122	64		
Psalm 133	115		
Psalm 133:3	115	Song of Solomon 4:16	112
Psalm 132:13	93	Song of Solomon 5:1	78, 112
Psalm 135:21	93	Song of Solomon 8:2	138
Psalm 143:5	14	Ecclesiastes 2:5	6
Psalm 148:4	139	Ecclesiastes 2:24-25	18
Psalm 150	28	Ecclesiastes 3:12-13	18
Proverbs 1:8	69	Ecclesiastes 5:18-20	18
Proverbs 3:1	69	Ecclesiastes 8:15	18
Proverbs 3:18	96	Ecclesiastes 9:9	18

Ecclesiastes 10:11	14	Isaiah 51:3	11, 63, 70, 144
Ecclesiastes 12:5	129		
Ecclesiastes 12:7	129	Isaiah 51:9-11	69
Isaiah 5:1-2	71	Isaiah 51:11	78, 152
Isaiah 5:2	35	Isaiah 52:11	60
Isaiah 5:1-7	38	Isaiah 53	126
Isaiah 5:7	71	Isaiah 53:2	95
Isaiah 5:11-12	38	Isaiah 53:3	126
Isaiah 6:5	153	Isaiah 53:8	130
Isaiah 8:18	93	Isaiah 55:1	iv
Isaiah 14	26	Isaiah 55:12-13	iv, 11, 145
Isaiah 14:9	129	Isaiah 61:1	80
Isaiah 14:12-15	26, 42	Isaiah 61:1-3	80
Isaiah 14:13	25	Isaiah 61:7	78
Isaiah 16:9	147	Isaiah 61:10-11	100
Isaiah 25:6	7, 17, 112, 114	Isaiah 63:10	108
		Isaiah 63:20-21	107
		Isaiah 65:25	5
Isaiah 25:6-8	132	Isaiah 66:1	140
Isaiah 25:8	152	Jeremiah 2:2	146
Isaiah 30:7	68	Jeremiah 2:13	98
Isaiah 30:33	13	Jeremiah 3:16	95
Isaiah 32:15	11	Jeremiah 8:7	145
Isaiah 32:15-16	80	Jeremiah 8:20	146
Isaiah 33:20	94	Jeremiah 17:12	13
Isaiah 35:10	78, 152	Jeremiah 17:13	98
		Jeremiah 23:29	107
Isaiah 37:16	49	Jeremiah 24	78
Isaiah 40:22	12	Jeremiah 24:5-7	79
Isaiah 40:23	49	Jeremiah 31:9	60
Isaiah 41:8	131	Jeremiah 31:12	99, 101
Isaiah 41:19	11, 76	Jeremiah 31:33	108
Isaiah 41:19-20	144	Jeremiah 32:22	76
Isaiah 44:3	80	Jeremiah 32:38	60
Isaiah 45:21	14	Jeremiah 39:4	24
Isaiah 46:10	14, 15	Jeremiah 48:32	147

Jeremiah 49:19	65	Ezekiel 43	104
Jeremiah 50:44	65	Ezekiel 43:1-5	104
Jeremiah 51:9	42	Ezekiel 43:1-7	81
Jeremiah 51:53	40	Ezekiel 43:1-23	101
Jeremiah 52:7	24	Ezekiel 43:3-5	106
Ezekiel 1	108	Ezekiel 44:4	106
Ezekiel 1:4	109	Ezekiel 48:35	67, 101
Ezekiel 10	27	Daniel 4:26	124
Ezekiel 10:3-4	104	Daniel 4:30	42
Ezekiel 13:9	109	Daniel 8:16	15
Ezekiel 13:19	109	Daniel 9:20-21	15
Ezekiel 27:27	26	Daniel 10:13	15, 16, 26
Ezekiel 28	9, 24, 26, 27, 140	Daniel 10:20	26
		Daniel 10:21	15, 26, 67
Ezekiel 28:12-19	24-25, 26	Daniel 12:1	15
Ezekiel 28:13-14	5, 8, 23, 25, 27	Daniel 12:1-3	114
		Daniel 12:3	152
Ezekiel 29:3	65	Hosea 4:13	75
Ezekiel 31	9	Hosea 6:7	72
Ezekiel 31:8-9	10, 76	Hosea 10:1	71
Ezekiel 31:15-18	10, 76	Hosea 14:4-7	71
Ezekiel 32:21	129	Joel 2:1-3	i
Ezekiel 36	9	Joel 2:20	47
Ezekiel 36:33-35	145	Amos 3:13	60
Ezekiel 37:27	60	Amos 4:13	60
Ezekiel 40:16	61	Amos 6:5	28
Ezekiel 40:22	61	Amos 9:11	94
Ezekiel 40:26	61	Obadiah 1:7	112
Ezekiel 40:31	61	Micah 4:4	147
Ezekiel 40:34	61	Micah 5:2	14
Ezekiel 40:37	61	Micah 5:11	109
Ezekiel 41:6-11	138	Habakkuk 1:12	14
Ezekiel 41:18-20	61	Hagai 2	145
Ezekiel 41:25-26	61	Zechariah 2:12	48
Ezekiel 42:1-14	138	Zechariah 3:10	147
Ezekiel 42:20	11	Zechariah 10:2	109

Zechariah 14:8	47	Matt. 26:36-46	84
Malachi 3:16	105	Matt. 27:33	84
Matt. 1:1-2	127	Matt. 27:52	130
Matt. 5:4	158	Matt. 27:59-60	83
Matt. 5:6	158	Matt. 28:1	89
Matt. 5:8	153	Matt. 28:5-6	88
Matt. 5:10	158	Matt. 28:18-20	127
Matt. 5:34	140	Mark 1:14-15	127
Matt. 6:11	21	Mark 6:13	98
Matt. 8:11	17, 112	Mark 10:17	115
Matt. 11:28	158	Mark 13:1	95
Matt. 12:28	108	Mark 13:28	148
Matt. 13:43	152	Mark 14:32	84
Matt. 14:19	20	Mark 15:22	84
Matt. 17:2	96	Mark 16:1	89
Matt. 18:8	132	Mark 16:6	88, 143
Matt. 18:20	104, 105	Mark 18:1	84
Matt. 19:29	80, 115	Mark 18:26	84
Matt. 20:29	115	Luke 1:19	15, 16
Matt. 22:29-30	17	Luke 1:26	15, 16
Matt. 24:27	46, 47	Luke 3:21-22	95
Matt. 24:32	144	Luke 4:1	95
Matt. 24:44	126	Luke 4:14	95
Matt. 24:50	126	Luke 7:32	30
Matt. 25:21	152	Luke 8:3	108
Matt. 25:23	152	Luke 10:18	27
Matt. 25:34	80, 115, 135	Luke 10:25	115
		Luke 11:20	108
Matt. 25:41	27, 132	Luke 12:19	154
Matt. 25:46	154	Luke 12:36	126
Matt. 26:26	iii, 19	Luke 12:37	16, 17, 154
Matt. 26:28	113		
Matt. 26:29	17, 113, 114, 154	Luke 12:37-38	154
		Luke 12:40	122, 126
Matt. 26:36	84	Luke 12:46	126

Reference	Pages
Luke 13:29	17
Luke 13:34	82
Luke 14:7-24	154
Luke 14:15	21
Luke 15:17	91
Luke 15:20	91
Luke 15:22-27	154
Luke 15:23	112
Luke 15:25	30
Luke 15:29	112
Luke 16	132
Luke 16:9	131, 150
Luke 16:19-23	154
Luke 16:19-31	128, 130
Luke 16:25	152
Luke 17:27-30	37
Luke 18:18	115
Luke 18:9-14	133
Luke 21:5	95
Luke 22:17	19, 113
Luke 22:19	19, 113
Luke 22:20	113
Luke 23	9
Luke 23:42-43	121
Luke 23:43	8, 128, 134, 151
Luke 23:45	58
Luke 23:46	136
Luke 24:30	20
Luke 24:43	112
Luke 24:53	108
John 1:1	16
John 1:4	99
John 1:14	94
John 1:18	16, 111, 131, 154
John 1:29	81
John 1:33	95
John 2:4	89
John 2:16	138, 155
John 2:19-21	95
John 3:5	98
John 3:15-16	99
John 3:36	99
John 4	64
John 4:22	40
John 4:23	149
John 4:36	116, 154
John 5:24	99
John 5:26	99
John 6:39-40	123
John 6:40	99
John 6:44	123
John 6:47	99
John 6:54	123
John 7:37-39	111
John 10:10	117
John 10:22	146, 147
John 11:24	123
John 12:13	61
John 12:25	154
John 12:48	123
John 13:23	16, 111, 131
John 13:28-29	131
John 14:1	138
John 14:1-3	117, 136, 155
John 14:2	138
John 14:2-3	127, 137, 148, 150

John 14:23	152	Acts 2:1	106
John 14:26	104, 108	Acts 2:2	104, 108
John 15:3	98, 107	Acts 2:2-3	109
John 15:11	78	Acts 2:2-4	107
John 15:26	104	Acts 2:3	107
John 16:8	108	Acts 2:4	109
John 16:13	108	Acts 2:6	107
John 16:21	131	Acts 2:17	109
John 16:22-23	131	Acts 2:42	113
John 17:3	137, 154	Acts 2:46	108, 112, 113
John 17:5	16		
John 17:24	14, 16, 153	Acts 2:47	112
		Acts 3:20-21	127
John 19:25	89, 108	Acts 4:31	106
John 19:26	89	Acts 5	70
John 19:41	10, 83	Acts 5:30	10, 92
John 19:41-42	85	Acts 7:38-51	108
John 19:42	143	Acts 7:49	140
John 20:11-13	87	Acts 9:9	113
John 20:13	91, 93	Acts 9:19	113
John 20:15	10, 83, 85, 89, 91, 93	Acts 9:20	127
		Acts 9:22	127
John 20:16	93	Acts 10:38	80, 94
John 20:17-18	91	Acts 10:39	10, 92
John 20:20	106	Acts 10:41	112
John 20:22	106	Acts 11:3	113
John 20:25	106	Acts 11:16-17	109
John 20:28	106	Acts 13:29	10, 92
Acts 1:3	127	Acts 15:10	69
Acts 1:4	112	Acts 15:16	94
Acts 1:5	109	Acts 16:7	105
Acts 1:13	108	Acts 16:34	113
Acts 1:15	108	Acts 20:7	113
Acts 2	104, 107, 108, 110	Acts 20:11	113
		Acts 20:25	127

Scripture Index

Reference	Page
Acts 24:15	128
Acts 26:13	95
Acts 26:14	72
Acts 27:21	113
Acts 27:33-38	113
Acts 28:23	127
Acts 28:31	127
Rom. 2:7	115
Rom. 3:20	108
Rom. 5:1	111
Rom. 5:2	59
Rom. 5:20	108
Rom. 5:21	115
Rom. 6:3-4	89
Rom. 6:20-23	80
Rom. 6:22	62, 116, 154
Rom. 6:22-23	115
Rom. 7:7-11	108
Rom. 8:4	108
Rom. 8:9	105
Rom. 8:14	108
Rom. 8:19-25	126
Rom. 8:22-25	ii
Rom. 8:23	128
Rom. 9:23	118
Rom. 10:12	118
Rom. 11:33	118
Rom. 14:10	133
Rom. 14:17	78
Rom. 15:4	115
1 Corinthians 1:7	126
1 Corinthians 2:9	152
1 Corinthians 3:1-2	118
1 Corinthians 3:16	103
1 Corinthians 5:7	113
1 Corinthians 5:11	38
1 Corinthians 6:9	115
1 Corinthians 6:10	38
1 Corinthians 6:19	94
1 Corinthians 10:1-11	110
1 Corinthians 10:5	117
1 Corinthians 10:11	115
1 Corinthians 10:16	20, 113
1 Corinthians 10:16-22	112
1 Corinthians 11:26	17, 113, 114
1 Corinthians 11:30	130
1 Corinthians 12:12	153
1 Corinthians 13:12	159
1 Corinthians 14:25	106
1 Corinthians 15:6	131
1 Corinthians 15:18	131
1 Corinthians 15:20	131
1 Corinthians 15:28	50
1 Corinthians 15:34	38
1 Corinthians 15:36-44	157
1 Corinthians 15:45	10
1 Corinthians 15:51	123, 131
1 Corinthians 15:51-54	138
1 Corinthians 24	96
2 Corinthians 1:20	99
2 Corinthians 1:21-22	80
2 Corinthians 3:3	108
2 Corinthians 3:6	108
2 Corinthians 3:7	69
2 Corinthians 3:17	108
2 Corinthians 3:18	153

2 Corinthians 4:6	32, 153	Ephesians 1:23	50
2 Corinthians 4:7	96	Ephesians 2:6	139
2 Corinthians 4:17	152	Ephesians 2:7	118
2 Corinthians 5:1	128	Ephesians 2:18	59
2 Corinthians 5:1-2	137	Ephesians 2:20-22	104
2 Corinthians 5:1-4	94	Ephesians 3:6	116
2 Corinthians 5:4	137	Ephesians 3:8	118
2 Corinthians 5:8	151	Ephesians 3:10	139
2 Corinthians 5:10	133	Ephesians 3:12	59
2 Corinthians 6:16	104	Ephesians 3:16	118
2 Corinthians 6:16-18	60	Ephesians 4:30	108
2 Corinthians 10:3-6	110	Ephesians 5:5	115
2 Corinthians 12	139	Ephesians 5:18	38, 104
2 Corinthians 12:2-4	8, 139	Ephesians 5:26	98, 107
Galatians 3:13	10	Ephesians 6:12	110, 116, 139
Galatians 3:19	108		
Galatians 4:6	105		
Galatians 4:21-31	115	Philippians 1:11	79
Galatians 4:26	51	Philippians 1:19	105
Galatians 5:6	133	Philippians 1:23	127, 135, 143, 151
Galatians 5:13	108		
Galatians 5:21	38, 115		
Galatians 5:22	78		
Galatians 5:22-23	80	Philippians 1:27-30	110
Galatians 6:2	108	Philippians 3:20	126
Galatians 6:7-8	110	Philippians 3:20-21	127, 138
Galatians 6:8	115, 116, 154	Philippians 4:7	111
Ephesians 1:3	115, 139	Colossians 1:12-13	116
		Colossians 1:27	118
		Colossians 2:2	118
Ephesians 1:3-5	14	Colossians 2:3	96
Ephesians 1:17-18	108	Colossians 2:10	50
Ephesians 1:18	118	Colossians 3:4	99
Ephesians 1:20	139	Colossians 3:15	111

Reference	Page
1 Thessalonians 1:10	126
1 Thessalonians 4:17	142
1 Thessalonians 4:13-15	131
1 Thessalonians 4:13-17	138
1 Thessalonians 4:16-17	127
1 Thessalonians 4:17	151
1 Thessalonians 5:7	38
1 Timothy 1:16	115
1 Timothy 3:3	38
1 Timothy 3:6	27
1 Timothy 3:15	104, 111
1 Timothy 4	20
1 Timothy 4:1-5	19
1 Timothy 6:12	110, 115
1 Timothy 6:19	96, 97
2 Timothy 1:1	116
2 Timothy 2:20	104
2 Timothy 4:18	124
Titus 1:2	99, 115, 116, 137
Titus 2:13	126
Titus 3:5-7	117
Titus 3:7	115
Hebrews 2:5	59, 73, 125
Hebrews 2:14-15	43
Hebrews 3	118
Hebrews 3:7	110
Hebrews 4	118
Hebrews 4:3-10	73
Hebrews 4:9-10	152
Hebrews 4:11	110
Hebrews 5:12	118
Hebrews 6:5	59, 73
Hebrews 7	34
Hebrews 8:1	140
Hebrews 8:5-6	51
Hebrews 8:10	108
Hebrews 9:5	49
Hebrews 9:11-14	59
Hebrews 9:23-24	148
Hebrews 9:28	126
Hebrews 10:7	14
Hebrews 10:13	126
Hebrews 10:19-22	58, 59, 148
Hebrews 11:5	129
Hebrews 11:10	122
Hebrews 11:10-16	41
Hebrews 11:16	122
Hebrews 12:11	79
Hebrews 12:14	153
Hebrews 12:16	81
Hebrews 12:22	26, 51, 123
Hebrews 13:14	74, 122
Hebrews 13:15	149
James 1:25	108
James 1:27	134
James 2:12	108
James 2:13-17	134
James 2:23	131
James 2:24	134
James 3:17-18	79
James 5:14-15	98
James 5:17-18	66

Reference	Pages
1 Peter 1:4	116
1 Peter 1:19-20	14
1 Peter 2:5	148, 149
1 Peter 2:9	103
1 Peter 2:24	10
1 Peter 3:3-4	105
1 Peter 4:3	38
1 Peter 4:17	104, 111
2 Peter 1	127
2 Peter 1:13-14	94
2 Peter 3	127
2 Peter 3:5-13	39
2 Peter 3:12-14	126, 128
1 John 1:1	95, 99
1 John 1:1-2	99, 154
1 John 1:1-4	116, 137
1 John 1:5	53
1 John 2:20	80
1 John 2:25	99, 116
1 John 2:27	80
1 John 3:2	153
1 John 3:6	153
1 John 3:8	42
1 John 5:11-13	99
1 John 5:20	97, 154
3 John 1:11	153
Jude 1:7	132
Jude 1:9	15
Jude 1:21	154
Revelation 1:6	58
Revelation 1:7	30
Revelation 1:15	33
Revelation 1:16	95
Revelation 2	133
Revelation 2:4	150
Revelation 2:6-10	133
Revelation 2:7	iii, 5, 8, 11, 17, 32, 39, 99, 133, 135, 141, 150, 154
Revelation 2:17	154
Revelation 2:18	33
Revelation 2:26-27	150
Revelation 3:12	123, 138, 150
Revelation 3:20	112
Revelation 3:21	150
Revelation 4:2	140
Revelation 4:3	39
Revelation 4:10-11	155
Revelation 5:8	30
Revelation 5:8-14	155
Revelation 5:9-10	58
Revelation 5:10	149
Revelation 7:9	151
Revelation 7:9-10	62
Revelation 7:11-12	156
Revelation 7:15	156
Revelation 7:15	138, 150
Revelation 7:15-17	4
Revelation 7:17	132, 152, 154
Revelation 10:1	39
Revelation 11:16	156
Revelation 11:19	138
Revelation 12:7	15, 27
Revelation 12:9	27, 42, 43
Revelation 13:6	51
Revelation 13:8	14

Scripture Index

Revelation 14:2	30	Revelation 21:9-10	18
Revelation 14:13	152	Revelation 21:9-11	153
Revelation 14:15	138	Revelation 21:10	123
Revelation 14:17	138	Revelation 21:21	137
Revelation 15:2	30, 150	Revelation 21:23	32, 53
Revelation 15:3	110	Revelation 22	127
Revelation 15:5	51	Revelation 22:1	97
Revelation 15:5-6	138	Revelation 22:1-2	98, 135, 141
Revelation 15:8	138		
Revelation 16:1	138	Revelation 22:2	99, 150
Revelation 16:17	138	Revelation 22:1-3	iii, 5, 7, 9, 11, 17, 34, 39
Revelation 17	42		
Revelation 17:2	38		
Revelation 17:6	38	Revelation 22:3	148, 155
Revelation 18	42	Revelation 22:1-5	149
Revelation 18:2	82	Revelation 22:4	153
Revelation 19	127	Revelation 22:4-5	5, 58
Revelation 19:1-7	156	Revelation 22:14	17, 150
Revelation 19:6-9	123	Revelation 22:17	97
Revelation 19:9	112, 154	Revelation 22:19	17, 123
Revelation 19:21	82		
Revelation 20	127		
Revelation 20:2	42		
Revelation 20:3	150, 151		
Revelation 20:10	43		
Revelation 20:11-15	132		
Revelation 20:12-13	133		
Revelation 20:14	81		
Revelation 21	127, 137		
Revelation 21:2	51, 123, 153		
Revelation 21:3	4, 67, 94		
Revelation 21:4	132, 151		
Revelation 21:6	97		
Revelation 21:8	82		

Subject Index

A
Aaron 49, 57, 68, 70, 115, 126
Abraham 41, 43, 63, 65, 67, 112, 130, 131, 166, 169, 170, 171
Adam ii, iii, 2, 3, 10, 11, 12, 17, 30, 31, 35, 36, 37, 38, 39, 56, 57, 58, 67, 70, 71, 72, 73, 81, 86, 87, 88, 89, 90, 91, 92, 93, 97, 98, 99, 106, 110, 111, 112, 153
Affliction 41, 42, 114, 134
Angelic 8, 15, 24, 26, 27, 42, 67, 68, 163, 169, 170, 171
Angels i, 15, 25, 26, 27, 43, 87, 88, 130, 155, 156, 165, 173
Animal 20, 21, 39, 43, 102
Assurance 59
Authority 166

B
Babel 34, 35, 40, 41, 42, 164
Babylon 26, 27, 40, 42, 81, 82, 145, 163, 164, 176
Baptism 88, 89, 96, 98, 109, 112
Beautiful iii, 4, 6, 10, 11, 23, 95, 100, 102, 111, 112, 142, 143, 144, 157, 158, 161, 176
Beauty 2, 9, 10, 24, 25, 66, 72, 94, 95, 101, 104, 105, 161, 162, 175, 176
Believers 14, 59, 73, 74, 78, 84, 88, 99, 104, 108, 110, 113, 115, 116, 117, 122, 123, 124,

Blessing 126, 130, 133, 135, 136, 137, 138, 149, 150, 152, 159, 167, 177

Body 18, 19, 20, 37, 39, 40, 55, 66, 77, 78, 80, 113, 115, 116, 117, 118, 119, 136, 137, 143, 149, 150, 151, 155, 156, 158

Body 7, 8, 10, 31, 77, 83, 86, 87, 94, 95, 96, 97, 116, 128, 129, 130, 133, 134, 137, 139, 140, 157

Book of Life 133

Booths, Feast of 54, 61, 151, 154, 169, 172

Bride 6, 18, 51, 62, 72, 77, 78, 90, 100, 111, 112, 137, 146, 147, 153, 157

Bridegroom 100

C

C.S. Lewis 82, 158

Cathedral 4, 46, 102

Celestial i, 5, 8, 14, 24, 26, 27, 30, 52, 54, 112, 123, 124, 140

Children 13, 23, 41, 43, 82, 140, 152, 156, 170, 176

Christ 5, 8, 10, 14, 17, 32, 42, 46, 50, 51, 58, 59, 79, 80, 86, 88, 89, 92, 94, 96, 99, 102, 104, 105, 106, 108, 115, 116, 118, 121, 122, 124, 126, 127, 133, 135, 136, 139, 148, 149, 150, 153, 154

Church ii, 1, 4, 5, 27, 45, 46, 47, 59, 70, 78, 84, 85, 86, 90, 92, 101, 102, 103, 104, 105, 107, 109, 110, 111, 113, 115, 117, 119, 121, 133, 150, 155, 172

City of God 32, 34, 41, 74

Cleansing 148

Clothing 57, 105

Consequences i, ii, 31, 42, 66, 71, 142, 166

Creation ii, 5, 14, 16, 24, 34, 35, 36, 39, 52, 53, 54, 55, 59, 68, 71, 73, 74, 106, 127, 152,

Subject Index

Creatures	173 35, 37, 68, 153, 155, 156	Destruction Dimension Divine	39, 106, 111, 145 113, 117 4, 16, 19, 25, 32,
Cross	8, 10, 40, 85, 86, 89, 92, 134		90, 95, 96, 99, 105, 106, 116,
Curse	iii, 5, 10, 37, 116, 149, 154	Dominion	121, 148 147
Culture	3, 33, 34	Dragon	42, 43, 65, 66, 68,
Curtain	5, 12, 59		82, 91
		Drama	iii
		Dwelling	4

D

Dancing	28, 30
Daniel	26, 114, 176
Dante	121, 122, 124
Darkness	i, 31, 32, 35, 103, 110, 116, 153
David	28, 29, 48, 50, 60, 93, 94, 98, 113, 126, 146, 147, 165, 166, 171
Dead	59, 88, 127, 129, 133, 134, 135, 152
Death	i, 9, 17, 24, 42, 43, 58, 69, 79, 81, 86, 88, 89, 92, 99, 107, 113, 115, 116, 117, 122, 123, 124, 125, 127, 128, 129, 130, 132, 133, 134, 150, 169
Desire	4, 38, 41, 51, 72, 82, 94, 95, 96, 127, 143

E

Eden	i, ii, iii, 1, 2, 3, 4, 5, 6, 7, 8, 9, 10, 11, 12, 13, 14, 15, 16, 17, 18, 19, 20, 21, 23, 24, 26, 27, 28, 30, 31, 32, 33, 36, 37, 38, 39, 40, 41, 42, 43, 46, 47, 48, 50, 51, 52, 54, 55, 56, 57, 58, 59, 60, 61, 63, 65, 66, 67, 68, 69, 70, 71, 72, 74, 76, 78, 80, 81, 82, 88, 89, 90, 91, 92, 93, 94, 96, 99, 101, 102, 103, 104, 110, 111, 112, 113, 114, 115, 117, 118, 119, 124, 125, 127, 132, 135, 136, 138, 140,

			142, 143, 144, 145, 146, 147, 148, 149, 150, 151, 152, 153, 154, 155, 157, 158, 159, 162, 163, 165, 166, 168, 169, 170, 171, 172, 174, 175, 177	Everlasting	iv, 11, 20, 52, 68, 78, 82, 97, 114, 115, 144, 149, 152
		Eyes	1, 4, 5, 7, 11, 25, 38, 63, 64, 65, 66, 75, 78, 79, 95, 108, 131, 134, 153, 157, 169, 172
Elijah	66, 125, 126, 129, 168, 169		
		F	
Enoch	15, 32, 33, 129, 164, 169	Faith	6, 17, 19, 39, 40, 41, 59, 69, 70, 72, 80, 81, 93, 117, 124, 133, 134, 146, 150, 152
Eschatological	30, 39, 61, 104, 113, 114, 115, 123, 126, 127, 143, 172, 176		
		Fall	i, ii, 2, 10, 11, 12, 15, 27, 30, 31, 38, 39, 42, 64, 70, 90, 92, 93, 94, 97, 98, 106, 153, 162, 163
Essence	142		
Eternal	5, 9, 13, 14, 16, 43, 52, 59, 74, 79, 80, 81, 82, 97, 99, 110, 114, 115, 116, 117, 128, 129, 130, 131, 132, 133, 135, 137, 149, 151, 152, 154, 168		
		Family	20, 21, 23, 64, 102, 113, 177
		Father	14, 16, 17, 29, 30, 38, 39, 40, 48, 58, 60, 69, 82, 87, 88, 91, 92, 95, 112, 130, 134, 135, 137, 142, 149, 152, 154, 175
Eternity	14, 52, 127, 130, 151, 152, 153		
Eve	iii, 10, 30, 38, 39, 56, 58, 71, 72, 86, 87, 89, 90, 91, 92, 93, 97, 99, 112, 153		
		Fear	15, 43, 85, 98, 156, 157
		Feast	7, 17, 25, 54, 61,

Subject Index

	106, 114, 132, 151, 154, 169, 172	Future	158, 159 4, 14, 29, 73, 80, 96, 115, 124, 170
Fellowship	4, 16, 20, 37, 59, 97, 98, 112, 116, 131, 137, 138, 154	**G** Gabriel Garden	15, 16 i, ii, 1, 2, 3, 4, 5,
Female	172		6, 7, 8, 9, 10, 11,
Figurative	i, 6, 8, 16, 17, 27, 31, 33, 43, 65, 89, 92, 99, 148, 157, 165, 168		12, 13, 14, 15, 17, 18, 19, 21, 23, 24, 27, 30, 31, 32, 33, 34, 36,
Fire	i, 8, 13, 24, 25, 37, 39, 43, 70, 72, 82, 88, 104, 107, 109, 122, 128, 132, 145		38, 39, 41, 43, 46, 47, 48, 51, 52, 55, 56, 57, 58, 62, 63, 65, 69, 70, 71, 72, 74, 76, 78,
Food	1, 5, 7, 9, 17, 18, 19, 20, 21, 37, 38, 54, 57, 68, 74, 75, 76, 77, 114, 118, 132, 134, 158, 167, 168, 169		80, 81, 82, 83, 84, 85, 86, 87, 88, 89, 90, 91, 92, 93, 95, 96, 97, 99, 100, 101, 110, 111, 112, 124,
Forever	3, 5, 29, 53, 58, 60, 81, 114, 131, 132, 136, 142, 143, 148, 149, 150, 151, 153, 154, 155, 156, 169	Gates Gethsemane Glory	140, 144, 145, 149, 150, 153, 161, 162, 163, 164 50, 64, 125, 131 83, 84, 86 10, 13, 14, 16, 29,
Foundation	14, 15, 16, 17, 27, 45, 73, 96, 104, 135		32, 42, 49, 52, 79, 81, 88, 95, 96, 106, 112, 124,
Freedom	108		130, 133, 134,
Friendship	138		136, 151, 152,
Fulfillment	34, 49, 109, 152,		153, 155, 156,

Term	Pages
God	162, i, ii, iii, 1, 2, 3, 4, 5, 6, 8, 9, 10, 11, 12, 13, 14, 15, 16, 17, 18, 19, 20, 21, 23, 24, 25, 26, 27, 29, 30, 31, 32, 33, 34, 35, 36, 37, 38, 39, 40, 41, 42, 43, 46, 47, 48, 49, 50, 51, 52, 53, 54, 55, 56, 57, 58, 59, 60, 61, 65, 66, 67, 68, 69, 70, 71, 72, 73, 74, 75, 76, 77, 78, 79, 80, 81, 82, 88, 89, 91, 92, 93, 94, 95, 96, 97, 98, 99, 100, 103, 104, 105, 106, 107, 108, 110, 111, 112, 113, 114, 116, 117, 118, 122, 124, 125, 126, 127, 128, 129, 131, 132, 133, 134, 136, 137, 139, 140, 141, 145, 146, 148, 149, 150, 151, 152, 153, 154, 155, 156, 157, 158, 161, 163, 164, 166, 167, 168, 169, 171, 172, 173, 176
Gold	8, 24, 27, 45, 50, 54, 55, 56, 61, 62, 70, 85, 86, 102, 105, 123, 126, 137
Good	iii, 1, 2, 5, 7, 9, 15, 18, 19, 26, 29, 31, 34, 35, 36, 38, 41, 55, 59, 66, 69, 71, 73, 74, 75, 76, 77, 78, 79, 80, 82, 90, 93, 96, 99, 103, 115, 118, 123, 133, 134, 152, 159, 170, 172
Guardian	8, 23, 24, 25, 26, 27

H

Term	Pages
Heaven	iii, 5, 8, 9, 11, 12, 20, 26, 35, 37, 39, 40, 41, 49, 51, 52, 53, 59, 60, 65, 66, 67, 72, 73, 75, 81, 94, 101, 102, 104, 109, 112, 115, 116, 118, 119, 121, 122, 123, 124, 126, 127, 128, 129, 132, 134, 135, 136, 137, 139, 140, 143, 145, 148,

Subject Index

	149, 150, 151, 154, 155, 156, 157, 161, 169, 173		136, 137, 138, 148, 149, 151, 154, 155, 166, 167, 173, 174, 177
Hell	13, 82, 102, 122, 124, 129, 131, 132, 163, 168	Human	i, ii, 2, 3, 5, 6, 9, 12, 13, 15, 16, 26, 27, 31, 32, 34, 35, 36, 37, 38, 39, 40, 42, 53, 55, 56, 58, 65, 66, 70, 71, 72, 73, 79, 84, 88, 95, 96, 98, 99, 102, 111, 122, 133, 153, 158, 165
Holy	i, iii, 3, 4, 5, 8, 12, 18, 19, 20, 23, 24, 25, 27, 29, 30, 47, 48, 49, 50, 51, 53, 54, 55, 57, 58, 59, 64, 67, 73, 78, 79, 80, 81, 84, 85, 86, 90, 94, 95, 101, 102, 103, 104, 105, 106, 107, 108, 109, 115, 116, 123, 126, 127, 134, 136, 144, 148, 149, 151, 164		
		I	
		Image	98, 102, 116, 154, 157
		Imagination	76
		Imperishable	105, 116
Home	23, 41, 48, 64, 104, 124, 128, 129, 130, 137, 146, 151, 152, 158, 166, 167, 173	Incarnation	117
		Influence	122
		Inheritance	67, 115, 116, 122
		Intermediate	9, 123, 130, 131, 132, 134, 135, 136, 137, 162
Honey	21, 36, 41, 69, 75, 76, 77, 78, 112	Interpretation	7, 139, 153, 174
House	12, 24, 29, 30, 50, 56, 59, 61, 64, 71, 72, 74, 94, 104, 108, 109, 111, 112, 117, 121, 127, 128,	Israel	ii, 12, 15, 20, 26, 28, 29, 30, 34, 35, 36, 37, 38, 40, 41, 42, 47, 48, 49, 50, 51, 53, 54, 55, 57, 59, 61, 64, 65,

66, 67, 68, 69, 70,
71, 72, 76, 77,
78, 81, 93, 98, 99,
106, 107, 109,
110, 111, 112,
116, 117, 118,
126, 138, 144,
145, 146, 147,
148, 150, 151,
166, 171, 172,
173

J

Jerusalem 3, 4, 7, 18, 26, 32,
34, 46, 48, 51,
52, 61, 64, 67,
83, 84, 85, 94, 98,
101, 103, 106,
114, 123, 137,
144, 149, 150,
155, 164

Jesus ii, iii, 5, 8, 9, 10,
11, 16, 17, 19,
20, 21, 30, 32,
42, 58, 59, 61, 78,
79, 80, 83, 84,
85, 86, 87, 88, 89,
90, 91, 92, 93,
94, 95, 96, 97, 99,
104, 105, 106,
108, 109, 111,
112, 113, 114,
116, 121, 127,
128, 130, 134,
135, 136, 137,
138, 143, 144,
146, 149, 153,
154, 164, 172,
173, 176

Jewish 8, 15, 26, 27, 40,
64, 76, 85, 86, 92,
106, 113, 116,
124, 125, 126,
128, 143, 153,
154

Judgment i, 13, 25, 39, 88,
89, 108, 111, 132,
133, 134, 156,
168, 172

Justice 80, 170

K

Kempis 121, 122, 123,
124

King iii, v, 3, 5, 6, 7, 10,
11, 14, 16, 17, 18,
19, 20, 21, 23, 24,
25, 26, 27, 28, 29,
38, 42, 48, 57, 58,
61, 70, 80, 93, 98,
112, 124, 135,
142, 146, 147,
149, 159, 161,
162, 163, 165,
166, 167, 171,
173

Kingdom 5, 11, 14, 17, 21,
33, 38, 58, 61,
69, 78, 79, 80, 94,
114, 115, 116,
121, 122, 123,
124, 125, 127,

Subject Index

Knowledge 130, 131, 134, 135, 136, 144, 146, 147, 148, 149, 151, 152, 154, 155, 169, 171, 172, 173
1, 9, 26, 32, 41, 54, 74, 128, 149, 153

L

Lamb iii, 4, 5, 14, 18, 32, 34, 43, 51, 58, 61, 62, 82, 110, 113, 123, 137, 141, 149, 151, 153, 154, 155, 156, 157

Lampstand 45, 53, 54, 55, 56

Language 17, 21, 30, 42, 43, 56, 58, 107, 109, 116, 117, 146, 154, 155, 157, 168

Lazarus 128, 130, 131, 132, 133, 134

Life iii, 1, 2, 3, 4, 5, 7, 9, 11, 17, 18, 19, 27, 32, 34, 39, 43, 46, 56, 69, 74, 79, 88, 89, 91, 92, 95, 96, 97, 98, 99, 101, 110, 114, 115, 116, 117, 123, 125, 132, 133, 136, 137, 141, 147, 149, 150, 154, 157, 158, 159, 164, 168, 169, 179

Light i, 4, 5, 32, 47, 53, 54, 79, 89, 96, 103, 105, 116, 125, 127, 138, 149, 153, 162

Literal iii, 3, 6, 7, 8, 10, 12, 16, 40, 47, 49, 52, 62, 69, 70, 71, 86, 92, 94, 96, 97, 98, 104, 105, 106, 107, 109, 130, 132, 139, 148, 163, 165

Literature 125

Love 14, 16, 18, 24, 29, 37, 48, 59, 60, 61, 64, 72, 75, 78, 80, 86, 99, 101, 102, 103, 110, 112, 133, 134, 143, 144, 146, 150, 152, 169, 174, 176, 179

M

Mankind 13, 15, 60, 67, 87

Marriage 18, 19, 37, 123, 154, 156, 157

Memory 11, 85

Messiah iii, 13, 14, 16, 72, 94, 107, 114, 125, 126, 130, 134,

Messianic 144, 147, 166, 171, 173, 176

5, 11, 14, 61, 69, 73, 74, 78, 79, 80, 94, 115, 122, 123, 125, 127, 130, 134, 135, 136, 144, 146, 148, 151, 169, 170, 171, 172, 173

Michael 15, 26, 67

Moses 40, 41, 49, 50, 51, 53, 55, 57, 65, 68, 70, 75, 109, 110, 112, 117, 126, 169

Mountain i, 5, 7, 8, 17, 23, 24, 25, 26, 27, 48, 51, 71, 114, 132, 169

Music 4, 7, 19, 28, 29, 30, 33, 76, 102, 157, 158, 179

N

Nations iii, 5, 10, 26, 35, 40, 67, 71, 84, 100, 106, 132, 141, 149, 161, 162, 163

Nature 36, 75, 76, 135, 145, 167

Natural 32, 97

Negative 77, 90, 107, 148, 155, 165, 166, 172

New Earth iii, 5, 6, 11, 12, 36, 39, 52, 67, 81, 94, 123, 127, 128, 135, 151

Noah ii, 35, 36, 37, 38, 39, 55, 67, 70, 110, 111

O

Oak 75, 167

Oasis 61, 142, 169

Observed 54, 88, 104, 107, 109

Offspring 33, 34, 39, 40, 57, 67, 80, 92, 163, 170

Olive 11, 36, 65, 69, 72, 75, 78, 80, 84, 110, 144, 165

Omen 46

P

Pain ii, 12, 79, 131, 152, 168

Parables 130, 133

Paradise iii, 2, 3, 4, 5, 6, 7, 8, 9, 11, 14, 15, 16, 17, 28, 31, 32, 55, 78, 90, 97, 121, 124, 125, 128, 131, 133, 134, 135, 136, 139, 140, 141, 150, 154, 174, 175

Paul 4, 8, 19, 32, 96, 102, 110, 113,

	115, 116, 127, 128, 137, 139, 152, 157, 168, 177	**Q**	
		Qodesh	11, 12
		Quality	14, 77
		Queen	23, 142, 159
Peace	iv, 20, 36, 63, 64, 70, 78, 79, 80, 94, 97, 111, 132, 133, 134, 144, 147, 152, 153, 171	**R**	
		Radiance	99, 101, 153
		Redemption	59, 99, 128, 146
		Redemptive	i, 11, 14, 16, 17, 32, 34, 67, 70, 74, 90, 104, 112
Perfect	24, 58, 59, 116, 149, 152, 157, 158	Reigning	5, 58, 149, 155, 156, 157
Perfection	24	Relationship	37, 90, 107, 112, 137
Physical	9, 15, 116, 128		
Picture	16, 25, 42, 80, 82, 85, 96, 111, 112, 115, 133, 134, 148, 151, 157, 158, 163, 164, 166, 173	Rest	7, 20, 24, 53, 72, 73, 74, 85, 86, 87, 94, 95, 96, 109, 111, 126, 141, 142, 149, 152, 157, 173
Pomegranates	6, 36, 60, 61, 62, 65, 69, 71, 72, 75, 78	Restoration	4, 11, 39, 72, 94, 127
Power	18, 26, 42, 43, 68, 80, 81, 95, 98, 108, 155, 156, 162, 163	Resurrection	9, 85, 88, 89, 92, 107, 112, 115, 117, 122, 123, 126, 127, 128, 129, 130, 132, 134, 135, 137, 143, 150, 157
Prophecy	i, 17, 164		
Prophets	7, 9, 68, 98, 106, 147, 166, 167, 168, 171, 172	Rule	11, 14, 20, 114, 124, 147, 171
Purgatory	122	**S**	
Purification	59, 128, 148	Sabbath	53, 72, 73, 74, 126, 152
		Salvation	61, 77, 89, 91, 99,

			113, 156
Satan	i, 27, 42, 43, 68, 86	**T**	
		Tears	132, 147, 152
		Technology	33
Senses	7, 104	Temptation	iii, 167
Sin	10, 15, 25, 27, 30, 36, 38, 39, 41, 42, 55, 57, 58, 70, 71, 79, 80, 81, 88, 90, 98, 99, 113, 148, 149, 167	Theology	33, 47, 126, 127
		Throne	iii, 4, 5, 13, 14, 26, 34, 47, 49, 61, 81, 132, 133, 140, 141, 149, 150, 151, 154, 155, 156, 163, 171
Sleep	114		
Society	33	Transfiguration	96, 169
Sorrow	69, 78, 126		
Soul	2, 3, 12, 73, 75, 128, 130, 143	Travel	6, 36, 86, 93
		Treasures	15, 86
Spirit	ii, 11, 19, 31, 54, 59, 78, 79, 80, 81, 90, 94, 95, 103, 104, 105, 106, 107, 108, 109, 110, 111, 113, 116, 129, 130, 134, 136, 141, 149, 150, 172	Tree of Knowledge	74
		Tree of Life	iii, 1, 2, 5, 9, 11, 17, 27, 32, 34, 39, 46, 56, 74, 88, 92, 96, 97, 98, 99, 102, 125, 136, 141, 149, 150, 154, 164
Spiritual	4, 7, 10, 32, 33, 34, 40, 65, 77, 78, 81, 86, 87, 92, 97, 98, 104, 105, 110, 111, 115, 116, 117, 118, 119, 144, 145, 146, 148, 149, 150, 157, 165	Tribulation	133
		U	
		Unity	115
		Universe	12, 47, 49, 50
		V	
		Valley	i, 11, 63, 65, 70, 71
Sports	158	Valuable	128
		Value	165

Vine	17, 36, 71, 72, 78, 110, 114, 147, 154, 165, 166, 176, 177
Vulgate	4, 8, 28

W

Waste	11, 63, 70, 144, 145
Water	iii, 1, 5, 6, 7, 9, 10, 34, 36, 39, 59, 61, 65, 66, 69, 75, 79, 80, 97, 98, 107, 109, 111, 141, 149, 161, 162, 164, 166, 167, 168, 170
Wealth	18, 65, 130, 142, 151, 155
Wedding	158
Worship	5, 58, 59, 148, 149, 150, 154, 155
Work	1, 2, 3, 12, 13, 15, 17, 31, 34, 35, 36, 37, 38, 40, 42, 53, 54, 55, 56, 58, 59, 60, 61, 68, 71, 73, 74, 79, 86, 88, 99, 122, 123, 133, 134, 146, 152, 157, 158

www.ingramcontent.com/pod-product-compliance
Lightning Source LLC
Chambersburg PA
CBHW050631300426
44112CB00012B/1756